RACE, REFORM AND REBELLION

THE SECOND RECONSTRUCTION IN BLACK AMERICA, 1945–1982

by

Manning Marable

University Press of Mississippi
Jackson

Printed in Hong Kong

Library of Congress Cataloging in Publication Data

Marable, Manning, 1950–
    Race, reform and rebellion.

    Bibliography: p.
    Includes index.
    1. Afro-Americans—Politics and government.
    2. Afro-Americans—Civil rights.   3. United
    States—Race relations.
    I. Title.
    E185.61.M32   1984   305.8′96073   84-7436
    ISBN 0-87805-225-9

Contents

Dedication

To all women of colour, everywhere, who embody the spirit of
freedom . . .
For Sojourner Truth,
For Harriet Tubman,
For Lucy Parsons,
For Ida B. Wells,
For Mary Church Terrell,
For Mary McLeod Bethune,
For Claudia Jones,
For Fannie Lou Hamer,
For the women fighters of the ANC, SWAPO, FRELIMO, PLO,
PAIGC, and the Sandinistas,
For Assata Shakur,
For Sonia Sanchez,
For Alice Walker,
For Joan Little,
For Angela Davis,
For Sandra Neely Smith,
For Toni Cade Bambara,
For Shirley Graham DuBois,
and for my friend, co-worker, lover and wife,
For Hazel Ann.

Acknowledgements

The author and publishers wish to thank the following who have kindly given permission for the use of copyright material:

Harper & Row, Publishers, Inc. for an extract from *Why We Can't Wait* by Martin Luther King, Jr. Copyright © 1963 by Martin Luther King, Jr.

Hughes Massie Ltd on behalf of the author, and Random House, Inc. for the poem 'Un-American Investigators' from *The Panther and the Lash* by Langston Hughes. Copyright © 1967 by Langston Hughes.

Hutchinson Publishing Group Ltd and Random House, Inc. for an extract from *The Autobiography of Malcolm X* by Malcolm X, with the assistance of Alex Haley.

Johnson Publishing Company Inc. for the poem 'Junglegrave' by S. E. Anderson from *Negro Digest*, 1968.

William Morrow & Company Inc., for an abridgement of the poem 'Nigger. Can You Kill' and extract from 'Ugly Honkies' from *Black Feeling, Black Talk, Black Judgement* by Nikki Giovanni. Copyright © 1968, 1970 by Nikki Giovanni.

Every effort has been made to trace all the copyright holders but if any have been inadvertently overlooked the publishers will be pleased to make the necessary arrangement at the first opportunity.

Editors' Preface

Mention the United States and few people respond with feelings of neutrality. Discussions about the role of the United States in the contemporary world typically evoke a sense of admiration or a shudder of dislike. Pundits and politicians alike make sweeping references to attributes of modern society deemed 'characteristically American'. Yet qualifications are in order, especially regarding the distinctiveness of American society and the uniqueness of American culture. True, American society has been shaped by the size of the country, the migratory habits of the people and the federal system of government. Certainly, American culture cannot be understood apart from its multi-cultural character, its irreverence for tradition and its worship of technological imagery. It is equally true, however, that life in the United States has been profoundly shaped by the dynamics of American capitalism and by the penetration of capitalist market imperatives into all aspects of daily life.

The series is designed to take advantage of the growth of specialised research about post-war America in order to foster understanding of the period as a whole as well as to offer a critical assessment of the leading developments of the post-war years. Coming to terms with the United States since 1945 requires a willingness to accept complexity and ambiguity, for the history encompasses conflict as well as consensus, hope as well as despair, progress as well as stagnation. Each book in the series offers an interpretation designed to spark discussion rather than a definite account intended to close debate. The series as a whole is meant to offer students, teachers and the general public fresh perspectives and new insights about the contemporary United States.

CHRISTOPHER BROOKEMAN

WILLIAM ISSEL

Preface

This book is a history of a people and a vision: the rise of
Afro-Americans in political struggles in the United States since 1945,
and their vision of biracial or multicultural democracy and social
transformation, in which other national racial minority groups
shared. Most readers will be quite familiar with the general
outline depicted here: the emergence of a powerful black industrial
working class and the demise of the black Southern peasantry; the
successful effort to abolish legal segregation; the outbreak of Black
Power, urban rebellion, and the renaissance of black, Chicano and
American Indian nationalisms in the 1960s; the contradictory legacy
of black electoral participation within the US political system,
culminating in the election of thousands of black officials in the 1970s;
and the white political backlash against black equality, the return of
vigilante racist violence, and the election of Ronald Reagan in 1980.

This introductory monograph departs from other standard essays
on the period in several critical respects. In Chapter 2, I give
particular attention to the relationship between the anti-communist
'Red Scare' of the late-1940s and 1950s with the evolution of the black
freedom movement. It is my view that the Cold War, and most black
leaders' accommodation to anti-communism, retarded desegregation
campaigns for at least a decade. Second, throughout the work I pay
close attention to the various black nationalist organisations of the
period, from the Nation of Islam to the Black Panther Party. Most of
the original and innovative political theory and programmes
advanced by blacks have come from the nationalists whose views on
integration are sharply divergent from those of more moderate black
spokesmen and women. Finally, I suggest that the central issue which
still confronts the black movement is not the narrow battle for
integration or political rights, but the effort to achieve economic
democracy, social justice, and a transformation of the entire American political economy and society. A Third Reconstruction at some

future point is historically probable, given the gross structural failures of the Second Reconstruction to abolish permanently high rates of unemployment for blacks, Latinos, and low-income whites, or to resolve the dire conditions of poor health care, inferior public schools, and urban decay which plague all national minorities and millions of white Americans. A vision of a culturally pluralist democracy, a non-racist society, was best expressed by the leaders of the black rebellion – W. E. B. DuBois, Paul Robeson, Fannie Lou Hamer, Malcolm X, Martin Luther King, Jr., and many more. This multicultural vision was also shared by national minority activitists – Dennis Banks, Cesar Chavez, José Angel Gutierrez and others. What remains unfinished is the realisation of a political strategy appropriate to the unique social contours of American society to implement that vision.

I owe a debt of gratitude to both Fisk University and Colgate University for providing me with the research resources and time needed to complete this monograph. Special thanks to Dr June Marable for assisting in the preparation of the manuscript, and to my wife, Hazel Ann, for her very special insights into the life and the mind of black folk.

MANNING MARABLE

14 June 1983

1. Prologue: The Legacy of the First Reconstruction

In two historic instances, Negro Americans have been beneficiaries – as well as victims – of the national compulsion to level or to blur distinctions. The first leveling ended the legal status of slavery, the second the legal system of segregation. Both abolitions left the beneficiaries still suffering under handicaps inflicted by the system abolished.

C. Vann Woodward, *The Strange Career of Jim Crow*

What is the object of writing the history of Reconstruction? Is it to wipe out the disgrace of a people which fought to make slaves of Negroes? Is it to show that the North had higher motives than freeing black men? Is it to prove that Negroes were black angels? No, it is simply to establish the Truth, on which Right in the future may be built.

W. E. B. DuBois, *Black Reconstruction in America, 1860–1880*

I

During two brief moments in history, the United States experienced major social movements which, at their core, expressed a powerful vision of multicultural democracy and human equality. The first was developed before the seminal conflict in American history, the Civil War (1861–65), and came to fruition in the twelve-year period of reunion, reconstruction and racial readjustment which followed (1865–77). Almost a century later, a 'Second Reconstruction' occurred. Like the former period, the Second Reconstruction was a series of massive confrontations concerning the status of the Afro-American and other national minorities (e.g. Indians, Chicanos, Puerto Ricans, Asians) in the nation's economic, social and political institutions.

Both movements brought about the end of rigid racial/caste structures which had been used to oppress blacks for many decades. Both elevated articulate and charismatic black leaders from the Afro-American working class and fragile middle class. Both were fought primarily in the Southern US, although in certain respects both inspired major socio-economic reforms in the Northern states as well. In both instances, the Federal government was viewed as a 'reluctant ally' of the blacks and their progressive white supporters, whereas the opponents to black equality were primarily white Southern Democrats and substantial numbers of white small-business and working-class people. Both movements pressured the Federal courts and Congress to ratify and to validate legislative measures which promoted greater racial equality and an improvement in the material status of blacks and poor whites. Finally, both movements eventually succumbed to internal contradictions, the loss of Northern white support, and the re-emergence of the South's tradition of inequality and racial prejudice as the dominant theme of US public policies *vis à vis* blacks. History never repeats itself exactly, so it would be foolish to view the period of racial rebellion from 1945 to the present strictly through the prism of the past. Nevertheless, no real understanding of modern America is possible without an analysis of this nation's ongoing burden of race and class, a social and economic dilemma which was created by almost 250 years of chattel slavery. The racial patterns of the present and the possibilities for the future are buried in that past, in the myriad of successes and failures of the Civil War, and the First Reconstruction. It is here that our assessment of modern American race relations must begin.

More than any other modern nation in the world, with the possible exception of South Africa, the United States developed from the beginning a unique socio-economic structure and a political apparatus which was simultaneously racist, stubbornly capitalist, and committed to a limited form of bourgeois democracy: a racist/capitalist state. In electoral politics, free blacks from the eighteenth century onward found it difficult if not impossible to exercise the franchise. North Carolina permitted some blacks to vote in 1667, for example, but repealed the measure in 1715. At the election of George Washington in 1789, no Southern state permitted blacks to vote. In the nineteenth century, Northern states passed anti-black voting restrictions as well. In 1823, New York established a stiff property qualification which effectively eliminated blacks from voting. Pennsylvania and Indiana denied black males the right to vote in 1838 and 1851, respectively. In most states, blacks were forbidden by law to pursue certain vocations. Free blacks in South Carolina, for example, could not work as clerks; Maryland blacks were forbidden to sell wheat, corn or tobacco without a state licence after 1805; Georgia's free blacks briefly lost the right to own or sell property in 1818. The primary source for all discriminatory legislation, North and South, prior to the Civil War, was the omnipresence of slavery. The 'peculiar institution' was the South's chief mode of agricultural production, and its existence, and the unquenching demand for servile black labour, directly and indirectly influenced the shape of every state's laws and relations with blacks. The growth of the slavery mode of production generated increasing political and social conflicts within American society over a period of eight decades, which culminated in the Civil War.

The white North did not wage the Civil War 'to free the slaves'. Most Republicans, including Lincoln, expressed absolutely no support for the idea of social and political equality between the races. This was, at first, clearly a 'white man's war', fought to preserve Federal authority. Throughout the conflict, blacks in the North continued to experience racist assaults. When blacks were hired to work on riverboats in 1862, for example, white residents of Cincinnati, Ohio, were so outraged that they looted and burned the city's black districts. In July 1863, white New Yorkers destroyed black-owned stores, burned a black orphanage, and lynched black women and men in a four-day racist rampage. It was only after white military casualty figures mounted that an alarmed white public began to accept the suggestion that Northern blacks should be permitted to join the Union army in combat units. The Enlistment Act of July 1862 ordered that black troops should receive half the amount of salary that whites received. Despite this insult, about 186,000 blacks enlisted in the Union army during the conflict. Half of these troops were from the South. In a series of bitter engagements with the Confederate army, they fought with courage and distinction which amazed racists on both sides of the struggle. Partially due to the brutal policy of 'no quarter' which many Southern troops exercised when fighting blacks, 38,000 black soldiers were killed in the war.

By the battle of Shiloh in April 1862, it became evident to the Lincoln administration that a disruption of the South's labour force was a necessity in order to win the war. In July 1862, Congress legally

freed any slaves who had run away from the plantations to join the
Union army. Three months earlier, Congress abolished slavery in
Washington, DC and provided up to $300 .per slave to the former
owners. On 1 January 1863, Lincoln freed all slaves who lived in rebel
territory not yet controlled by the Union army. Technically, slavery
as a legal institution did not end in the United States until the
ratification of the Thirteenth Amendment in December 1865. Practi-
cally, black emancipation occurred not by fiat, but by the direct
actions of the slaves themselves. Thousands waited, watching for the
first opportunity to escape. Northern and Southern whites began to
understand what virtually every black American, slave or free, had
first comprehended. 'After the first few months', noted black scholar
W. E. B. DuBois observed, 'everybody knew that slavery was done
with; that no matter who won, the condition of the slave could never
be the same after this disaster of war.'[1] As nameless chattels, they had
been raped, whipped, sold on the auction block, worked in the hot
fields of endless cotton rows from dawn to dreary dusk. As men and
women, they departed defiantly, with every expectation that their
ordeal would soon end, and the freedom was close at hand. 'To win
the war', DuBois wrote, 'America freed the slave and armed him; and
the threat to arm the mass of black workers of the Confederacy
stopped the war.'[2]

Reconstruction actually began barely one year after the conflict
started, when in July 1862, one Union general, Rufus Saxon,
confiscated plantations along the Carolina coast and promoted the
development of black-owned family farms. General William T.
Sherman issued Order No. 15 in January 1865, which seemed to
promise land to the former slaves. Other Union officers and
politicians held property rights as superior to whatever claims blacks
made for a just return for 250 years of unpaid labour power. General
Nathaniel P. Banks ordered Louisiana blacks to return to their
masters and to accept absurdly low wages. After Lincoln's assassination, President Andrew Johnson, a Southerner, promptly voided most
of the land transfers to blacks, and returned the property to wealthy
whites. In 1866, the Governor of Mississippi complained that the
presence of 9000 black troops in his state promoted the rumour that
former slaves would be given property. President Johnson ordered all
black troops out of the state within five months. Despite these and
other problems, blacks attempted to purchase land wherever and
whenever possible. By the early 1870s, Virginia black farmers had

purchased 80,000 to 100,000 acres. A decade after the war, Georgia blacks owned approximately 400,000 acres, worth $1.3 million. The failure of the Federal government to recognise the necessity for massive land redistribution, along the lines of what blacks themselves called 'forty acres and a mule', would be the principal reason for the failure of the First Reconstruction. In most Southern counties by the mid-1870s, 5 per cent of the white farmers controlled at least 40 per cent of the productive agricultural land. The upper one-tenth of the white farmers in most states owned anything from one-half to two-thirds of the farmland. Racial equality could not occur in political and social relations when economic power was held in relatively few hands.

In non-economic matters, however, Reconstruction produced major changes in the social status of blacks. The Federal government launched the Freedmen's Bureau, which provided food and clothing to millions. The Bureau opened 46 hospitals for blacks across the South. By 1870, its educational institutions claimed one-quarter of a million students and almost 10,000 instructors. A number of Bureau-sponsored colleges became the basis for Afro-American higher education: Howard University of Washington, DC, Atlanta University, Fisk University, and Hampton Institute, are among the most prominent examples. Prior to the Civil War, most Southern states had no real public school systems. With blacks as voters and legislators, the public school was made accessible to the poor of both races. Mississippi's constitution of 1868 created a biracial public school system for the entire state, and legislators set about the task of constructing hundreds of school buildings. The delegates at South Carolina's constitutional convention that same year ratified a proposal for universal education, and proposed $900,000 in expenditures for the public schools. Black religious organisations, notably the African Methodist Episcopal Church, were actively involved in educational and health care efforts. From 1865 to 1869, black churches established 257 black schools in North Carolina alone, which served 15,600 black students. State legislatures passed legislation creating orphanages and other public charities for blacks and whites.

The electoral defeat of Congressional Democrats in November 1866, and the subsequent impeachment of Johnson, shifted effective power from the President to the 'Radical Republicans'. The effect of this political transition was felt almost at once: the passage of the

Fourteenth Amendment, which guaranteed blacks civil rights; the Fifteenth Amendment, which allowed black male adults the electoral franchise; and the Federal government's acceptance of black legislative representation, both in the state and nation. Reconstruction state governments, as a rule, tended to have a smaller percentage of blacks as merited by their respective numbers in each state. Only one Southern state, Mississippi, appointed or elected blacks to the US Senate. Only fourteen blacks were elected to the US House of Representatives during Reconstruction. Most of the states' top offices were filled by white Southerners. White historians, dismayed by the phantom of 'Negro rule', have tried to claim that these men were unfit for public office. Even their white contemporaries, influenced by the deep racism of the day, knew otherwise. Four of the sixteen elected to Congress had received college diplomas; five were prominent lawyers. Francis L. Cardozo, who served as South Carolina's secretary of state from 1868 to 1872, was a former student of the University of Glasgow. Mississippi's two black US Senators, Hiram R. Revels and Blanche K. Bruce, were superior in intellect and political acumen to most of their counterparts. Revels was trained in an Ohio seminary, and attended Knox College in Illinois. During the war he served as a chaplain in the Union army, and in the late 1860s he emerged as the leader of Natchez, Mississippi's black community. Bruce had served as tax collector, sheriff and state superintendent of schools before his election to the US Senate in 1874. He purchased hundreds of acres of farmland in the state's 'blackbelt' region and became one of the most affluent public figures in the South. Between 1869 and 1901, a total of 816 black men were elected as Federal and state legislators. Of these, 63 per cent came from just four Southern states: South Carolina (218); Virginia (93); North Carolina (82); and Louisiana (122). Some Southern and border states with substantial black populations had few or no black elected officials: Kentucky (0); Maryland (0); Tennessee (12); West Virginia (1).

The drive for biracial democracy could not be contained in the South. Northern blacks fought for the repeal of every law which discriminated by race. Gradually, Northern states were forced to amend or abolish many racist regulations. In 1865, Illinois finally permitted blacks to testify in courtrooms. Blacks in Washington, DC, in 1865, led by the fiery abolitionist Sojourner Truth, led a boycott of public transportation facilities which practised Jim Crow. Philadelphia blacks fought successfully to bar segregation in the city's streetcars. Rhode Island blacks forced state officials to desegregate public schools in 1866. Northern blacks pressured their white Congressmen to ratify the Enforcement Act of May 1870, and the Civil Rights Act of March 1875, which further protected blacks' civil liberties. The period even brought black women leaders to the centre of national attention. Frances Ellen Watkins Harper, for instance, travelled and spoke throughout the South from 1865 to 1871, raising capital for black schools and hospitals. In the 1870s, she became Assistant Superintendent of the YMCA school in Philadelphia, and subsequently helped to establish the National Association of Colored Women. Across the nation, blacks in commerce, politics and education were building new institutions with incredible energy. Between 1865 and 1900, to take a single example, over 1200 black-owned newspapers were established. This fact alone, from a population which was 90–95 per cent illiterate in 1860, is awesome.

The decline and demise of the First Reconstruction grew apparent before the Panic of 1873 and the economic recession which lasted for four years afterwards. Northern capitalists recognised that they did not have to condone biracial rule in the South in order to develop the predominantly rural region. Conservatives in the Republican Party found that their own interests converged with those of the former planter class to a greater extent than they did with poor blacks. As historian Lawrence Goodwyn observes, 'the bankers, manufacturers, shippers, and merchants' who ran the Republican Party 'soon wearied of their attempt to build a postwar party in the South based on black suffrage. As elected victories in the 1860s and 1870s proved that the [Republicans] could rule with a basically Northern constituency, Negroes, their morale declining, and white radical abolitionists, their numbers thinning, lost the intra-party debate over Southern policy'.[3] White Southern hostility towards blacks expressed itself dramatically with race riots in Meridian, Mississippi, in 1871, and in Savannah, Georgia, and Hamburg, South Carolina, in 1872. White terrorists organised a series of vigilante groups, including the Ku Klux Klan and the Knights of the White Camelia, to intimidate black voters and elected officials. In the disputed presidential election of 1876, the Republicans secured their narrow victory by promising to curtail civil rights measures and to allow the re-establishment of white supremacy in the South. After the so-called Compromise of 1877, Federal troops were eventually ordered to leave the South.

The end of Reconstruction produced a political and social climate of fear and intimidation for every black person in the South. Despite a brief period from the late 1880s, to the mid-1890s when black and white Southern farmers attempted to develop a biracial opposition to the planters through the Populist Party, the conditions of black life and labour deteriorated rapidly. Politically, the Federal government abandoned any commitment to biracial democracy. In 1883, the Supreme Court declared the Civil Rights Act of 1875 unconstitutional. The principle of 'separate but equal', America's legal justification for domestic *apartheid*, was ordained by the Supreme Court in the *Plessy v. Ferguson* decision of 1896. By the 1890s, Southern states had begun to rewrite their Reconstruction-era constitutions, denying blacks and many poor whites the right to vote. The effect of these new state constitutions was as striking as it was undemocratic. In Alabama, for example, there were 181,000 blacks who were eligible to vote in 1900; two years later, merely 3000 were noted as registered voters. Republican presidents supported the creation of a 'Lily White' wing of their party in the South, which would deny blacks the right to participate even in their own political organisations. Political disfranchisement was also facilitated by extra-legal means. Between 1882 and 1903, 2060 blacks were lynched in the United States. Some of the black victims were children and pregnant women; many were burned alive at the stake; others were castrated with axes or knives, blinded with hot pokers, or decapitated.

II

The experiment in biracial democracy was effectively at an end. For many millions of black farmers, the only hope for political survival and economic self-sufficiency was in an exodus from the South. The earliest migrants left in the 1870s. Benjamin 'Pap' Singleton, a black mortician, led over 7000 blacks from Kentucky and Tennessee into Kansas. In 1879, a second wave of 60,000 black farm families walked and rode from the lower Mississippi River Valley into Kansas. Many blacks later migrated to Oklahoma Territory; between 1891 and 1910 more than two dozen all-black settlements were established in the state. The vast majority who fled, however, moved to the North. The flood of black humanity increased steadily: 170,000 migrants in 1900–10; 454,000 in 1910–20; 749,000 in 1920–30. Black migration dropped during the Great Depression decade, 1930–40, with only

349,000. From 1940–50, the movement accelerated again, totalling 1,599,000 for the decade. In the thirty years between 1910 and 1940, the black population in Illinois increased from 109,000 to 387,000; in New York from 134,000 to 571,000; in Pennsylvania from 194,000 to 470,000. In 1940, 22 per cent of all blacks lived in the North, compared to 10 per cent in 1910. This major demographic shift produced dramatic changes in the labour patterns of blacks. In 1890, 63 per cent of all black males were agricultural workers, 22 per cent were domestic servants, and only 14 per cent worked in transportation, communications, and/or manufacturing. In 1930, the percentage of black male agricultural workers declined to 42 per cent. Only 11 per cent were domestics, but 36 per cent were employed in manufacturing, transportation and communications. The small, black middle class which emerged after slavery had begun to multiply. The number of black public and private schoolteachers more than doubled from 1910–40. The number of black-owned businesses between 1904 and 1929 grew from 20,000 to over 70,000. Between 1900 and 1914, 47 black-owned banks were established. The percentage of black youth between the ages of 5 to 20 enrolled in school increased from 33 per cent in 1890 to 65 per cent 50 years later. In the same period, black illiteracy dropped from 61 per cent to 15 per cent. The migration from the rural South to the urban Northeast and Midwest, and the growth of a black urban working class throughout the nation, brought an improvement in health care, education, economic and political life for millions of black people. Nevertheless, the substantial gap between the socio-economic and political status of whites and blacks still existed, and was reinforced across the nation by the rule of Jim Crow.

Even these marginal improvements in the material existence of many blacks did nothing to halt the proliferation of brutal white violence. The Jim Crow system of racial exploitation was, like slavery, both a caste/social order for regimenting cultural and political relations, and an economic structure which facilitated the superexploitation of blacks' labour power. Unlike slavery, Jim Crow was much more clearly capitalistic, since white owners of factories did not have to purchase entire black families in order to obtain the services of a single wage-earner. However, in caste/racial relations, both systems were dependent upon the omnipresence of violence or coercion. Throughout the early twentieth century, white politicians, business leaders and most workers defended the necessity to discipline the black working class via lynchings, public executions, and the like. One particularly brutal moment occurred immediately after World War I, when whites across the country committed an array of bestial acts against blacks, unheard of even in salvery. In the 'Red Summer of 1919' 70 blacks were lynched, including ten soldiers who had fought 'to preserve democracy against the Kaiser'. Eleven of these blacks were burned alive. In the Chicago race riot of 1919, 38 persons were killed, and 537 were injured. Up to 1000 black families were burned out of their homes in the city. Whites in Knoxville, Tennessee, destroyed black property worth $50,000. Dozens of black cotton-farmers and labourers were shot in Elaine, Arkansas. An Omaha, Nebraska, white mob attacked a black man suspect accused of raping a white woman. The man was shot over 1000 times, and the corpse was lynched in the city's central district. Throughout the carnage, the Federal government remained blind and mute. State governments increased stringent segregation laws to the point of high absurdity. South Carolina insisted that black and white textile workers could not use the same doorways, pay windows, bathrooms or even the same water buckets. Many cities passed ordinances which kept blacks out of public parks and white residential districts. Atlanta outlawed black barbers from clipping the hair of white children and women in 1926. There were soon segregated zoos, baseball clubs, buses, taxicabs, restaurants, and race tracks. Historian C. Vann Woodward noted one extreme case: A Birmingham ordinance got down to particulars in 1930 by making it "unlawful for a Negro and a white person to play together or in company with each other" at dominoes or checkers'.[4] For all practical purposes, the black American was proscribed by the state from any meaningful political and social activity for two generations. Behind this powerful proscription, as always, was the use of force.

The first four decades of the twentieth century witnessed major social, cultural and economic changes for most black Americans. Yet after two world wars and a devastating economic depression, the barrier of the colour line still existed in the United States. Most white Americans, looking backward at Reconstruction, cautioned Negroes not to demand abrupt changes in their caste status too quickly. Jim Crow would gradually be allowed to decline after another century or two of racial improvement and social adjustment. But in growing numbers, blacks and other national minorities looked at America's experiment in multicultural democracy as the harbinger for a better life in the immediate future. In the prophetic words of W. E. B. DuBois, the campaign for freedom had hardly begun:

This the American black man knows: his fight here is a fight to the finish. Either he dies or wins. If he wins it will be by no subterfuge or evasion of amalgamation. He will enter modern civilization here in America as a black man on terms of perfect and unlimited equality with any white man, or he will enter not at all. Either extermination root and branch, or absolute equality. There can be no compromise. This is the last great battle of the West.[5]

2. The Cold War in Black America, 1945–1954

It is the problem of the Russian People to make changes there. We cannot advance a progressive development by threatening Russia from the outside. . . . America is incomparably less endangered by its own Communists than by the hysterical hunt for the few Communists there are here. In my eyes, the 'Communist conspiracy' is principally a slogan used in order to put those who have no judgment and who are cowards into a condition which makes them entirely defenseless. Again, I must think back to the Germany of 1932, whose democratic social body had already been weakened by similar means. . . .

Albert Einstein, open letter to Norman Thomas, 1954

There are class divisions among Negroes, and it is misleading to maintain that the interests of the Negro working and middle classes are identical. To be sure, a middle-class NAACP leader and an illiterate farmhand in Mississippi or a porter who lives in Harlem all want civil rights. However, it would be enlightening to examine why the NAACP is not composed of Negro porters and farmhands, but only of Negroes of a certain type.

Harold Cruse, *Rebellion or Revolution*

I

The aftermath of any war affects those on the side of its victors even more than it does those who have lost. For many Afro-Americans who celebrated V-J Day in the late summer of 1945, there was an intense sense of joy and dread: fears that there might be another anti-black 'Red Summer' such as had swept the nation in 1919; hopes that the progressive economic changes that had occurred for blacks during the wartime era could be expanded; unanswered questions about the new administration of Harry S. Truman, its commitment to the modest social democratic policies of Franklin D. Roosevelt and to the limited pursuit of civil rights. Two decades later, black social critic Harold Cruse described his feelings at that ambiguous moment in history:

> World War II shattered a world irrevocably. But people who thought as I did were called upon in 1945 to treat the postwar era with intellectual and critical tools more applicable to the vanished world of the thirties – a world we had never had time to understand as we lived it. I spent the years from 1945 to about 1952 wrestling with this perplexity. . . .[1]

The crimes of the Third Reich against European Jews had shocked the nation, and the popular ideology which inspired public opposition to Hitler was rooted in an anti-racist and democratic context. The blatant contradiction between the country's opposition to fascism and the *herrenvolk* state and the continued existence of Jim Crow in the States after 1945 was made perfectly clear to all. Blacks and an increasing sector of liberal white America came out of the war with a fresh determination to uproot racist ideologies and institutions at home. But few at the time were precisely clear as to what measures were required to turn this egalitarian commitment into public policy.

Part of the dilemma which confronted black leaders resided in the ambiguous legacy of the late president, Franklin D. Roosevelt (1933–45). By most standards, the Democrat had been the most liberal chief executive in regard to the civil rights of national minorities in American history. The number of black Federal employees was increased from 50,000 in 1933 to 200,000 by 1946. Roosevelt had appointed a small group of prominent middle-class blacks, including lawyers Robert C. Weaver and William H. Hastie, journalist Robert L. Vann, and educator Mary McLeod Bethune, to administrative posts. Government agencies in the 'New Deal' administration of Roosevelt were organised on strictly segregated lines. Youths who worked in the Civilian Conservation Corps camps were segregated by race; provisions in the Public Works Administration which mandated certain percentages of black workers in the construction of buildings were blatantly ignored; benefits from the Agricultural Adjustment Administration were often denied to black rural farmers through fraud and outright corruption. Roosevelt resisted blacks' demands that the Federal government should pressure defence contractors to hire greater numbers of minorities. It was only under the direct threat of a black workers' march on Washington, DC, co-ordinated by black labour leader A. Philip Randolph in 1941, that Roosevelt signed Executive Order 8802 which met the blacks' concerns in a limited respect.

In a real sense, the watershed of Afro-American history occurred during the 1940s. Thousands of black men working as sharecroppers and farm labourers were drafted into the army with the outbreak of World War II. Over three million black men registered for the service, and about 500,000 were stationed in Africa, the Pacific, and in Europe. Fighting as customary in segregated units, black troops again distinguished themselves on every front. At home, the war effort brought another million black women and men into factory lines of production. Some white workers viewed this racial turn of events with greater alarm than the spectre of fascism. Between March and June 1943, a series of 'hate strikes' against the upgrading of blacks in industries contributed to a total 100,000 man-days lost. Philadelphia street-car workers refused to work with blacks in 1944, and Roosevelt was forced to order 5000 Federal troops into the city to restore order. Partially through the militant labour-organising efforts of the American Communist Party, the number of black union members rose from 150,000 in 1935 to 1.25 million by the end of the war. Even in many Southern cities black and white workers formed biracial unions and fought for higher wages and improved working conditions. In 1943–44, 11,000 black and white tobacco workers at the R. J. Reynolds plant in North Carolina struck successfully to upgrade the salaries of black employees. In politics, blacks evinced for the first time since the demise of Reconstruction a growing leverage on state and national affairs. Northern black voters had largely shifted their political allegiances from the Republican to the Democratic party during the Great Depression. In 1934, Arthur W. Mitchell of Chicago became the first black Democrat elected to Congress in American history. Ten years later, a Harlem minister and militant political activitist, Adam Clayton Powell, was elected to the House. Black Northern votes for Roosevelt in the presidential election of 1944 accounted for his margin of victory over Republican New York Governor Thomas Dewey in eight states, including Michigan and Maryland. The major civil rights organisations in the country, the

National Association for the Advancement of Colored People (NAACP), founded by DuBois in 1910, more than tripled its membership in 1934–44. The NAACP Legal Defense Fund had gained considerable success in the repeal of Jim Crow state legislation through its appeals to the Supreme Court. By 1945, a growing number of white Americans in the North had concluded that the system of racial segregation would have to be modified, if not entirely overthrown.

In the months immediately following World War II, blacks made decisive cracks in the citadel of white supremacy. By 1946, there were over two dozen blacks who were serving in state legislatures in Northeastern states (New York, Massachusetts, Pennsylvania, New Jersey, and Vermont), in the Midwest (Illinois, Kansas, Nebraska), the West (California and Colorado) and even in border states (West Virginia and Kentucky). In 1945, Truman appointed a black attorney, Irvin C. Mollison, as Associate Judge of the US Customs Court. In 1946, William H. Hastie was named Governor of the Virgin Islands, and black sociologist Charles S. Johnson was appointed to the National Commission advising the US State Department on participation in the United Nations Education, Scientific, and Cultural Organisations (UNESCO). Ralph J. Bunche, a former socialist and co-organiser of the militant National Negro Congress in the 1930s, was named to the Anglo-American Caribbean Commission of the State Department. Across the country, blacks were participating openly in electoral politics in heretofore unprecedented numbers. In Harlem, black Communist Party leader Benjamin J. Davis was elected to the New York City Council. By 1947, 12 per cent of all voting-age blacks in the South were registered, up from only 2 per cent in 1940. Blacks in the upper South – Virginia, North Carolina, and Tennessee – began to be elected in small numbers on city councils and school board posts. Congress reflected this trend towards a more liberal to moderate segregationist policy. Against 1937–38, when only 10 bills which were considered favourable to desegregation and civil rights were introduced to Congress, by 1949–50, 72 bills were being proposed. After 1946, several Northern states passed local restrictions against racial discrimination in employment.

During the 1940s, there was also a marked improvement in the quality and accessibility of black education. In the 1930s, the incomes of private black colleges had decreased by 16 per cent, and private gifts declined by 50 per cent. In October 1943, a group of black college presidents, led by Tuskegee Institute president Frederick D. Patterson, established the United Negro College Fund to save these institutions. During 1944, 1945 and 1946, about a million dollars a year was raised. Black public schoolteachers campaigned to equalise the pay schedules between blacks and whites in a number of states and cities. In 1943, black teachers in Tampa, Florida, sued successfully in Federal court to overturn unequal salary schedules. This was followed by similar legal actions by black teachers in Charleston, South Carolina, in 1944, and in Columbia, South Carolina, Newport News, Virginia, Little Rock, Arkansas, and Birmingham, Alabama, in 1945. Black parents attempted, with less success, to increase state allocations in support of black segregated public schools. On balance, greater progress in improving black educational prospects was achieved in these few years than during the previous three decades. By 1950, 83,000 black women and men between the ages of 18 to 24 were enrolled in universities, 4.5 per cent of their age group.

In the labour force, a similar picture of change emerged. Philip S. Foner notes that 'the median income of nonwhite wage- and salary-earners had risen from 41 percent of the white median in 1939 to 60 percent in 1950; the percentage of male black workers in white-collar and professional jobs had risen from 5.6 in 1940 to 7.2 in 1950, and that of craftsmen and operatives from 16.6 percent of the total in 1940 to 28.8 percent in 1950'.[2] By 1946, there were 450,000 black members of the American Federation of Labor (AFL) in the South, and another 200,000 in the rest of the country. Substantial numbers of blacks were in many sectors of the workforce that were unionised before the war and afterwards: 17 percent of all semi-skilled meatpacking workers were black, 9.2 percent of the coalminers, and 68 percent of the tobacco workers. By 1946, blacks were also well represented in the more progressive Congress of Industrial Organizations (CIO). The largest numbers of black workers who were organised were in the Steelworkers of America-CIO (95,000 blacks); the Automobile, Aircraft, Agricultural Implement Workers of America-CIO (90,000); Hodcarriers and Common Labor-AFL (55,000); Marine and Shipbuilding Workers-CIO (40,000); and the United Electrical, Radio and Machine Workers-CIO (40,000). The nation's most influential black trade unionist, A. Philip Randolph, was a leading force for desegregation both inside the House of Labor and within the largest society. By 1955, he was named vice-president of the merged AFL-CIO.

The growing social and economic power of the black working and middle classes seemed to many to provide the basis for an entirely new political relationship between blacks and whites. In early 1948, NAACP political theorist Henry Lee Moon predicted with stunning accuracy that the potential weight of this emerging black force could no longer be ignored by either the Democratic or the Republican parties. The ballot is 'the indispensable weapon in the persistent fight for full citizenship . . . a tool to be used [against] Jim Crow', Moon declared in *Balance of Power: The Negro Vote*. 'By 1936, after four years of the New Deal, colored voters in the urban centers of the North and East had caught up with the procession. The mass migration out of the Republican camp was in response to the Roosevelt program which . . . made an effort to meet some of their urgent needs'.[3] Moon observed that the black vote would be delivered in the future only to those candidates of either party who addressed civil rights issues and strengthened the social and economic reform programmes initiated by the Roosevelt administration. He also cautioned Democrats not to take the black voter for granted, and sensed that, even in any election year, blacks could easily move their allegiances. In retrospect, Moon seriously overemphasised the volatility of the black electorate; but at the time, no white candidate could be absolutely certain that blacks would remain basically Democrats. During the early post-war years, blacks had occupied positions of minor-level influence in the trade unions, in municipal and state politics, and were in many formerly all-white universities. It was apparent to every observer, particularly the national leaders of the Democratic Party, that the black electorate's interests would have to be accommodated at the expense of the South and Jim Crow.

II

The democratic upsurge of black people which characterised the late 1950s could have happened ten years earlier. With the notable exception of the *Brown* decision of 17 May 1954, which ordered the desegregation of public schools, most of the important Supreme Court decisions which aided civil rights proponents had been passed some years before. In May 1946, for example, the high court ruled that state laws requiring segregation on inter-state buses were unconstitutional. In *Smith v. Allwright*, delivered 3 April 1944, by an eight to one margin, the Supreme Court ended the use of the all-white primary election. By the spring of 1946, there were 75,000 black registered voters in Texas and 100,000 black voters in Georgia. Yet the sit-ins, the non-violence street demonstrations, did not yet occur; the façade of white supremacy was crumbling, yet for almost ten years there was no overt and mass movement which challenged racism in the streets. This interim decade, between World War II and the Montgomery County, Alabama, bus boycott of December 1955, has also generally been ignored by black social historians. I think that the answer to the question, 'Why were mass popular protests for desegregation relatively weak or non-existent in the period 1945–54?' is precisely the answer to the second question, 'Why have historians of the black Movement done so little research on the post-war period?' The impact of the Cold War, the anti-communist purges and near-totalitarian social environment, had a devastating effect upon the cause of blacks' civil rights and civil liberties. As this chapter will illustrate, the paranoid mood of anti-communist America made it difficult for any other reasonable reform movement to exist. The sterile legacy of anti-communism, felt even today, has so influenced many American historians that they are not even able to comment on the facts before them.

By the end of 1946, the Soviet Union and the United States had reached a clear breaking point in their relations. From the Soviets' perspective, the Americans were ungrateful for their pre-eminent role in the anti-fascist war effort, and lacked any critical understanding of their domestic and foreign requirements needed to restore peace and economic order. The Soviets had lost 20 million men and women in World War II. During the summer of 1946, the worst drought of the twentieth century dried up all the crops in the Ukraine and Volga lands, and millions were on the verge of starvation. Urban consumption declined to only 40 per cent of 1940 totals. 'In the coal-mines of the Donetz Basin men were still pumping water out of the shafts. . . . The steel mills, rattling with wear and tear, turned out only 12 million tons of ingot, a fraction of the American output. Engineering plants were worked by adolescent semi-skilled labour. People were dressed in rags; many were barefoot.'[4] The Soviet Union was simply in no condition to fight another war, but it did feel that its national interests had to be preserved. The Americans were driven by other motives.

For many political conservatives and emigrants from Eastern Europe, World War II had been 'the wrong war against the wrong enemy', writes social historian David Caute. 'These groups were joined after 1944 by others initially favorable to the war but subsequently appalled by the spread of Soviet Communism in Eastern Europe and by the reduction of [these] nations to satellite status. Here Catholic indignation ran high.' Anti-communist liberals in both major political parties 'soon developed a determination to halt Soviet encroachment by every available means and to deal roughly with elements at home – Communists, fellow travelers, Progressives – who foolishly or wickedly adopted the Soviet point of view'.[5] American corporate interests were concerned about expanding investments abroad and reducing or eliminating all pro-labour legislation sponsored by the New Deal at home. The anti-communist campaign permitted them to do both, as well as to flush suspected leftists out of positions of trade union authority. A great many post-war politicians, such as Wisconsin Senator Joe McCarthy and California Senator Richard M. Nixon, simply 'recognized a good thing when they saw it, [and] cynically manipulated public hysteria for their own political purposes'.[6]

Noted playwright Lillian Hellman accurately describes the post-war 'Red Scare' period as a 'Scoundrel Time':

It was not the first time in history that the confusions of honest people were picked up in space by cheap baddies who, hearing a few bars of popular notes, made them into an opera of public disorder, staged and sung, as much of the congressional testimony shows, in the wards of an insane asylum. A theme is always necessary, a plain, simple, unadorned theme to confuse the ignorant. The anti-Red theme was easily chosen ... not alone because we were frightened of socialism, but chiefly, I think, to destroy the remains of Roosevelt and his sometimes advanced work. The McCarthy group ... chose the anti-Red scare with perhaps more cynicism than Hitler picked anti-Semitism.[7]

In March 1947, Truman asked Congress to spend $400 million in economic aid and military hardware to halt leftist movements in Turkey and Greece. In the following years, five million investigations of public employees suspected of communist sympathies were held. Trade unions were pressured to purge all communists and anti-racist activists with leftist credentials. By July 1947, union leader Philip

Murray ordered the CIO executive committee, 'If communism is an issue in your unions, throw it to hell out, and throw its advocates out along with it'.[8] The CIO convention of 1949 expelled the 50,000-member United Electrical, Radio, and Machine Workers union for being dominated by leftists; within months, eleven progressive unions with nearly one million members were purged from the CIO. In 1949, 15 states passed 'anti-subversion laws'. 'Writing or speaking subversive words' in Michigan was a crime punishable by a life sentence in prison. In 1951, Tennessee mandated the death penalty for the espousal of revolutionary Marxist ideas. That same year, Massachusetts required a three-year term in the state prison for anyone who allowed a Communist Party meeting to be held in their homes. Georgia, Indiana, Pennsylvania and Washington outlawed the Communist Party. The US Attorney General, Tom Clark of Texas, warned all Americans in January 1948: 'Those who do not believe in the ideology of the United States, shall not be allowed to stay in the United States'.[9]

'The wealthiest, most secure nation in the world was sweat-drenched in fear', Caute writes. 'Federal, state and municipal employees worried about their pasts, their student indiscretions, their slenderest associations. . . . Some hastened to save their own skin by denouncing a colleague. In schools, universities, town halls and local professional associations, a continuous, pious mumbling of oaths was heard – the liturgy of fear.'[10] For black America, the 'Scoundrel Time' was refracted through the prism of race, and was viewed in the light of their own particular class interests. For many black industrial and rural agricultural workers, the communists were the most dedicated proponents of racial equality and desegregation. In the 1930s, they had organised a vigorous defence of the Scottsboro Nine, a group of young black men unjustly convicted of rape in Alabama. The Party had sponsored Unemployed Councils, and provided the major force to desegregate American labour unions. For the aspiring black middle class, the image of the Communist Party was entirely different. Many black preachers had often denounced Marxism because of its philosophical atheism. Black entrepreneurs were dedicated to the free enterprise system, and sought to enrich themselves through the existing economic order. Many black leaders had condemned the Party during World War II for urging blacks to maintain labour's 'no strike' pledges. Foner notes, 'It was to be exceedingly difficult for the Communists to overcome the resentment among blacks created by the Party's wartime policies. The Communists never completely erased the feeling in sections of the black community that they had placed the Soviet Union's survival above the battle for black equality.'[11] In general, black middle-class leaders attempted to divorce themselves from the communists as the reactionary trend was building across the country.

The most prominent black leaders were affected in different ways by the outbreak of the domestic Cold War. Randolph was the doyen of the black labour movement. During World War I, he and his radical associate Chandler Owen had edited the militantly socialist journal the *Messenger*, and were known throughout Harlem as the 'Lenin and Trotsky' of the black movement. During the Red Summer of 1919, President Woodrow Wilson had denounced Randolph as 'the most dangerous Negro in America'. During the mid-1920s Randolph had organised the Brotherhood of Sleeping Car Porters, and began to moderate his leftist views considerably. His fierce struggle with the Communist Party over the leadership of the National Negro Congress from 1935 and 1939 left a bitter anti-communist bias in his entire political outlook. During the war, he had continued to urge black workers to adopt a 'strategy and maneuver (of) mass civil disobedience and non-cooperation' to fight racism.[12] But Randolph opposed, certainly from this point onward, any co-operation or 'united front' activity with the communists. In 1947, he organised the Committee Against Jim Crow in Military Service and Training, and threatened the Senate Armed Services Committee that he would direct a massive civil disobedience effort if the US armed forces were not promptly desegregated. But in the post-war years, Randolph deliberately eschewed any political or organisational links with revolutionary Marxists. In his speeches and writings, he denounced the domestic communist 'conspiracy' at every opportunity. By clearly separating the interests of black labour from the radical left, he believed that he could gain the political support of many anti-communist liberals and the Truman Administration. As Randolph declared before a Congressional committee in 1948, racial segregation 'is the greatest single propaganda and political weapon in the hands of Russia and international communism today'.[13]

Although elected to Congress only in 1944, Adam Clayton Powell, Jr., quickly emerged as the most influential black public official for the next two decades. Almost twenty years younger than Randolph, Powell had acquired his reputation as a dedicated militant during the

Great Depression. As the son of the leader of one of the largest black churches in the nation, Harlem's Abyssinian Baptist Church, Powell led a series of popular boycotts which called for black jobs and greater welfare and social services. A charismatic speaker whose entire 'way of life' was 'an act of rebellion', Powell had at first no reservations about joining with the communists who defended the interests of black poor and working people.[14] The practical contributions of the Party were praised by Powell in a 1945 statement: 'There is no group in America, including the Christian church, that practices racial brotherhood one-tenth as much as the Communist Party'.[15] Once in Congress, Powell led the fight against anti-communism. In early 1947, when two Congressional contempt citations were passed against communists who refused to divulge information to the House Un-American Activities Committee (HUAC) by votes of 370 to 1 and 357 to 2, only Powell and progressive New York Congressman Vito Marcantonio voted against the majority. Powell recognised that every defender of racial segregation in Congress was also a devout proponent of anti-communist legislation, and that the Negro had no other alternative except to champion the civil liberties of the left in order to protect the black community's own interests. This advanced perspective, which would prove to be correct in later years, found little support among the black middle class, despite Powell's continued personal popularity. Within Congress itself, Powell was contemptuously dismissed as a political pariah for fifteen years.

Since 1930, the leader of the NAACP had been Walter White. Under his direction the organisation had grown in numbers and political influence. During the 1920s, he had written a provocative investigative report on lynchings in the South. As an assistant secretary to James Weldon Johnson, he had served tirelessly and with Johnson's retirement, White slowly moved the NAACP to the right. Internally, co-workers who resisted any of White's initiatives were soon fired. In DuBois' words, White 'was absolutely self-centered and egotistical to the point that he was almost unconscious of it. He seemed really to believe that his personal interests and the interest of the race and organization were identical. This led to curious complications, because to attain his objects he was often absolutely unscrupulous.'[16] In 1933–34, White feuded with DuBois over the NAACP's lack of a coherent economic policy for blacks to deal with the Great Depression. In despair and outrage, DuBois resigned as editor of the NAACP journal, the *Crisis*, in June 1934, after 24 years of service. DuBois returned to the NAACP after an absence of ten years as research director, but with the outbreak of the Cold War, White pressured the board to fire him within three years because of DuBois' 'radical thought' and progressive activities in international peace and Pan-Africanist movements. White's bitter relationship with DuBois was manifested towards his opposition to the entire American left generally. From the beginning of his tenure at the NAACP, he had fought any influence of communists or independent radicals in the organisation. He supported the early 'witch-hunts' to exclude communists from all levels of the Federal government. When in late 1947, a poll of the NAACP national office revealed that 70 per cent of the staff intended to support former vice president Henry Wallace on the Progressive Party ticket in opposition to Truman, White warned DuBois and other Wallace-advocates not to take part in any electoral campaign. Simultaneously, White was already 'making a nationwide drive for Truman, by letter, newspaper articles, telegrams and public speech'. Like Randolph, White attempted to identify the struggle for black equality with the anti-communist impulse.[17]

The most prominent black supporters of progressive and leftist politics were DuBois and the famous cultural artist-activist Paul Robeson. DuBois had been an independent socialist since 1904, but had experienced a series of volatile confrontations with revolutionary Marxists. In the wake of the Bolshevik Revolution, he denounced the entire concept of the 'dictatorship of the proletariat', and told the readers of the *Crisis* that he was 'not prepared to dogmatize with Marx and Lenin'.[18] As late as 1944, DuBois had written that 'the program of the American Communist Party was suicidal'.[19] Yet after extensive travels in the Soviet Union in 1926, 1936 and 1949, DuBois' view on matters shifted considerably. He concluded that the Soviets' anti-imperialist positions promoting the necessity for African political independence from European colonial rule were genuinely progressive; he was impressed with the Soviet Union's extensive domestic educational, social and technological gains. By the late 1940s, he believed that the black liberation movement in America had to incorporate a socialist perspective, and that blacks had to be in the forefront in promoting peaceful co-existence with the Soviet bloc. Robeson was politically closer to the communist movement for a greater period of time. In the late 1930s, he supported the progressive government of Spain against the Nazi-backed Spanish fascists in that country's bloody civil war. He recognised earlier than DuBois that the rise in domestic anti-communism would become a force to stifle progressive change and the civil rights of blacks. In early 1949, in a controversial address in Paris, he declared that US policies toward Africa were 'similar to that of Hitler and Goebbels'. The Soviet Union 'has raised our people to full human dignity'. These and other statements led to Robeson's wide public censure. His noted career as a Shakespearean actor and singer, which was described by American critics as the most gifted of his generation before 1945, crashed in short order. To muffle Robeson's impact, HUAC quickly called black baseball player Jackie Robinson before the committee to denounce him. Robeson had been a 'famous ex-athlete and a great singer and actor', Robinson admitted, but his subversive statements gave support to the communist cause. 'We can win the fight [against segregation] without the Communists and we don't want their help.'[20]

As the presidential election of 1948 approached, the Truman Administration recognised that the Negro electorate would play an unusually decisive role in the campaign. More than Roosevelt, Truman privately viewed the blacks' goals of social and political equality with great contempt. But the administration's aggressively anti-communist polemics could not create a sufficient electoral bloc among white voters which would guarantee victory that November. Democratic party disaffections grew on the left and right, with Wallace's Progressive Party and the Southern-based States' Rights Party, which nominated hard-line segregationist Strom Thurmond of South Carolina. The Republicans renominated popular New York governor Thomas Dewey as their standard-bearer, a politician who had run a very creditable race against Roosevelt in 1944. Presidential advisers informed Truman that he might even win the popular vote, but without critical black support in the industrial Northeast, the Midwest, and California, he would lose the electoral college count to Dewey – or, as in 1800 and 1824, a disastrous statement could occur and the House of Representatives might have to select a president in 1949. Thus, for the first time since 1876, it seemed apparent that blacks would decide the national election. Truman immediately responded to blacks' interests by publicly calling for new civil rights legislation. He promised to promote fair employment procedures and to press federal contractors aggressively to comply with desegregation guidelines. On 26 July 1948, the president issued an executive order to the effect 'that there shall be equality of treatment and opportunity for all persons in the armed forces without regard to race, color, religion or national origin'.[21] Randolph promptly suspended the Committee Against Jim Crow in Military Service and Training's plans for a proposed boycott. White and his NAACP supporters exhorted blacks to reject the Wallace campaign, and urged them to vote for Truman in the interests of civil rights. White's efforts were a triumph for Cold War liberalism. In Harlem, Truman received 90,000 votes to Wallace's 21,000 votes, even though the Progressive Party's anti-racist platform was far superior to that of Truman's. In Pittsburgh, only 2000 blacks cast ballots for Wallace. In California, Ohio and Illinois, black voters provided the decisive electoral edge for Truman over Dewey. Overall, Truman carried about two-thirds of the black vote, and with that margin, he won the election. True to his campaign promises, in 1949 Truman continued to promote modest biracial reform efforts at the Federal level, while at the same time escalating the Cold War at home. Truman's victory silenced and isolated black progressives for many years, and committed the NAACP and most middle-class black leaders to an alliance with Democratic presidents who did not usually share black workers' interests, except in ways which would promote their own needs at a given moment. Accommodation, anti-communism, and tacit allegiance to white liberals and labour bureaucrats became the principal tenets of black middle-class politics for the next decade.

III

Without much public fanfare or notice, a series of new political formations created by blacks and liberal whites began to emerge at this time. Blacks in South Carolina formed the Progressive Democratic Party to challenge the whites-only state Democratic Party. By May 1944, the Progressive Democrats had organised chapters in 39 of the state's 46 counties, and had begun an independent electoral strategy to expand the number of registered black voters in South Carolina. That same year, the biracial Southern Regional Council was formed in Atlanta, a coalition of clergy and professionals who supported the gradual but steady abolition of Jim Crow. The most important new biracial group, however, was the Congress of Racial Equality (CORE), established in 1942 by the pacifist Fellowship of Reconciliation, directed by A. J. Muste. Of CORE's 50 charter members, at least a dozen were black, including a Howard University divinity school graduate, James Farmer. The black youth secretary for the Fellowship of Reconciliation, social democrat and pacifist Bayard Rustin, gave political purpose and direction to the young formation. One of CORE's first actions was a confrontation with barbers at the University of Chicago who in November 1942 refused to cut Rustin's hair. From these modest beginnings, CORE developed into a civil rights group which emphasised non-violent direct action, rather than the litigation and moral suasion techniques of Walter White and the NAACP. Unlike the older organisation, it was democratic, and most funds raised by chapters remained at the local level. By 1947, there were 13 CORE chapters, mostly in Ohio, New York, Illinois, Kansas, and Minnesota. CORE chapters staged a series of non-violent boycotts to desegregate lunchcounters and schools in a series of Northern and Midwest cities. White Methodist student leader George Houser and Rustin developed a plan for CORE to test desegregation laws on inter-state buses in the upper South during the late autumn of 1946. Perhaps hearing about the proposed 'Journeys of Reconciliation', NAACP leaders, including attorney Thurgood Marshall, warned that: 'A disobedience movement on the part of Negroes and their white allies, if employed in the South, would result in wholesale slaughter with no good achieved'.[22] Walter White, true to form, refused to provide any financial support for the effort. On 9 April 1947, a small party of 8 blacks and 8 whites left Washington, DC, determined to sit in whites-only sections of the buses. In the journeys, CORE members were repeatedly arrested and intimidated by Southern police, bus drivers, and the local courts. Rustin and other activists were sentenced to serve 30 days on North Carolina's jail gang. The Journeys of Reconciliation failed to overturn the South's racial codes, but in the process, they established a pattern of civil rights protest which would be revived with greater effectiveness as the Freedom Ride movement in the 1960s.

By the early 1950s, the progress towards civil rights began to slow down perceptibly. The number of registered black Southern voters reached 1.2 million by 1952. Yet 'in the lower South, apart from a very few cities', C. Vann Woodward writes, 'little change in Negro voting or office-holding could be detected. By one means or another, including intimidation and terror, Negroes were effectively prevented from registering even when they had the courage to try'.[23] On 2 June 1946, a black army veteran, Etoy Fletcher, was flogged publicly in Brandon, Mississippi for attempting to register. Senator Theodore

Bilbo of Mississippi boasted that only 1500 out of 500,000 black potential voters were registered in his state. 'The best way to keep a nigger away from a white primary is to see him the night before', Bilbo declared. The *Jackson Daily News* (Mississippi) warned the state's few registered black voters: 'Don't attempt to participate in the Democratic primary anywhere in Mississippi. . . . Staying away from the polls will be the best way to prevent unhealthy and unhappy results'.[24] Southern registrars employed Kafkaesque tests to determine whether blacks were 'literate' enough to vote. One white registrar in Forest County, Mississippi, asked black potential voters this question: 'How many bubbles are in a bar of soap?'[25] As one Alabama political leader explained, the vote of even one black person in the deep South was an intolerable threat to the entire structure of Jim Crow. 'If it was necessary to eliminate the Negro in 1901, because of certain inherent characteristics, it is even more necessary now because some intellectual progress makes the Negro more dangerous to our political structure now than in 1901. The Negro has the same disposition to live without working that his ancestors had in the jungle 10,000 years ago.'[26] Most of these racist politicians were still leading figures in the national Democratic Party, and were represented in powerful posts in the Truman Administration.

Truman himself was virtually silent from 1946–53 as white racist vigilante groups proliferated. As the black population in Los Angeles County, California, reached 200,000 by 1946, the Ku Klux Klan began to appear on the West Coast. Klan organisations were formed throughout the South, and were reported active in Pennsylvania and New Jersey. In New York, the state attorney general estimated that there were 1000 Klansmen in his state alone in the late 1940s. In the face of growing racist opposition, the NAACP counselled continued reliance upon the Truman Administration, legal challenges to segregation laws, and a general policy which spurned direct action. The failure and tragedy of this conservative approach to social change was in its parochial vision and tacit acceptance of the Cold War politics. By refusing to work with Marxists, the NAACP lost the most principled anti-racist organisers and activists. Instead of confronting the racists politically, with the commitment of a Robeson or a DuBois, they accepted the prevailing xenophobia of the times, and in the end undercut their own efforts to segregate society. The anti-communist impulse even affected CORE, to its detriment. A few CORE chapters, in Columbus, Ohio, and Chicago, encouraged Marxist participation

in the early 1940s. In 1949, however, when Trotskyists joined the San
Francisco chapter, the national office voided its affiliation. In 1948,
Houser and CORE's executive committee drafted a 'Statement on
Communism', which was passed unanimously by its convention that
year. CORE denounced any ties with 'Communist-controlled'
groups, and CORE members were ordered not to co-operate or work
with so-called communist-front organisations. As CORE's historians
noted, this action did not prevent 'conservatives and racists from
continuing to attack CORE as Communist-controlled. Despite its
vigorous anticommunist position, CORE suffered considerably from
the McCarthyite hysteria of the period. The Red Scare, by labeling
radical reform groups subversive, seriously impeded CORE's
growth.'[27] By 1954, CORE had all but ceased to exist as an
organisation.

IV

As the Cold War intensified, the repression of black progressives
increased. Aided by local and state police, a gang of whites disrupted
a concert given by Paul Robeson in Peekskill, New York in 1948.
HUAC witnesses declared that Robeson was 'the black Stalin among
Negroes'.[28] in August 1950, the US government revoked his passport
for eight years. Officials prevented Robeson entering Canada in 1952,
although no passport was necessary to visit that country. DuBois ran
for the US Senate in New York in the autumn of 1950 on the
progressive American Labor Party ticket, and denounced the anti-
communist policies of both major parties. Despite wide public
censure, he received 206,000 votes, and polled 15 per cent of Harlem's
ballots. The Truman Administration finally moved to eliminate
DuBois' still considerable prestige within the black community. On 8
February 1951, DuBois was indicted for allegedly serving as an 'agent
of a foreign principal' in his anti-war work with the Peace Information
Center in New York. The 82-year-old black man was handcuffed,
fingerprinted, and portrayed in the national media as a common
criminal. Before his trial, the New York *Herald-Tribune* convicted him
in a prominent editorial: 'The DuBois outfit was set up to promote a
tricky appeal of Soviet origin, poisonous in its surface innocence,
which made it appear that a signature against the use of atomic
weapons would forthwith insure world peace. It was, in short, an
attempt to disarm America and yet ignore every form of Communist

aggression.'[29] An international committee was formed to defend
DuBois and his colleagues at the Peace Information Center.
Threatened with a fine of $100,000 and a five-year jail term, DuBois
continued to denounce the Truman Administration while out on bail.
In November 1951, a Federal judge dismissed all charges against
DuBois, when the government failed to introduce a single piece of
evidence that implied that he was a communist agent.

Despite DuBois' acquittal, the government had accomplished its
primary objectives. DuBois' voluminous writings on Negro sociology,
history and politics were removed from thousands of libraries and
universities. The State Department illegally withheld his passport for
seven years. Black public opinion moved even further to the right.
One leading black newspaper which had carried DuBois' essays for
decades, the *Chicago Defender*, declared that 'it is a supreme tragedy
that he should have become embroiled in activities that have been
exposed as subversive in the twilight of his years'. The oldest Negro
fraternity, which DuBois had helped to found in 1906, Alpha Phi
Alpha, did not rally to his defence. Only one of thirty Alpha Phi Alpha
chapters expressed public support for DuBois. Virtually every black
college president except Charles S. Johnson of Fisk University,
DuBois' *alma mater*, said nothing about the case. The NAACP was
especially conspicuous in its moral cowardice. White told NAACP
board members that the government had definite proof which would
convict DuBois. The NAACP Legal Defense lawyers made no
overtures to provide assistance. The central office contacted NAACP
local chapters with strongly worded advice about 'not touching'
DuBois' case. Black schoolteachers' groups and the black National
Baptist Convention took no action. The entire ordeal left DuBois in
bitter doubt about the political future of the Negro middle class:

The reaction of Negroes [to the case] revealed a distinct cleavage
not hitherto clear in American Negro opinion. The intelligentsia,
the successful business and professional men, were . . . either silent
or actually antagonistic. The reasons were clear; many believed
that the government had actual proof of subversive activities on our
part; until the very end they awaited their disclosure. [These
blacks] had become American in their acception of exploitation as
defensible, and in their imitation of American 'conspicuous
expenditure.' They proposed to make money and spend it as
pleased them. They had beautiful homes, large and expensive cars

and fur coats. They hated 'communism' and 'socialism' as much as any white American.[30]

On many black college campuses, the Red Scare was reflected in a growing exclusion of radical views from classroom discourse. Any faculty member who had a history of militant activism, either in the Communist Party or in other suspicious groups, could be fired. Two examples from Fisk University can be cited. Giovanni Rossi Lomanitz had been an active Party member in the early 1940s, working in the Federation of Architects, Engineers, Chemists and Technicians. A former associate of J. Robert Oppenheimer, Lomanitz taught at Cornell and in the late 1940s began an appointment at Fisk. In 1949 HUAC subpoenaed Lomanitz, and before the committee he refused to testify against himself, citing the Fifth Amendment. In twenty-four hours, despite the support of faculty and students, president Charles S. Johnson dismissed Lomanitz without due process. Five years later, Fisk mathematics professor Lee Lorch was summoned before HUAC. Lorch pointedly denied being a member of the Communist Party during his tenure at Fisk, and refused to answer questions about his alleged Party membership before 1941 by evoking the First Amendment. Johnson issued a public statement stating that Lorch's position before HUAC 'is for all practical purposes tantamount to admission of membership (in the Communist Party)'. Out of a faculty of 70, 48 urged Fisk's Board of Trustees to retain him, as did 22 student leaders and 150 alumni. Fisk instead ended Lorch's contract, as of June 1955.[31]

A number of black former activists agreed to become informers against the communists. In the federal trial of twelve leading Party officials, which included two blacks, New York City Councilman Benjamin J. Davis and Henry Winston, staged in New York City during July and August 1948, one of the government's black witnesses was an autoworker, William Cummings. Cummings joined the Party in 1943 for the FBI in Toledo, Ohio, and told the jury that communists 'taught militants that one day the streets would run with blood'. The defendants received sentences ranging from three to five years in Federal prisons, and were ordered to pay fines of $5000 each. Some of the Party's oldest black recruits turned into agents for the government. William O. Nowell, born in a Southern sharecropper's family, joined the Party in the late 1920s. Trained in the Soviet Union, he rose as a Party leader in Detroit's trade union struggles.

When he was expelled from the Party in 1936, he promptly worked as an agent in Henry Ford's 'goon squad', threatening and beating other autoworkers. From 1948 until 1954, Nowell became a 'professional anti-communist', testifying in approximately 40 trials and hearings. Manning Johnson entered the Party in 1930, and quickly climbed to its national committee in the ten years before his departure. Johnson repeatedly perjured himself at numerous trials, later claiming with pride that he would lie 'a thousand times' to protect 'the security of the government'. The US Justice Department paid Johnson $4500 a year for his services. Ex-communist Leonard Patterson received $3800 a year for two years, testifying against his former comrades before HUAC and in the courts. North Carolina black attorney Clayton Clontz joined the Party after the war, and covertly informed the FBI on its activities from August 1948 until February 1953. In the trial of one communist, Clontz made the astonishing claim that he was told that Soviet troops would land in the US if America 'declared war on [U.S.] communists in the revolution'.[32]

The purge of communists and radicals from organised labour in 1947–50 was the principal reason for the decline in the AFL–CIO's commitment to the struggle against racial segregation. In the wake of the NAACP's stampede to the right, a left of centre space on the political spectrum was open, and militant black workers took advantage of the opportunity. In June 1950, nearly 1000 delegates met in Chicago at the National Labor Conference for Negro Rights. Robeson gave a moving plenary address which condemned the Cold War and supported deténte with the Soviet bloc countries. Black delegates from AFL unions noted that the federation still maintained all-white unions, and black veterans of the CIO argued that their organisation had all but abandoned the struggle for Negro rights. The Chicago conference established a steering committee for the co-ordination of future work, which included Coleman Young, a Detroit leader of the Amalgamated Clothing Workers, UAW activist William R. Hood, and Cleveland Robinson, vice president of the Distributive, Processing, and Office Workers Union. In 1950 and 1951, the committee helped to develop 23 Negro Labor Councils, each fighting to end segregated facilities at the workplace, expanding black job opportunities, and attacking racism in the unions. The militant Detroit Council, led by Hood, inspired the call for the creation of a new black progressive labour organisation. In October 1951, the National Negro Labor Council was formed in Cincinnati, Ohio. The delegates at the convention represented unions expelled from the CIO for retaining communists, as well as members of both the AFL and CIO. Hood emerged as the president, and Young was elected executive secretary. Almost immediately, the National Negro Labor Council came under direct attack. CIO leaders denounced Hood, Young and other black labour activists as the 'tool(s) of the Soviet Union'. Lester Granger of the National Urban League criticised the Council as 'subversive'. In its brief history, the organisation pressured to desegregate jobs in major US firms; organised campaigns to increase black workers' salaries and to upgrade their job ranks; led pickets against hotels and companies practising Jim Crow; and challenged the unions to advance more black workers into leadership positions. The pressure against the Congress' pickets and protest activities was enormous. By December 1954, HUAC denounced the 'pro-Communist ideology' of the organisation. It is true that communists participated in the National Negro Labor Council, but in no way were the desegregationist programmes it carried out dictated or even directly influenced by the Party. By 1956, however, due to political pressures from the US government, corporations and white labour leaders, the National Negro Labor Council had disappeared.[33]

Besides Robeson, DuBois, and the militant workers of the National Negro Labor Council, few examples or models of black resistance existed, except in the Communist Party. Black communist leader Henry Winston was confined during his 1948 trial in a poorly ventilated, closet-like cell. Despite two heart attacks, and following this, the judge's denial that he be seen by his family doctor, Winston's will to fight remained strong. At the April 1952 trial of black communists Pettis Perry and Claudia Jones, Perry described himself 'as a victim of a frameup so enormous as to resemble the Reichstag Fire trial' of 1933. Secretary of the Party's Negro Commission, Perry defiantly asked the court, 'How could a Negro get justice from a white jury?' A native West Indian Marxist, Jones 'delivered a long indictment of America's treatment of black people'. Convicted, Perry received three years and a $5000 fine; Jones, one year and one day in jail, and a $2000 fine. Claude Lightfoot, secretary of the Illinois party, was arrested in June 1954, and had to stay in jail four months until $30,000 bail money could be collected. Convicted in January 1955, the black World War II veteran was given five years and a $5000 fine. Prison life for these black revolutionaries was difficult physically, but their resistance remained uncompromised. Claudia Jones' acute asthmatic and cardiac conditions were made worse by having to work at a prison loom. In ten months she was sent to a hospital, and she died not long after her release. Prison doctors refused to treat Winston's eyesight, and as a result he became blind. Confronted with segregated accommodation in the Federal prison at Terre Haute, Indiana, Benjamin Davis filed a suit against prison officials. Despite being placed on 'round-the-clock administrative segregation', Davis refused to be defeated.[34]

The black middle class's almost complete capitulation to anti-communism not only liquidated the moderately progressive impulse of the New Deal years and 1945–46; it made the Negroes unwitting accomplices of a Cold War domestic policy which was, directly, both racist and politically reactionary. When paranoid librarians took DuBois' works off their shelves, they did not stop there – banned literature often included black publications such as the *Negro Digest* and the NAACP's *Crisis*, as well as the *New Republic*, *The Nation*, and other white-oriented liberal journals friendly to desegregation causes. When Robeson was blacklisted along with Lillian Hellman, director Dalton Trumbo and the 'Hollywood Ten', did blacks think their feeble voices praising American patriotism would save black actors and artists? The wife of Adam Clayton Powell, Hazel Scott, a talented singer and pianist, could not obtain employment for years. Black television actor William Marshall, stage performer Canada Lee, and others were victimised by blacklists. When Randolph defended anti-communism at home, did he not recognise that in doing so, he became a tool for American interests and power abroad? In 1952, Randolph travelled with Socialist leader Norman Thomas to Asia under the auspices of the Congress for Cultural Freedom. Speaking in Japan and Burma, he denounced Russia's 'slavery' and emphasised the progress made in US race relations. In 1967, it was revealed that the Congress for Cultural Freedom was a subsidised front for the US Central Intelligence Agency (CIA). Historian Christopher Lasch's criticisms of Thomas could be made with equal vigour of Randolph: 'He does not see that he was being used [for different purposes] from the ones he thought he was advancing. He thought he was working for democratic reform . . . whereas the CIA valued him as a showpiece, an anti-Communist who happened to be a Socialist'.[35] By serving as the 'left wing of McCarthyism', Randolph, White and other Negro leaders retarded the black movement for a decade or more.

V

Another dimension to America's traditional racial dilemma became more prominent after the war. Blacks were by far the largest single racial minority group in the nation, but they were not alone. In the Far West, Chinese peasants were brought into California to labour in the mines and for railroad companies after the Civil War. Before the Depression of 1893 roughly 30,000 worked as lowly-paid labourers on Californian ranches and farms. In the 1890s, a trickle of Japanese immigrants expanded into a flood. By 1898, 60,000 Japanese lived in Hawaii; between 1886 and 1908 the number of Japanese on the mainland increased from 4000 to over 100,000. The 1924 immigration legislation passed under President Calvin Coolidge effectively prevented Japanese entering the US mainland, but new waves of cheap workers were found by American businesses in the Philippines. By the end of the 1920s, about 25,000 impoverished Filipino farm-workers were employed in California's Salinas and San Joaquin valleys. At the beginning of World War II, some 78,000 Chinese-Americans and 127,000 Japanese-Americans were living on the West Coast. In the eastern US, coloured workers were drawn from the Caribbean. The Puerto Rican population in New York City alone increased from barely 60,000 in 1940 to 240,000 in 1950. The majority of these newer national minority groups experienced a system of rigid racial segregation, residential discrimination, political oppression and low wages which blacks had known intimately for generations. As early as 1906–7, anti-Japanese riots erupted in San Francisco, as racist whites pillaged the Japanese community. In 1942 over 100,000 Japanese-Americans, mostly native-born US citizens, or Nisei, were forcibly removed to internment camps for the duration of World War II. Most lost their homes and all of their personal belongings. The American general who supervised their mass arrests justified US policy in bluntly racist language: 'A Jap's a Jap. It makes no difference whether he is an American citizen or not'.[36] Puerto Rican workers were often victimised by policies of crude racial discrimination by unions and managers alike. Compounding this problem of ethnic competition for jobs was a fresh influx of European and Asian immigrants after 1945. Between 1948 and 1953, the Displaced Persons Act brought 410,000 Slavic and Germanic people into the country. Another 50,000 Hungarians and 31,000 Dutch-Indonesians arrived several years later. Thus by the Cold War period, the problem of the colour line was not simply a social equation of black and white.

Despite the wide diversity of the national minorities which lived and laboured in the US, there were two specific oppressed groups with which blacks had a special relationship, by both historical experience and economic status – Mexican-Americans (or Chicanos) and American Indians. The Spanish had colonised the American Southwest almost 200 years before slavery effectively took root in the Carolinas and Virginia. Slavery was officially abolished by Mexico in 1829, a move designed primarily to halt the immigration of white slaveholders into Texas. After the Mexican War of 1846–48, the United States seized roughly half of the nation of Mexico as its territory, and within a generation, thousands of Mexican peasants worked as peons and wage-labourers for white American settlers. The 'Anglos' systematically weakened or destroyed the Spanish-built missions and other institutions of Mexican culture. Mexican ranches were seized, usually by illegal means, and became the property of white Americans. Mexican sheep-herders were often denied access to pasture lands and water for their flocks, and in the early 1880s scores were murdered by rampaging white ranchers in the Graham–Tewksbury War in Arizona. As heavy industry moved into the region by 1900 – railroads, mining, smelting – white corporations relied upon the Mexican population as their principal reservoir of cheap labour. In times of economic expansion, Mexicans were used as strike-breakers or scabs during periodic conflicts between white labourers and managers. In periods of recession and depression, they became the 'reserve army of labour', the first to be fired from their jobs, as blacks were in the South. During the 1930s, almost half a million Mexicans were forcibly deported 'as unemployed Anglos claimed Mexican jobs'.[37] Racist and nativist groups, including the American Federation of Labor, the American Legion, the Daughters of the American Revolution and the Veterans of Foreign Wars, fought vigorously for the exclusion of additional Mexican workers from the country. The Ku Klux Klan in Texas, New Mexico and Arizona attacked and sometimes killed Chicano men and women with legal impunity. Despite these assaults and legal restrictions, the number of Mexican-Americans continued to increase. Between 1900 and 1930, approximately 1.5 million Mexicans settled in the United States – more than the total number of Europeans who colonised the US east coast between 1607 and 1790.

Throughout the early twentieth century, the political, economic and social status of Mexican-Americans was scarcely distinguishable from that of blacks. Like Afro-Americans, Chicanos attempted to improve their economic status by joining trade unions. Mexican-Americans participated in the Knights of Labor and several, including Manuel Lopez, a master workman of the Fort Worth, Texas local, emerged as key leaders. During the Great Depression, Chicano working-class activists were part of the Congress of Industrial Organizations, and were particularly influential in fighting racial prejudice as leaders of the United Cannery, Agricultural, Packing, and Allied Workers Union. Generally, however, the social controls imposed by both capital and the Anglo political and caste system remained effectively to check Mexican-American resistance. A dual pay structure in Arizona mines and in Southwestern ranches perpetuated the income gap between Chicanos and Anglos. Chicanos were generally denied basic constitutional rights and civil liberties even when they had been born inside the US. In electoral politics, their votes were often manipulated or discounted. One typical example of this occurred routinely during the 1930s and 1940s in southern Texas. Political bosses, or 'jefes', determined whether Chicanos were 'qualified' to vote on a case-by-case basis. As political scientist V. O. Key observed in 1949, the jefe often paid the Chicano voter's 'poll taxes' and held 'the tax receipts until election day to insure discipline and orderly procedure. Economic dependency often makes the control easier, and in south Texas there are large landholdings with whole communities employed on a single ranch'. In Duval County, Texas, such regimentation of the Chicano vote ensured electoral margins for favoured Democratic Party candidates of at least 90 per cent. The Duval vote in the Democratic Party Senatorial primary of 1948, for example, was 4622 votes for the then Congressman Lyndon Johnson to 40 votes for his opponent. The common judgement among most white Texas politicians, therefore, was that the Mexican-American electorate had 'only the most remote conception of Anglo-Saxon governmental institutions'. Among Chicanos, Key wrote, one finds 'a high incidence of political indifference, ignorance, timidity, and sometimes venality'.[38] People subjected to such racist contempt are inevitably the victims of violence. During August 1942, Los Angeles police illegally raided the growing Latino barrio (ghetto) of that city and arrested 600 Chicanos. In June 1943, fourteen off-duty policemen established a

'Vengeance Squad' and began attacking Los Angeles Chicanos at random. Joined by hundreds of white sailors and tourists, they 'toured the barrios in convoys of taxi cabs, in bars and restaurants and movie houses' as white police officers 'looked the other way'. History records the incident as the 'Zoot Suit Riots', named for the style of clothing then worn by young Chicano males: in fact, it was a racist pogrom not unlike that waged by whites against the black community of Atlanta in 1906, or against Chicago blacks in 1919.[39]

The special plight of the Native Americans at the hands of European settlers pre-dated American slavery itself. A succession of colonial, state and federal government treaties with various Indian nations, from the seventeenth century to the mid-nineteenth century, were invariably violated by whites in an effort to eradicate the Indian from the frontier. By the end of President Andrew Jackson's Administration, the majority of Native American nations had been defeated militarily and forcibly removed west of the Mississippi. After the Civil War, the US government pursued a policy against the Indians of the west which can only be termed genocidal. General William T. Sherman's 1866 orders to his troops were specific: 'At least 10 Indians are to be killed for each white life lost. You should not allow the troops to settle down on the defensive but carry the war to the Indian camps, where the women and children are . . . [You] should not delay the punishment of the Indians as a people.'[40] The contemporary Indian nationalist movement of the 1970s and 1980s was born here, over a century ago, in the fierce determination of Native American people to resist their own extermination. The Athabascan people of the Southwest (Apaches and Navajos) waged an unrelenting campaign to maintain their way of life and culture, as did the Sioux and other Indian nations of the Great Plains. By the end of the century, however, the sheer numbers of settlers and the superiority of white military power overwhelmed and crushed the Indian resistance movement. Indian leaders and guerrilla generals – Sitting Bull, Crazy Horse, Geronimo – were imprisoned, murdered or assassinated. Women and children were butchered by government troops at the Wounded Knee massacre of 1890. Unique cultural forms of resistance, such as the Native American Church, were criticised by American officials for fostering Indian unity. The role of Afro-Americans in the political and territorial suppression of the Indian people is, at best, mixed. There were numerous instances of Black-Indian military and political co-operation along the American frontier, most notably among the Seminoles of Florida. For several decades, runaway slaves and Indians fought successfully against federal troops, defeating white soldiers decisively in several battles, before they succumbed in the 1840s. Conversely, black soldiers in the Ninth and Tenth Regiments of the US army were used against Indians on the Great Plains in the 1870s and 1880s. At one point, about one out of five American troops ordered to 'suppress civil disorders', to chase 'Indians who left the reservation out of frustration or in search of food', 'arrest rustlers and guard stagecoaches' were black. Called the 'Buffalo Soldiers', these black troops 'paradoxically helped bring the white man's law and order to the frontier', and in doing so, aided the process of destroying Indian civilisation.[41] Over the entire century, the Indian population was cut from two million to barely 200,000.

A crude type of 'American apartheid' was imposed upon Indians, with the expressed purpose of destroying Indian political unity and regimenting indigenous culture. Indians were scattered across the country, designated to live in so-called tribal areas or reservations. The Dawes Act of 1887 divested Indians of huge tracts of land, 'impoverish[ing] large numbers of people who then became beggars or wards of the various states'. The Reorganization Act of 1934 'enabled tribes to achieve corporate status through charters, thereby enabling them to continue their existence in a collective form'. Still, all major power was controlled in Washington, DC by the paternalistic Bureau of Indian Affairs.[42] By World War II, the 350,000 Indians had become the most marginalised of all national minority groups. Alcoholism, high rates of infant mortality and severe malnutrition were prevalent in the reservations. Desperate young Indian men by the thousands left the reservation in search of work in major cities. Conditions for Native Americans became even worse with Cold War domestic policies aimed at minorities. In 1953, upon Congressional orders, the Bureau of Indian Affairs proposed the 'termination' of thirteen Indian 'groupings'. The Termination Act was a modern version of Sherman's policies towards the Indian. In brutal violation of existing treaties, thousands of Indians were swiftly relocated to specific urban enclaves or centres in Los Angeles, San Francisco, Denver, Phoenix, and Cleveland. As Indian scholar Roxanne Dunbar Ortiz notes, 'in the cities, the mostly young Indian relocatees experienced grueling urban poverty and unemployment in place of the grinding rural poverty and unemployment, with the added inevitability of losing their homelands and their existence as people'.[43] Tens of thousands of Indians were 'thrown into white society without the skills or means to survive; a sizeable proportion of Indian land was again appropriated and most of it sold to whites; and those tribes that were terminated were subject to state and local taxation without an economic base from which to pay the taxes'.[44]

With the growth of the post-war black freedom movement, however, came a concomitant awakening of political and social consciousness among all other national minorities. Among Chicanos, the American GI Forum and the Community Service Organisation were created to register voters and to urge members of their community to take a more active role in the electoral system. The Mexican-American Political Association was founded in California in 1958, and four years later, the Political Association of Spanish-Speaking Organisations was established in Texas. The major political forum of the Mexican-American middle class remained the League of United Latin American Citizens (LULAC), which had been established three decades before. Assimilationist in cultural outlook and inclined towards the liberal wing of the Democratic Party, LULAC shared many characteristics of the NAACP. LULAC members eschewed political militancy of any type. Their construction prohibited 'any radical and violent demonstrations which may tend to create conflicts and disturb the peace and tranquility of our country'. LULAC leaders 'always emphasized American citizenship, education, equality, and the use of the English language rather than the Spanish language'.[45] Puerto Rican immigrants had begun to establish a series of small businesses in New York City's boroughs, and Puerto Rican workers soon emerged in increasing numbers as trade union officials, civic and neighbourhood political leaders. On the West Coast, Japanese-American leaders, supported by progressive whites, led a successful fight in 1946 to defeat an anti-Nisei constitutional provision. Despite the loss of millions of dollars worth of property, Nisei pooled their meagre resources collectively to compete with whites in both business and professional fields. Between 1945 and 1960, the percentage of Japanese-American professionals among their male workforce had increased four times, reaching roughly the level among whites. Due to their strenuous opposition, Indian leaders forced the federal government to halt the Termination Act by 1961, giving Indian activists a renewed sense of their potential power. The forces of racial repression had not been halted, and like the Afro-American, other national minorities continued to labour beneath the burden of caste oppression and economic exploitation. But between the lines, a new level of political courage and commitment among all people of colour had been achieved, even during the period of McCarthyism.

VI

In the early spring of 1946, an event of symbolic significance occurred which, in time, would touch the lives of several million rural Afro-Americans and Chicanos. In Montgomery County, Alabama, on the 7700 acre plantation of the McLemore Brothers, black fieldhands were busy preparing for the new year's crop. The McLemores proposed to have an experiment. Setting aside a 150-acre tract, the white planters decided to see whether cotton could be processed from seed to market 'without touching human hands'. In a one-man operation, newly purchased farm machinery prepared the land, and subsequently 'planted, fertilized, chopped, weeded, defoliated and picked' every boll of cotton on the 150-acre plot. Tuskegee Institute social scientists noted, 'this is probably the first time that the human hand rarely touched the cotton from the time plans were made until the burlap-wrapped bale of cotton was delivered from the gin process'.[46] The South had traditionally lagged well behind the rest of the nation in agricultural technology. By 1945, 30.5 per cent of all US farmers had tractors; tractor-ownership percentages in the South were considerably lower – South Carolina, 5.4 per cent; Georgia, 5.9 per cent; Alabama, 4.5 per cent; Mississippi, 4.1 per cent. A typical Southern white owner-operated farm averaged only 122 acres; but farms owned by corporations and managed by whites averaged 2126 acres. In the past, large and small white farmers kept black farmworkers' wages at subsistence levels; but low salaries allowed them to hire the maximum numbers of black workers. As late as 1945, the average hourly salaries of non-white men on Southern farms was only 0.23 cents, compared to 0.66 cents for white males. The larger farms increasingly relied upon machines to replace black labour in the cotton fields during the 1940s. Within ten to fifteen years, the smaller white farms would follow their lead. Expendable, despite his/her low wages and long hours (an average workday of 9.7 hours), the black farmworker was rapidly becoming extinct. 'Labour-intensive' farming was giving way to 'capital-intensive' farming.

The mechanisation of Southern agriculture was a decisive reason why the black migration north continued. From 1940–50, the number of non-Southern blacks increased from 2.4 million to 6.4 million. In most industrial cities in the Midwest, the black population growth rate was between 500 to 1000 per cent above that for whites. The drive to the North was inspired also by the promise of higher wages and better working conditions; but these factors were dependent upon the availability of employment. During the last five years of Truman's Administration, non-white unemployment averaged 6.9 per cent, compared to 4 per cent for white workers. By 1954 and 1955, non-white unemployment had jumped to 9.3 per cent v. 4.5 per cent for whites. In 1954, 16.5 per cent of all non-white youths in the job market were unemployed. The black ghettoes of the North, first taking shape with the industrial demand for Negro labour a half century before, were beginning to become stagnant centres for joblessness and despair.

By the spring of 1954, nine years after Roosevelt's death, there was a feeling of unfulfilled ambitions and expectations among many blacks. The legalistic strategy of the NAACP had proved successful, yet there was still much dissatisfaction with the now elderly Walter White's authoritarian style and dependence on the anti-communist liberal wing of the Democratic party. CORE and the National Negro Labor Council had almost disappeared from public view, for very different reasons. Republican Dwight David Eisenhower had been elected president in 1952. No friend of the armed forces desegregation decision of 1948, the former five-star general wanted to slow down the pace and retard the movement for civil rights. Dewey's vice presidential running mate of 1948, California Governor Earl Warren, had been named Chief Justice of the Supreme Court. For blacks, he was best known for placing 100,000 Japanese-Americans into concentration centres during World War II. Neither Eisenhower, the NAACP, nor black America would yet discover that this same Republican politician would become the strongest defender of blacks' rights in Supreme Court history. No one could realise completely the new phase of American history that would dawn on 17 May 1954, in a legal decision which would mark the real beginning of the Second Reconstruction.

3. The Demand for Reform, 1954–1960

... a little rebellion, now and then, is a good thing. ... It is a medicine necessary for the sound health of government.

Thomas Jefferson to James Madison, 1787

Racial integration, [is] a great myth which the ideologues of the system and the Liberal Establishment expound, but which they cannot deliver into reality. ... The melting-pot has never included the Negro.

Harold Cruse

I

Black parents and civil rights lawyers in Virginia, Kansas, Washington, DC, South Carolina, and Delaware had challenged the legality of segregated public school systems during the early 1950s. By late 1952, all these cases had reached the Supreme Court. After a year and a half of hearings, the high court finally handed down a unanimous decision in what was popularly known as *Brown v. Board of Education of Topeka, Kansas*. The Court ruled that 'we cannot turn the clock back ... to 1896 when *Plessy vs. Ferguson* [the decision which validated the separate-but-equal principle] was written. We must consider public education in the light of its full development and its present place in American life'. Chief Justice Earl Warren and other justices were persuaded by the writings of black sociologists that racial segregation did irreparable damage to black schoolchildren both socially and psychologically. 'In the field of public education the doctrine of "separate but equal" has no place. Separate educational facilities are inherently unequal.' Warren and his colleagues thus overturned the legal justification for one of the principal pillars of white supremacy.[1]

The *Brown* decision marked the end of a long phase in the legal war of attrition between the NAACP and the defenders of racial inequality. As early as 1938, the Supreme Court had ordered Missouri to guarantee its black residents who applied to state schools that equal educational provisions would exist. In 1948, the Court voided any real estate agreements which racially discriminated against purchasers. One year later, *Sweatt v. Painter* ruled that Texas' segregated law school for blacks was inherently unequal and inferior in every respect to its law school for whites. *McLaurin v. Oklahoma* declared in 1950 that Oklahoma had to desegregate its law school. The Supreme Court stated that racial restrictions of this type 'impair and inhibit' the Negro student's 'ability to study, engage in discussions and exchange views with other students and, in general, to learn his profession'.[2] Thus, even before *Brown*, a pattern of desegregation had been set into motion by the Court. By 1953, blacks attended 10 formerly all-white public colleges and 23 graduate schools in the South. By Truman's second term, many Southern Democrats understood that they could forestall court-ordered desegregation only if they spent millions of dollars in upgrading all-black public schools. Expenditures soared 800 per cent between 1939 and 1952 in the South's futile efforts to build new black schools. After *Brown*, it became apparent that the all-black public school system was legally intolerable. Upper South states led the way in desegregation efforts. Baltimore, Washington, DC, cities in Delaware and West Virginia desegregated their public schools by September 1954. On 31 May 1955, the Supreme Court ordered boards of education to draw up desegregation plans 'with all deliberate speed'. Within the next twelve months 350 school boards representing nine Southern states had desegregated without much white opposition. By January 1956, the Supreme Court had overturned segregation laws in Tennessee, Arkansas, Florida, and Texas. Lower courts generally tried to cater to Southern whites by interpreting the timeframe for desegregation as indefinite; but they had no legal recourse except to carry out desegregation mandates of the high court. By the 1956–57 school year, 723 Southern school districts had been desegregated, and 300,000 black children were either attending formerly white schools or were part of a 'desegregated' school district. Despite these gains, there were at this point 2.4 million black Southern children still enrolled in Jim Crow schools, and 3000 white school boards expressed every intention of maintaining the colour line in spite of the Supreme Court's mandates.

Within several years Congress reinforced the Supreme Court's desegregation initiatives with the passage of the first civil rights legislation since the demise of Reconstruction. The Civil Rights Act of 1957, as first designed, was a fairly strong federal commitment to blacks' rights. One section of the Act required federal guarantees for the voting rights of blacks, and authorised the Justice Department to sue states and local interests which supported segregated schools or perpetuated racial restrictions in elections. The Democratic majority leader in the Senate, Texas Senator Lyndon B. Johnson, a former segregationist, was chiefly responsible for manoeuvring the bill through fierce Southern and conservative opposition in the upper house. In the weakened version which was eventually passed, federal judges were permitted to arrest state and local officials who kept blacks from voting. The act also mandated a Commission on Civil Rights which developed an agenda for federal action. In May 1960, a second Civil Rights Act was passed over bitter opposition and a filibuster led by Southern Democrats, or Dixiecrats. Federal judges were now permitted to select 'referees' who could by-pass local white registrars who kept blacks from voting. These referees were empowered to register black voters. The law also included federal sanctions and penalties for racists who used violent measures to disrupt the orderly process of voting and desegregation.

II

For many blacks, the drive for desegregation still seemed agonisingly slow. In Deep South cities steeped in *apartheid*-style social relations, the black population was humiliated and exploited to the breaking point. In Montgomery, Alabama, the median annual income for the average black worker was under $1000 in 1956; only 2000 black adults were registered to vote. In early December 1955, when Mrs Rosa Parks was arrested for sitting in a 'whites-only' section of a municipal bus, black civic leaders led by E. D. Nixon decided to act. A boycott of local buses was held to protest against the city's segregation code, and this challenge to racism blossomed into an international event. Emerging as the principal leader of the boycott was a young black doctor of divinity, the Reverend Martin Luther King, Jr. Ably assisted by the Reverend Ralph David Abernathy and activist Bayard Rustin, King urged local blacks to employ non-violent protest tactics. Throughout 1956, approximately 95 per cent of Montgomery's blacks refused to use the buses. White police and local officials arrested 92 black organisers on a variety of charges in the effort to frustrate the boycott. Black and white liberal activists were vindicated by a Supreme Court ruling of 13 November 1956, which outlawed segregation on Montgomery buses. Overnight, King became the charismatic symbol of the political aspirations of millions of coloured people across the world. Domestically, the success of the Montgomery bus boycott reinforced a similar effort begun in Tallahassee, Florida, and sparked a fresh boycott in nearby Birmingham, Alabama.

In Little Rock, Arkansas, blacks seemed to be making greater progress towards desegregation. Integration had occurred in some of the state's schools, and the capital city of Little Rock had begun to implement plans for a gradual, grade by grade desegregation of its public schools The state governor was a racial moderate, Orval E. Faubus, who had defeated a rigid racist named James D. Johnson in the 1956 Democratic primary elections. Indeed, Faubus's greatest electoral support came from blacks and middle-to-upper-class whites. Less than a week before the schools opened, the Arkansas state court ordered Little Rock not to initiate the desegregation plan. A federal court overruled the state jurists, but Governor Faubus ordered the state's national guard to forbid nine black children to enter the high school. Armed with automatic rifles, the soldiers and a mob of unruly whites pelted and pushed blacks away from the schoolhouse before national television cameras. Arkansas's militant defiance of federal authority forced Eisenhower reluctantly to support the civil rights of blacks. In late September 1956, the president ordered the state's 10,000 guardsmen to submit to federal authority, and US army troops were called to disperse the angry whites blocking the high school. Little Rock schools were closed in 1958–59, and blacks did not actually attend the high school until August 1959.

By 1956, Southern white opposition to desegregation had begun to mushroom at every level of society. In Congress, North Carolina Senator Sam Ervin, Jr., drafted a racist polemic, the 'Southern Manifesto', on 12 March 1956, which vowed to fight to maintain Jim Crow by all legal means. Ervin succeeded in obtaining the support of 101 out of 128 members of Congress from the eleven original

Confederate states. In electoral politics, rabid segregationists attacked moderate to liberal New Deal Democrats as the white public shifted increasingly to the far right. Two moderate Democrats in Congress from North Carolina who did not support the Southern Manifesto were thrown out of office in the 1956 election. That same year, the white supremacy States' Rights Party collected 7.2 per cent of the popular vote in Louisiana, 17.3 per cent in Mississippi, and 29.5 per cent in South Carolina. National and state politicians in both the Democratic and Republican Parties catered to the militantly white racist trend. In a crass attempt to win some segregationist votes, Eisenhower campaigned throughout Dixie. In one South Carolina appearance, he evoked 'rebel yells' by standing smartly to attention when the band played the Confederate anthem 'Dixie'. A few Southern populists tried to resist the racist tide. In 1958, circuit judge George C. Wallace ran for governor of Alabama as a moderate on racial issues and a progressive on economic policies. His opponent, Attorney General John Patterson, campaigned as an advocate of an American-version of *apartheid*, and won easily. Wallace had received the support of the meagre black electorate, and had even won the quiet backing of the state's NAACP. In the wake of his defeat, Wallace swore, 'they out-niggered me that time, but they'll never do it again'. Four years later, Wallace won the state's gubernatorial election by taking the most extreme racist position since the capitulation of populist Tom Watson to racism a half century before. Ironically, by the 1960s, it was Wallace who personified the white South's commitment to racial bigotry, more than any other major public figure.[3]

A reign of white terror was hurled at the proponents of black freedom in the guise of new organisations and regulations. In 1955–59, White Citizens' Councils were initiated in almost every Southern city, comprised chiefly of middle-to-upper income whites in business, white-collar professions and the clergy, who vigorously opposed desegregation. In early 1956, five Southern legislatures passed at least 42 Jim Crow laws reinforcing separate black public schools. In Mississippi, state laws declared that it was illegal for a black child to enter a white primary, elementary, or secondary school. Georgia laws required that 'any school official of the state or any municipal or county schools' which 'spend tax money for public schools in which the races are mixed' was committing a felony. South Carolina's legislature publicly condemned 'the illegal encroachment of the central government' by its demands for black equality. Alabama politicians overwhelmingly voted to 'nullify' the Supreme Court's *Brown* decision for any schools within its borders. Mississippi and Louisiana even 'amended their state constitution to provide that to promote public health and morals their schools be operated separately for white and Negro children'.[4]

As the movement towards desegregation gained momentum, the measures employed by white supremacists and terrorists became more violent. In December 1951, civil rights proponents received a foretaste of events to come with the bombing in Miami, Florida, of the home of state NAACP leader Harry T. Moore. Moore was murdered in the attack, and many Christian, veterans' and civil rights agencies asked the Truman Administration to investigate the killing. But Truman, who could not be a candidate in the next election, had little political motivation to co-operate, so the Federal government did nothing. Thousands of local black leaders were threatened, arrested, intimidated and harassed. Mississippi assumed its traditional role in this respect as the South's crucible for racist violence. NAACP leaders were bludgeoned, pistol-whipped and shot at. The president of the Belzoni, Mississippi, NAACP chapter was assassinated on the city's courthouse lawn in 1955. In other Southern states, a similar pattern of overt violence occurred. Louisiana courts ordered the NAACP to halt all public meetings in the state. South Carolina legislators declared the NAACP a 'subversive organisation'. The Ku Klux Klan re-asserted itself as a powerful secret organisation, committing a series of castrations, killings, and the bombing of black homes and churches.

Woodward accurately describes this period as a time when 'all over the South the lights of reason and tolerance and moderation began to go out':

A fever of rebellion and malaise of fear spread over the region. Books were banned, libraries were purged, newspapers were slanted, magazines disappeared from stands, television programs were withheld, films were excluded. Teachers, preachers, and college professors were questioned, and many were driven out of the South. . . . Words began to shift their significance and lose their common meaning. A 'moderate' became a man who dared open his mouth, an 'extremist' one who favored eventual compliance with the law, and 'compliance' took on the connotations of treason.

Politicians who had once spoken for moderation began to vie with each other in defiance of the government.[5]

Desegregation across the South ground to a standstill. In 1958, 13 school systems were desegregated; in 1960, only 17. Despite their concessions, white racists in the government and other institutions began to perceive dimly that the forces for biracial democracy could be defeated, and that legal segregation in most civic relations might continue for many decades to come.

III

Beyond the civil rights battlefield, new trends in black culture and intellectual thought began to reveal themselves during the 1950s. For some white sociologists and cultural historians, the decade under Eisenhower and the Cold War has seemed a sterile and vacuous period of social conformity. The 'Silent Generation' of the white middle class began moving from the urban centres to the suburbs; the populace and politicians alike were preoccupied with televisions, automobiles, and other mass consumer goods. For black America, however, this conservative cultural description does not apply. In the creative arts, in literature, in intellectual work, there was a significant outpouring of energy, talent and hope for the future.

Some of the most provocative contributions to black culture occurred in literature. As early as 1937, black novelist Richard Wright, who was at the time a member of the Communist Party, predicted the new cultural directions which black writers would later pursue, in the essay, 'Blueprint for Negro Writing'. Wright declared that the real goal of black writing was political and social advocacy, 'molding the lives and consciousness of [the black] masses towards new goals'. It should not simply be 'the voice of the educated Negro pleading with white America for justice'.[6] Wright would become in many respects the seminal new Negro intellectual: breaking with the Communist Party in 1944; authoring the searing *Native Son* (1941), *Black Boy* (1945), and *The Outsider* (1953). Turning bitterly against the left during the Cold War, Wright was increasingly influenced by the European existentialist movement. From his exile in Paris during the 1950s, Wright spoke through his character Cross Damon on his fears for the oppressed:

There is no escaping what the future holds. We are going back to something earlier, maybe better, maybe worse, maybe something more terrifyingly human? These few hundred years of freedom, empire building, voting, liberty, democracy – these will be regarded as the *romantic* centuries in human history. There will be in that future no trial by jury, no writs of habeas corpus, no freedom of speech of religion – all of this being buried and not by Communists or Fascists alone, but by their opponents as well. All hands are shoveling clay onto the body of freedom before it even dies, while it lies breathing its last. . . .[7]

Most black intellectuals did not share Wright's pessimistic and even nihilistic vision of a world thrown into political chaos. Yet the generation of black writers born during the 1920s and coming into maturity during the post-war era were all influenced by his sweeping style and idealism.

The two black intellectuals most affected by Wright were undoubtedly Ralph Ellison and James Baldwin. Ellison's *Invisible Man* (1952), which evoked the existential tones of Doestoevsky and Camus, was viewed by many white critics as the most powerful fiction work written by an American in the post-war period. In *Go Tell It on the Mountain* (1953), Baldwin described the black exodus from the rural South into the North's ghettoes. After the *Brown* decision, Baldwin's considerable talent as a political critic was revealed in *Notes of a Native Son* (1955), *Nobody Knows My Name* (1960), and *The Fire Next Time* (1963). Other black novelists began to find a new audience for their work. Chester Himes' *If He Hollers, Let Him Go* (1945) discussed the intense racism of white workers levelled against blacks during World War II. Arna Bontemps, a veteran novelist of the Harlem Renaissance, a productive period of black cultural creativity in the 1920s, wrote a moving study of black adjustment in the North in *They Seek a City* (1945). Harlem novelist and cultural critic John Oliver Killens' novel of black Southern society and struggle, *Youngblood* (1954), won critical praise. As in the Harlem Renaissance, black women writers also played a critical cultural role in the 1950s. Ann Petry, a journalist in Harlem during the war, described the outrage and frustrations of inner city black youth in her first novel, *The Street* (1946). Petry subsequently produced two more novels, *Country Place* (1947), and *The Narrows* (1953), as well as a series of works for children and black teenagers.

In the field of black poetry, the two most popular intellectuals were Langston Hughes and Gwendolyn Brooks. Hughes, like Bontemps, was a product of the Harlem Renaissance, and his position as the 'poet laureate' of the Afro-American people was secure well before the 1950s. As a political progressive, Hughes could scarcely tolerate the growing climate of fear and repression which existed during the Cold War. In one poem entitled 'Un-American Investigators', Hughes revealed his long commitment to human freedom and democracy:

> The Committee's fat,
> Smug, almost secure
> Co-religionists
> Shiver with delight
> In warm manure
> As those investigated –
> Too brave to name a name –
> Have pseudonyms revealed
> In Gentile game
>   Of who,
>   Born Jew,
>   Is who?
> Is not your name Lipshitz?
>   Yes.
> Did you not change it
> For subversive purposes?
>   No.
> For nefarious gain?
>   Not so.
> Are you sure?
> The committee shivers
> With delight in
> Its manure.[8]

Brooks' first collection of poetry appeared in 1943, *A Street in Bronzeville*. Her second collection, *Annie Allen* (1949), won a Pulitzer prize in literature. Brooks' other works of the period include a short novel, *Maud Martha* (1953), two poetry volumes, *The Bean Eaters* (1960) and *Selected Poems* (1963), and a children's book, *Bronzeville Boys and Girls* (1956). Other significant black novelists and poets of the 1940s–50s included Margaret Walker; Melvin B. Tolson, author of

Heart-Shape in the Dust (1940) and *Rendezvous with America* (1944); the witty and prolific Zora Neal Hurston, author of the autobiographical *Dust Tracks on a Road* (1942), and the novels *Moses, Man of the Mountain* (1942) and *Seraph on the Suwannee* (1948); novelist Paule Marshall, *Browngirl, Brownstones* (1959); and poets Robert Hayden and Sterling A. Brown.

An even younger group of black writers emerged during the mid-to-late 1950s, born in the Depression, and developed politically during the outbreak of the Second Reconstruction. Chief among them was Lorraine Hansberry. The daughter of a prosperous, upper-middle-class black Chicago household, Hansberry attended school at the University of Wisconsin, Mexico's University of Guadalajara, and Chicago's Roosevelt University. In the mid-1950s she became a young writer for Harlem's radical *Freedom* newspaper. Her meteoric rise to prominence came with the production of her acclaimed play on the struggle of a poor black Chicago family seeking to move into a white neighbourhood, *A Raisin in the Sun* (1959). Hansberry described herself as part 'of the generation that grew up in the swirl and dash of the Sartre–Camus debate of the postwar years. The silhouette of the Western intellectual poised in hesitation before the flames of involvement was an accurate symbolism of some of my closest friends, some of whom crossed each other leaping in and out, for instance, of the Communist party'. Hansberry had come to reject Wright's existentialism as an exaltation of 'brutality and nothingness', because he had abandoned 'the reality of our struggle for freedom'. For her, and for many other young black intellectuals, the decisive human conflict was not against communism, but with Jim Crow and America's racial stereotypes of black life. Ironically, her call for a politically relevant black art echoed Wright's own 1937 essay.[9]

In black music, the post-war era also brought powerful changes to many aspects of popular culture. During the war, several 'poor, unknown and unprepossessing' black musicians developed a group that played in Harlem nightclubs – a set whose members included trumpeter Dizzy Gillespie, saxophonist Charlie Parker, and pianist Thelonius Monk. These men would revolutionise America's most creative indigenous music tradition, jazz. Before his death at the age of 35, Parker would become a living legend among musicians. As critic LeRoi Jones wrote in 1963, 'Parker was the soul and fire of the bebop era. After Parker, trumpet players, piano players, guitar players, bass players, etc., all tried to sound like him, in much the same fashion as all kinds of instrumentalists had once tried to sound like Louis Armstrong'. Both Gillespie and Monk developed popular bands which featured, at different times, Parker's worthy successor on the saxophone, the innovative stylist John Coltrane. Other brilliant black musicians making their stamp on jazz in the 1950s included trumpet soloist Miles Davis, tenor saxophonist Sonny Rollins, also saxophonist Ornette Coleman, and pianist Cecil Taylor. It cannot be emphasised too strongly that jazz played a powerful role in the cultural education of millions of young blacks and whites during this time. Listening to the beauty of Coltrane and Parker, established critics were often at a loss for words. The 'bebop' of the 1940s had given way, by the late 1950s, to an *avant-garde* described by some as 'the new music'. Coltrane was viewed in the last ten years of his brief life as a musical 'James Joyce', a man whose pre-eminence as an artist was 'being acclaimed great by fellow artists, critics and the public . . . not only while he [was] alive, but when he [was] also just *beginning* to prove that greatness concretely'.[10] For white American youth, especially from the suburban homes of the upper classes, jazz symbolised a cultural creativity they could not find within their own placid lives. It inspired the literature and lifestyle of a white 'beat' subculture which consciously rejected the 'Silent Generation's' crass materialism and political apathy. For blacks, jazz represented on the 'cultural front' what the Montgomery boycott, demonstrations and the new militant mood were in politics. It shattered established conventions; it mocked traditions; in form and grace, it transcended old boundaries to life and thought. It became the appropriate cultural background for their activities to destroy Jim Crow.

In the 1950s, the image of Africa as a cultural and political entity began to reassert its impact upon Afro-American intellectuals and artists. Prior to 1950, the general relationship between black Americans and Africans had taken three very different forms. Black Christian missionaries from the Congregationalist American Board of Commissioners for Foreign Missions had been sent to Liberia by 1821. During the nineteenth and early twentieth century, hundreds of black Baptists, Episcopalians, Methodists and Presbyterians were sent to proselytise across the continent. These religious missions served as a bridge for young Africans who came to the United States to attend universities and professional schools. During the 1920s, the militant black nationalist movement of Marcus Garvey embraced Africa as the symbolic home of all New World blacks. Garvey's organisation of several millions, the Universal Negro Improvement Association, attempted unsuccessfully to establish a beachhead in Liberia for the emigration of US and West Indian blacks. Two decades earlier, DuBois had initiated a series of political meetings between Afro-Americans, West Indians and Africans, the Pan-African Conferences of 1900, 1919, 1921, 1923, 1927 and 1945. The final conference, held in Manchester, England, brought DuBois together with some of the African intellectuals who would soon become the leaders of their nations' anti-colonialist movements. By the late 1950s, economic and political pressures had finally forced France, Belgium and England to end their direct rule over the continent. Many of the new African leaders were familiar to black American intellectuals, politicians, and civil rights leaders: Nnamdi Azikiwe of Nigeria had attended Howard University, and in 1932 received an MA degree in philosophy and religion at Lincoln University of Pennsylvania; Ghana's Kwame Nkrumah, another Lincoln University graduate, was the protegé of New World Pan-Africanist scholar/activists C. L. R. James, George Padmore and, to a lesser extent, DuBois.

Black American newspapers during the Cold War gave prominent coverage to the battle to end European colonialism. Richard Wright travelled across Africa to observe the groundswell of activism, and produced his strongest political statement from his experiences in *Black Power*. Black politicians, including Adam Clayton Powell, writers and journalists went to the conference of Third World and non-aligned nations at Bandung, Indonesia, in 1955. Hundreds of black professionals trained in the natural and social sciences emigrated to African nations to support the cause. The most significant African political events during the decade, the development of Nkrumah's Convention People's Party of Ghana and that nation's independence in 1957, and the rise of Egypt's Gamal Nasser as the leader of the Third World, influenced almost every Afro-American intellectual and activist. For King, Egypt's 1956 defiance of England seemed to have direct parallels to the US struggle for desegregation. 'They have broken loose from the Egypt of colonialism and imperialism, and they are now moving through the wilderness of adjustment toward the promised land of cultural integration', King wrote in 1957. 'As they look back they see the old order of colonialism and imperialism passing away and the new order of freedom and justice coming into being.'[11] DuBois saw Africa quite differently. In his

private correspondence with Nkrumah in 1957, he urged that
Ghana's leader should 'avoid subjection to and ownership by foreign
capitalists who seek to get rich on African labor and raw material, and
should try to build a socialism on old African communal life'. An
independent, non-aligned Africa could 'teach mankind what Non-
violence and Courtesy, Literature and Art, Music and Dancing can
do for this greedy, selfish, and war-stricken world'.[12] Even black
middle-class groups such as the NAACP, who had traditionally
eschewed any programmatic links with black Africa, began to
perceive the necessity for close co-operation. The contradiction of a
'free' Africa and their 'unfree' descendants in the US was an
immediate and important parallel which was reiterated by many civil
rights advocates.

IV

In the aftermath of the destruction of the National Negro Labor
Council, black workers had few organisational tools to protest against
the AFL–CIO's institutional racism. At the founding convention of
the merged AFL–CIO in 1955, delegates ratified Article 11 to their
constitution, which declared that the organisation would 'encourage
all workers, without regard to race, creed, color, national origin or
ancestry, to share equally in the full benefits of union organization'.
Another section of the constitution mandated the creation of a
Committee on Civil Rights which would have 'the duty and
responsibility to bring about at the earliest possible date the effective
implementation of the principle . . . of non-discrimination'. Black
delegates led by Randolph fought to obtain a greater commitment to
racial equality from the labour bureaucrats. Many pointed out that
the constitution authorised the AFL–CIO's Executive Council to
expel any labour affiliate which was 'dominated, controlled or
influenced in the conduct of its affairs' by Marxists, yet made no
comparable statement on unions which deliberately excluded blacks
from membership. AFL–CIO president George Meany opposed the
ban of overtly racist unions, and the proposal was easily defeated. At
the convention, Michael J. Quill, president of the Transport Workers
Union – CIO, condemned the constitution as 'a license for discrimination against minority groups'.[13] The delegates did attempt to make
token concessions to blacks, however, by appointing Randolph and
Willard S. Townsend, president of the United Transport Service

Employees – CIO as the only two blacks on the Executive Council. James B. Carney, Secretary-Treasurer of the CIO, was appointed to chair the AFL–CIO Committee on Civil Rights. Carney was not permitted, however, to deliver a blistering address on desegregation before the convention.[14]

In public, the white leaders of the AFL–CIO gave liberal 'lip-service' to desegregation. In April 1960, for example, Meany criticised the moderate Civil Rights Bill before Congress as an insult to 'the will of the vast majority of Americans who believe in, and wish to implement, the basic constitutional rights which properly belong to all Americans regardless of race or color or national origin'. Meany demanded that the federal authorities 'press forward vigorously in the full enforcement of civil rights laws, both old and new'.[15] Privately, it was clear to black trade unionists that Meany and many other white labour leaders would do virtually nothing to support the desegregation struggle both within organised labour and within the general society. Apologists for Meany argued that the AFL–CIO could not expel racist unions, because in the words of socialist Gus Tyler, 'the power of the Federation is moral, resting on consensus and persuasion'.[16] Even if this was the case – and the rigidly anti-communist directives on expulsion proved that it was not – it did not explain the AFL–CIO's tepid stance towards the desegregation campaigns in the South during the 1950s. The only unions which actively assisted the Montgomery bus boycott of 1955–56 were Randolph's Brotherhood of Sleeping Car Porters; several small United Auto Workers locals; the United Packinghouse Workers, District 65; and Local 1199 of New York. Southern union members played visible and active roles in the Massive Resistance. In Montgomery, the all-white Bus Drivers Union and the Montgomery Building Trades Council took part in the vigilante attacks against civil rights leaders. Southern locals refused to process grievances of black members. When AFL–CIO unions were invited to participate in Martin Luther King's 'Prayer Pilgrimage for Freedom' in Washington, DC, in May 1957, most refused or simply ignored the event.

Inside the AFL–CIO, the lack of union support for desegregation led Carney and another black member of the Civil Rights Committee to resign from their positions. The AFL–CIO did nothing, they complained, effectively to combat union racism even in the North. In Detroit, for example, a city with a major black working class population, less than 2 per cent of all apprentices in craft unions were black. Kansas City, Missouri, blacks were effectively barred from employment as steam fitters, plumbers, electricians, operating engineers, and sheet metal workers. In 1957, a black electrician in Cleveland, Ohio, was forced to sue Local 38 in an unsuccessful attempt to gain admittance. Unions aggressively removed black activists on the grounds that they were Communists or subversives. In March 1952, UAW leader Walter Reuther, a liberal proponent of desegregation, purged five militant anti-racists from leadership of Detroit's Local 600 and barred them from seeking re-election. Several industrial unions, including the Communications Workers of America and the Steelworkers Union, concluded blatantly segregationist provisions in their contracts with many factories. A number of unions continued to exclude blacks from membership, such as the Brotherhood of Railroad Trainmen, or deliberately kept black participation to a minimum. In December 1958, NAACP leader Roy Wilkins issued an open memorandum to Meany, declaring that:

> Three years after the merger agreement there is clear evidence that many unions continue discriminatory practices. . . . [Some] AFL–CIO affiliates limit Negro membership to segregated or 'auxiliary' locals. . . . Increasingly, we are receiving complaints against trade unions from our members and from Negro workers throughout the country charging racial discrimination and segregation. Careful investigation by our staff has in most instances sustained these individual charges and, in addition, has revealed a pattern of racial discrimination and segregation in many affiliate unions.[17]

Under considerable attack, Meany and other racist labour officials' actions became even more outrageous towards desegregation proponents within the unions. At the 1959 San Francisco convention of the AFL–CIO, Randolph urged that the Brotherhood of Railroad Trainmen and the Brotherhood of Locomotive Firemen and Enginemen be ordered to remove their anti-black exclusion clauses from their constitutions. Randolph also demanded that the AFL–CIO expand the programmes and effectiveness of their Civil Rights Commission. These and other anti-discrimination measures were promptly defeated. During the debate, Meany was so enraged with Randolph that he shouted, 'Who in hell appointed you as guardian of the Negro members in America?' Willie Baxter, vice president and director of civil rights of the Trade Union Leadership Conference of Detroit, responded, 'Brother Randolph was accorded this position by the acclamation of the Negro people in recognition of his having devoted almost half a century of his life in freedom's cause'.[18] Relations between Meany and Randolph, long sour, reached a new low two years later. On 12 October 1961, the Executive Council censured Randolph for creating a 'gap that has developed between organized labor and the Negro community'. In a classic instance of blaming-the-victim, Meany explained to the press that Randolph was too impatient, and that he had 'gotten close to those militant groups'. Roy Wilkins' response to Randolph's censure was shared by virtually every black American:

> The NAACP believes that the AFL–CIO's 'censure' of A. Philip Randolph is an incredible cover up . . . a refusal to recognize the unassailable facts of racial discrimination and segregation inside organized labor, as well as an evasion on the part of the AFL–CIO leadership of its own responsibility in fighting racism within affiliate unions. . . . Meany and the AFL–CIO Executive Council have not taken the required action to eliminate the broad national pattern of anti-Negro practices that continues to exist in many significant sections of the American labor movement, even after five and a half years of the merger and the endless promises to banish Jim Crow.[19]

The struggle of Randolph to uproot racism within organised labour assumed special significance in the 1950s, as the political economy of black America was being rapidly transformed. Between 1950–60, the black civilian labour force increased from 5.8 million to 6.7 million workers and 83 per cent of all black males and 48 per cent of black females over the age of 16 in 1960 were actively seeking jobs. Between 1940–60, the percentage of blacks involved in farm labour had declined sharply, 32 per cent to 8 per cent: 38 per cent of all black workers were classified as blue-collar workers, up 10 per cent in twenty years. By 1960, 9 per cent of all construction workers were black, as were 7 per cent of all manufacturing workers and 34 per cent of all employees engaged in personal services. Unions which practised a deliberate policy of racial exclusion thwarted blacks' efforts to find employment suitable to their training and talents. Blacks in unions

which excluded them from leadership positions had little incentive to
support their unions during strikes.

Many rural black families had left the South during the decade
with the expectation that their incomes and standard of living would
improve dramatically. Incomes for blue-collar jobs were higher in
Northern states, to be sure, but membership and apprentice positions
in many unions were not readily available to all black workers. In the
early post-war years, black families nationwide experienced a rise in
real incomes. Non-white median income in 1947 was $3563; by 1952,
the median income figure reached $4344, 57 per cent of white median
income of $7643. Between 1952 and 1959, the trend was towards greater
income inequality. By that later year, the black median income of
$5156 was only 52 per cent of the white median income level – roughly
where it had been in 1948. In 1959, 19 per cent of all white American
families earned over $15,000 annually, compared to 4 per cent of all
non-white families: 51 per cent of all white families earned $7000 to
$15,000 each year; for non-whites in that income range, only 29 per
cent. One-fifth of all non-white families earned a meagre median
income in 1959 of $1207, and one-third of all black families earned less
than $3000 annually, compared to 7.5 per cent for whites. Even as late
as 1962, the median income of all non-white males was below the 1960
figure.

The AFL–CIO's refusal to desegregate unions contributed in some
degree to the growing rates of unemployment among black workers in
the North in these years. During the Truman Administration,
non-white unemployment rates peaked at 9 per cent in 1950,
dropping to 5.4 per cent by 1952. Under Eisenhower, the unemployment rates for non-whites reached new highs. In the 1958 recession,
12.6 per cent of all non-white workers were unemployed, more than
twice the level experienced by whites. In 1960, 24.4 per cent of all
non-white youth in the labour force were without jobs; 802,000
non-white workers were unemployed during the year, 30 per cent of
them being laid off for more than 15 weeks. A growing army of idle
and desperate black men and women began to appear in the
industrial centres of the nation, driven to the edge of poverty. In 1960
55.9 per cent of all non-whites lived below the 'poverty level', a
Federal government index which indicates a severe lack of the income
necessary to provide food, clothing and shelter for any family. For the
1.5 million black families without a husband present, the situation
was even more severe: 65.4 per cent of such families in 1959 were

below the poverty level. Of all black female-headed households in rural areas, 82.2 per cent were also under the poverty level. Increasingly, as the economic situation worsened, blacks began to demand the inclusion of specific economic reforms within the overall goals of the civil rights struggle. It was no victory for black men to be allowed to sit in a formerly whites-only theatre or to rent hotel accommodation which had been segregated, when they had no jobs. It was cruel to permit black children to sit in all-white schools, when their mothers had no money to provide their lunches.

V

For most historians, the struggle for Negro equality since the Civil War has been characterised as an attempt at cultural assimilation on the part of blacks, into the great social mainstream of American life. Certainly part of the Afro-American struggle involved a fierce belief by many, particularly within the middle classes, that any form of racial separation was intolerable. But it would be a mistake to equate the battle against Jim Crow with a cultural affinity for the aesthetics and social norms of the Anglo-Saxon, Protestant majority. Almost every black person resisted segregation, because it was imposed upon him/her by a powerful white capitalist order. Beyond that, the black consensus for building alternative institutions which addressed the critical needs of black workers and the poor fell apart. Since the 1850s, a significant portion of the Afro-American people have tended to support the ideals of black nationalism, defined here, in part, as: a rejection of racial integration; a desire to develop all-black socio-economic institutions; an affinity for the cultural and political heritage of black Africa; a commitment to create all-black political structures to fight against white racism; a deep reluctance to participate in coalitions which involved a white majority; the advocacy of armed self-defence of the black community; and in religion and culture, an ethos and spirituality which consciously rejected the imposition of white western dogmas. At certain historical moments, such as in the 1850s and the 1920s, a majority of the black working class, rural farmers and the poor were in their political and social behaviour extremely nationalistic. Marcus Garvey was only one of a great tradition of black leaders who expressed that nationalistic tendency, and developed a political programme which won the support of thousands and in some instances millions of

advocates. By the 1950s, Garveyism had long since disappeared from
the black urban North, except in a handful of ghetto communities.
Yet the vision of Garveyites remained long after their institutions had
crumbled. Many blacks could clearly separate the fight for desegregation from a NAACP-promoted policy which might lead to the
eventual cultural and ethnic extinction of their national minority
group. Black nationalists of the post-war era were both *anti-racist and
anti-integrationist*, in the sense that they opposed Jim Crow laws and
simultaneously advocated all-black economic, political and social
institutions.

The Nation of Islam was the dominant black nationalist formation
of the period. Born in Detroit's black neighbourhoods during the
Great Depression, its creator and first 'divine' prophet was an
obscure pedlar of uncertain racial identity, W. D. Fard. After
preaching for four years an eclectic mythology of Sunni Islam
doctrine and black racial supremacy, Fard succeeded in recruiting
8000 blacks. He established the Fruit of Islam, a para-military force;
the Muslim Girls Training Class, a school specifically for women
members of the Nation; and a University of Islam. After Fard's
somewhat mysterious disappearance, his chief lieutenant Elijah
Muhammad became the leader of the religious movement. During
the 1930s, the Nation declined in membership, and by 1945 only four
Muslim temples and about 1000 adherents were still followers of
Muhammad. At this point, an event intervened which greatly
accelerated the growth of the Nation. Muhammad was convicted and
imprisoned briefly during World War II for resisting the draft. While
in a federal penitentiary, Muhammad recognised that black churches
and civil rights organisations had no programmes to recruit and to
transform the most oppressed members of the race: convicts, dope
addicts, pimps, young delinquents, prostitutes, criminals, and the
permanently unemployed. During the post-war period, the efforts of
the Nation shifted towards these lower-income strata. The results
were astonishing: by 1960, the Nation's membership was between
65,000 to 100,000 nationwide. Under Muhammad's tight discipline
and pro-black nationalist creed, thousands of drug addicts quit their
dependence on narcotics; prostitutes in the Nation were transformed
into so-called 'respectable women'. Educational and social programmes directed at ghetto youth also produced similar results. By
1960, over three-fourths of the Nation's members were between 17 to
35 years-old. Members donated one-quarter to one-third of their

annual incomes to the Nation, which was used to construct Islamic schools, temples, and businesses. In Chicago alone, the Nation owned half a million dollars' worth of real estate by 1960. The political programme of the group provided a striking contrast to that of the NAACP: racial separation; the ultimate creation of an all-black nation state; and capitalist economic development along racial lines.

The Nation's success during these years was also attributable to Muhammad's recruitment of a gifted and very charismatic spokesman named Malcolm Little. Converted to the Nation of Islam while in prison, Little had been a pimp and small-time criminal in the Boston and New York City ghettoes. Leaving prison in 1952, Little was renamed Malcolm X – the 'X' symbolically repudiating the 'white man's name'. Muhammad carefully nurtured Malcolm X's career upwards into the organisation's hierarchy. By 1954 Malcolm X became the minister of Harlem's Temple No. 7. Travelling across the country, Malcolm X was the articulate mouthpiece, as Aaron was for Moses, in a sense, to deliver the 'truth' to the race. Political leaders began to relate to the Muslims, recognising that Muhammad's absolute control over so many thousands of voters represented an important political bloc. Adam Clayton Powell attended a 'Leadership Conference' staged by Malcolm X in Harlem in January 1960. The leader of the Cuban Revolution, Fidel Castro, met with Malcolm X in a private discussion during his travels to the US that same year. Simultaneously, the FBI, and state and local police began to infiltrate the Nation, keeping closer surveillance of its actions.

As the Nation of Islam prospered, white liberals and Negro integrationists alike became fearful of the movement's stunning success in attracting lower-class blacks. Scholars studied the Nation, and drew parallels with the rise of fascism and anti-semitism in Europe. White sociologist Gordon W. Allport described the Nation as 'the hate that hate produced', a racial supremacist cult similar to 'Hitler [and] the White Citizens' Council'. In C. Eric Lincoln's *The Black Muslims in America*, the black social philosopher expressed concern that 'the Black Muslims' virulent attacks on the white man' might 'threaten the security of the white majority and lead those in power to tighten the barriers which already divide America'.[20] Civil rights leaders committed to racial assimilation were appalled by the Nation. In August 1959, Roy Wilkins of the NAACP declared that the Muslims had a 'hate-white doctrine' which was 'as dangerous as [any] group' of white racists. The Nation was clearly 'furnishing ammunition for the use' of white supremacists. NAACP chief counsel Thurgood Marshall, speaking at Princeton University, stated that the Nation of Islam was 'run by a bunch of thugs organized from prisons and jails, and financed, I am sure, by Nasser or some Arab group'.[21] James Farmer of CORE denounced the Nation as 'utterly impractical' and dangerous. 'After the black culture was taken away from us, we had to adapt the culture that was here, adopt it, and adapt to it.' By rejecting integration, Farmer reasoned, the Muslims were aiding Jim Crow. With a surer grasp of racial history, Malcolm X responded to these criticims. 'We who are Muslims, followers of the honorable Elijah Muhammad', he explained, 'don't think that an integrated cup of coffee is sufficient payment for 310 years of slave labor.' Malcolm X made the simple distinction between desegregation and integration which Farmer, Randolph, Wilkins, Marshall and other Negro leaders could never grasp. 'It is not a case of [dark mankind] wanting integration or separation, it is a case of wanting freedom, justice, and equality. It is not integration that Negroes in America want, it is human dignity.'[22]

The black nationalist current which Elijah Muhammad and Malcolm X had generated could not be contained in the Nation of Islam. Within a few local branches of the NAACP, similar tendencies developed. Robert Williams, an ex-marine and black militant, had become the leader of the Monroe, North Carolina, NAACP chapter. Viewing King's non-violent campaigns as ineffectual, he preached that the racist order would have to be overthrown with force. Blacks must 'convict their attackers on the spot. They must meet violence with violence', he told the press in May 1959. Within one month, the NAACP suspended Williams for six months for making statements which could 'be used by segregationists to spread the false impression that the NAACP supported lynching and violence'. Williams' response was that 'Negroes should have the right of armed self-defense against attack'.[23] Eventually expelled by Wilkins from the NAACP, Williams organised a militant local group. He saved the lives of 17 passive demonstrators who were threatened at Monroe's county courthouse by armed gangs of white racists. After a series of confrontations, Williams and his family fled to Canada, and finally received political asylum in Cuba. For many young blacks, Williams' bitter denunciations of racism and the placid Negro middle-class leadership were inspirational and provocative. As Williams observed, 'the forces with a vested interest in the equilibrium of the US master-slave society . . . are more than willing to point out to our miserably exploited and dehumanized masses that violent resistance and self-defense will mean total annihilation and extermination. This is in itself an unwitting admission of the beastly nature of the oppressor.'[24] The NAACP could banish Williams, but they could not silence him; neither could they stop the escalation of nationalist sentiment within the black rural South and urban North. With every white racist atrocity, the black nationalists' supporters grew; for every failure of the Federal government in protecting blacks' lives and liberties, the black reaction to white authority became more refined; with every press statement of Wilkins and Randolph calling for black passivism and restraint, more blacks were recruited into the Nation of Islam.

VI

It is not an historical accident that the demand for racial reform in the late 1950s paralleled the temporary decline of the Cold War. Civil rights workers in the South were constantly 'red-baited', but by Eisenhower's second presidential term in office (1957–61) the international climate of superpower confrontation had diminished to a degree. Desegregation advocates were not generally anti-capitalists, and the fierce anti-communism of Wilkins, Randolph and other Negro spokespersons made their views somewhat more acceptable to corporate and political power brokers. The Red Scare had silenced the black left, and had made the NAACP and Urban League less 'relevant', to use the expression current at the time, to many younger black activists. Eisenhower had done little to advance the cause of desegregation, activists argued, and moderate civil rights organisations had indirectly contributed to the reaction against racial justice by failing to advance a more 'direct-action' oriented programme.

One issue on which all major tendencies of the black movement could agree was the importance of the forthcoming presidential election of 1960. The two major candidates, Republican Vice President Richard M. Nixon of California and Democratic Senator John F. Kennedy of Massachusetts, were both remarkably alike. Elected to Congress in 1946, both became militant red-baiters on the House Committee on Education and Labor, chaired by McCarthyite Fred Hartley. Nixon excelled Kennedy in his opportunistic denouncement of the red menace, and as a result, rose to political power much more rapidly than the Cold War Democrat. In his successful bid for a California senate seat in 1950, Nixon pilloried liberal Democratic Congresswoman Helen Gahagan Douglass as a Communist Party sympathiser. From 1953–61 he served as vice president under Eisenhower. During his fourteen years in national politics, he acquired the popular epithet 'Tricky Dick' for his endless attacks against liberals, leftists, and the trade unions. In his central position at HUAC, for example, he fumed at one point that one suspected 'red' ought to be 'boiled in oil'.[25] Kennedy was only marginally to the left of Nixon on most issues, and in his actual international policies was more of an anti-communist.

Most political observers in the fall of 1960 thought that Nixon, who was the more widely known, should defeat the two-term Democratic Senator. Kennedy was 'a member of an emergent Irish upper class in America'. A Catholic, he was close to certain Eastern corporate interests, including the influential Committee for Economic Development, and the 'Ivy League'-trained intelligentsia.[26] The white South was traditionally anti-Catholic, and Kennedy's failure to protest against the Civil Rights Acts of 1957 and 1960 undermined traditional Democratic support he would have received in the region.

Black staff workers in Kennedy's campaign urged the Senator to assume Truman's strategy of 1948 by appealing directly to black voters. The Senator attacked the Republicans for perpetuating segregation in public housing, although as president, Kennedy would not pursue this issue for almost two years. He campaigned in urban areas with heavy concentrations of black voters. As in 1948, most civil rights leaders favoured the Democratic candidate, and the NAACP actively registered thousands of black voters. Several weeks before the election took place, King was sentenced to four months in prison for leading a non-violent protest in downtown Atlanta. Kennedy wisely telephoned King's wife, Coretta, and offered his support. Robert F. Kennedy, the Senator's chief strategist, used his influence to obtain King's release. This event, more than anything else, won the presidency for Kennedy. In most cities and states, three-fourths of all black votes went to the Democratic nominee. In Mobile, Alabama, 72.2 per cent of the blacks voted for Kennedy, while only 36.2 per cent of upper-income whites had supported him. In Houston, 85.3 per cent of all blacks and 50.8 per cent of the low-income whites favoured Kennedy, compared to only 16.7 per cent of the suburban white voters. In several states, the overwhelming black mandate made the difference in the electoral vote. In Illinois, for example, with black voters casting 250,000 ballots for Kennedy, the Democrat carried the state by merely 9000 votes. Since Kennedy's popular margin over Nixon was only 100,000 votes out of 68.8 million total votes, it seemed clear that the new administration would have to commit itself aggressively to the cause of desegregation.

Given America's racist history, it is not surprising that Kennedy fell far short of blacks' expectations. Kennedy pleased the black élite by nominating Thurgood Marshall to the New York Circuit Court. Black journalist Carl Rowan was named Deputy Assistant Secretary of State. Other blacks in the new administration included Robert Weaver, director of the Housing and Home Finance Agency; Mercer Cook, Ambassador to Norway; and George L. P. Weaver, Assistant Secretary of Labor. Publicly, Kennedy supported the gradual desegregation of American society, but he took few concrete steps at first to promote civil rights. Indeed, almost all of Kennedy's initial appointments to federal district courts in the Southern states were either uniformly hard-line racists or quiet proponents of Massive Resistance. This action made it difficult if not impossible for Southern blacks and civil rights activists to appeal to the federal courts for prompt justice. The administration did little to attack the South's opposition to blacks voting or registering. Cold War Liberalism, under Truman and later Kennedy, offered blacks only token concessions in the battle with Jim Crow. This recognition, by 1960, led to a new and more militant campaign to end racist hegemony over black people.

4. We Shall Overcome, 1960–1965

> We will soon wear you down by our capacity to suffer, and in winning our freedom we will so appeal to your heart and conscience that we will win you in the process.
>
> Martin Luther King, Jr.

> Ain't gonna let nobody turn me 'round
> turn me 'round, turn me 'round,
> Ain't gonna let nobody turn me 'round
> I'm gonna keep on walkin', keep on a-talkin'
> Marching up to freedom land.
>
> SNCC workers' song, summer, 1962

> When the Constitution said all men are created equal, it wasn't talking about niggers.
>
> J. B. Stoner, white racist leader

I

The Second Reconstruction actually began in earnest on the afternoon of 1 February 1960. Four young black students from North Carolina Agricultural and Technical College, Joseph McNeil, David Richmond, Franklin McCain and Izell Blair, sat at a drugstore lunchcounter in the 'whites only' section. Politely, but firmly, they refused to move until the store was closed. The next day about 30 students joined the desegregation protest, in what would become known as a 'sit-in'. On 3 February, over 50 black students and 3 white students participated in the demonstration. News of this form of non-violent, direct action protest spread quickly across North

→ *origins and emergence of SNCC*

Carolina, and then over the country. Within a week, sit-ins were being staged or planned in High Point, Charlotte, Winston-Salem, Elizabeth City, Concord and other North Carolina cities and towns. By the last week of February black students held sit-ins in Richmond, Virginia; Tallahassee, Florida; Baltimore, Maryland; Nashville and Chattanooga, Tennessee, and in two dozen or more cities in Southern and border states. The student revolt of February 1960 was, for the NAACP leadership, a completely unpredicted event. As historians August Meier and Elliott Rudwick observed, the early sit-ins

> speeded up incalculably the rate of social change in the sphere of race relations; broke decisively the NAACP's hegemony in the civil rights arena and inaugurated a period of unprecedented rivalry among the racial advancement groups; and made nonviolent direct action the dominant strategy in the struggle for racial equality during the next half-decade.[1]

With the spring of the year, the number of sit-ins rapidly increased. New forms of non-violent direct action protests using the Greensboro strategy developed: stand-ins at theatres refusing to sell tickets to blacks; wade-ins at municipal pools and segregated beaches; pray-ins at Jim Crow churches. By April 1960, 50,000 black and white students had joined the sit-in movement. A core of new activists emerged from the campuses in the process. The son of a noted black educator, Julian Bond, co-ordinated a major sit-in action, by closing down ten of Atlanta's major restaurants on 15 March. A Harvard graduate student majoring in mathematical logic, Bob Moses, travelled south to become part of the demonstrations in Newport News, Virginia. Ruby Doris Smith, a 17-year-old undergraduate at Spelman College in Atlanta, quickly assumed a leadership role among her peers. Marion Barry, Paul LePrad, Diane Nash and John Lewis left Fisk University's campus to lead the desegregation campaign in Nashville. Other prominent student leaders included Charles Jones of Charlotte, North Carolina; Charles Sherrod of Virginia Union University, Richmond, Virginia; and Chuck McDew of South Carolina State College, Orangeburg, South Carolina. Northern students responded favourably to the demonstrations by holding sympathy rallies. The students who engaged in the protests evoked different kinds of responses from local whites. In some cities, whites offered little or no direct resistance, and after a period of demonstrations, agreed to modify or abolish segregation practices in public accommodations. In many other instances, however, whites were bewildered and outraged. Non-violent black protestors were beaten and cut with razors and knives; hot cigarettes and cigars were burned into their arms and faces; they were spat upon and kicked to the floor; policemen locked them by the thousands into cramped, unsanitary jails. What is truly astonishing, given the white South's near-universal commitment to Massive Resistance, is that the number of students who were permanently injured or crippled was comparatively small.

It was inevitable that the leaders of the growing student movement would attempt to co-ordinate strategies and tactics on a national scale. Ella Baker, the perceptive and courageous executive director of King's Southern Christian Leadership Conference (SCLC), sponsored the founding meeting of what became the Student Nonviolent Coordinating Committee (SNCC) on 16–18 April 1960, in Raleigh, North Carolina. Barry was elected chairman of the new group, and in the next four months, Moses, Bond, and the other Fisk student leaders became dominant figures in SNCC. Like most of the NAACP and Urban League leaders, SNCC members were afflicted with an anti-leftist political bias which influenced them to resist any aid from socialists or radicals. At the 14–16 October SNCC conference in Atlanta, for instance, Bayard Rustin's 'radical' identification with social democracy so worried key student organisers that his invitation to speak there was rescinded. It was only in mid-1961 that SNCC accepted a grant of $5000 from the progressive Southern Conference Educational Fund through the intervention of socialist Southern activist Anne Braden. Coming of political age ten years after the silencing of DuBois and Robeson, the mostly lower-to-middle-class black students in SNCC had no identification with traditional black working-class struggles. They could not comprehend the meaning of the Cold War, the capitulation of the NAACP to the anti-communist Red Scare, and the devastation of legitimate black activism during the 1950s. They were, at this point, militant reformers and not revolutionaries, much like the black freedmen and politicians of the First Reconstruction. As participant Debbie Louis writes, 'their perspective was toward ending segregation. Their involvement from the very beginning was based on a decision that this equality was important enough to suffer heavily for. . . .' The students 'were motivated by a determination to secure the means for their own economic and social mobility, which in the circumstance clearly necessitated a direct assault on the tradition and law which limited them absolutely'.[2]

From other quarters, the NAACP was also challenged into action by the renaissance of CORE. At the high point of the Cold War, CORE had almost ceased to exist. Gradually, local chapters began to be restructured, new members were recruited, and some level of activism developed. CORE's Los Angeles chapter, which contained only ten members in 1955, initiated a modest but successful local effort to win jobs for black barbers and clerks. In 1958 Nashville's CORE provided leadership in the city's school desegregation efforts. In 1959 CORE co-sponsored a non-violent protest in Richmond, Virginia. Small CORE chapters in South Carolina had staged boycotts against racist local merchants. In St. Louis, CORE activist William Clay led the black community's efforts to win desegregation in public accommodations. From 1958 to 1960 the number of CORE locals increased from 8 to 19, and the number of individuals providing financial support to the organisation had grown from 4500 to 12,000. When the sit-in movement began, therefore, CORE was in a position to provide immediate support and direction. On 12 February, just twelve days after the first Greensboro demonstration, every CORE chapter across the country picketed drug and retail stores who allowed segregated services in their Southern-based facilities. North Carolina CORE activist Floyd McKissick led non-violent workshops across the state. Unrestrained by the gradualistic directives of the NAACP, Tallahassee CORE leaders led local blacks to wage the first 'jail-in' – filling the city's jails with large numbers of black and white demonstrators, during February 1960.

CORE's next move was to revise its tactics of 1948 to the 1960s – the 'Freedom Rides'. In December 1960, the Supreme Court ruled in *Boynton v. Virginia* that racial segregation was illegal on all interstate buses and trains, and in transportation terminals. James Farmer assumed the post as CORE's national director in February 1961, and soon began to plan for another 'journey of reconciliation'. Thirteen persons, including Farmer and SNCC activist John Lewis, travelled into the South, leaving Washington, DC on 4 May 1961. Predictably, the biracial group encountered violent resistance. Lewis and another Freedom Rider were assaulted in Rock Hill, South Carolina on 9 May. White mobs in Anniston, Alabama, attacked and burned one bus. In Montgomery, Alabama, white racists pulled Freedom Riders off the bus and administered a brutal beating. In Jackson, Mississippi, Farmer and a group of 26 other Freedom Riders representing SNCC and SCLC were given 67-day jail sentences for sitting in the whites-only sections of the city's bus depot. Farmer's jail term served to mobilise every CORE chapter; hundreds made the journey south to join the Freedom Rides. By July, CORE had spent almost $140,000 on bail and legal fees. Despite the legal burden, the Freedom Rides established CORE's credentials as a militant force for desegregation, winning for the group the enthusiastic support of SNCC and the grudging respect of the NAACP. From fiscal 1960–61 to 1961–62, CORE's national income soared from $240,000 to over $600,000; membership climbed from 26,000 in May 1961 to 52,000 in December 1962. By late 1961, CORE had established chapters in the most segregated counties of the Deep South, and the organisation was mounting a series of non-violent protests, pickets and activities in dozens of rural areas.

The desegregation battles of the early 1960s were conceived, planned, and carried out by young people – and all the impatience and idealism which characterises youth was an organic and integral aspect of this campaign for racial justice. Farmer, 41-years-old when the Freedom Rides began, was viewed by black students as a veritable sage and 'distinguished elder'. King was only 31, but even he seemed rather remote from the mind and mood that simmered across the black college campuses. The vast majority of black youth who were arrested, imprisoned and beaten were teenagers, or scarcely into their twenties. They viewed the legalistic manoeuvres of the NAACP with a politely hidden contempt, and judged the Urban League as being in the 'enemy's camp'. They knew little, if anything, of DuBois, the National Negro Congress, the 1941 March on Washington Movement, or Randolph's futile battles in the AFL–CIO. Many young whites who joined the sit-ins came from parents who had been members of the Socialist and Communist Parties. Others came from upper-class suburban homes, and had turned against the pampered affluence which their parents had showered upon them as children. They saw what blacks had always understood: the hypocrisy, the contradiction of America's democracy which was based upon the continued subjugation of the Negro. 'They captured and held on to the traditional democratic ideals they had been taught, eliminating the inconsistencies between doctrine and reality that they felt had crept into the preceding generation's practical values in relation to those ideals.'[3] Thus, racial reform in the South was not an aberration of bourgeois democracy; it was its fulfilment. Sit-ins were no rejection of the American Dream; they were the necessary although ambiguous steps taken towards its culmination. Historian Vincent Harding writes of this generation in the following manner:

> They were believers. When they sang in jail, in mass meetings, in front of policemen and state troopers, 'We Shall Overcome,' they meant it. Few were certain about details, but they *would* overcome. Vaguely, overcoming meant 'freedom' and 'rights' and 'dignity' and 'justice', and black and white together, and many other things that people in a movement feel more than they define. But they knew they were part of a revolution, and they believed that if they only persisted in courage, determination, and willingness to suffer, they would make it over.[4]

II

If the movement seemed at times to be a modern great awakening, or revival of the spirit, this was due in part to the religious character of its leadership. At every level of organisation, and in almost every small town where sit-ins or jail-ins occurred, black ministers were at the very centre of the struggle. In Tallahassee, the Reverend C. K. Steele had founded the Inter-Civic Council, a desegregation coalition which was designed after King's original Montgomery Improvement Association. Black minister and historian Vincent Harding led a prayer vigil at Atlanta's City Hall to protest against the vicious beating of Mrs Coretta Scott King, which resulted in her miscarriage. The Reverend C. T. Vivian of Chattanooga was a prominent SCLC organiser across Tennessee. The Reverend Walter Fauntroy supported desegregation activities by directing SCLC's Washington, DC bureau office. The Reverend Wyatt Tee Walker, the articulate black Baptist leader of Petersburg, Virginia, served as SCLC's executive director for a time, and was a constant thorn in the sides of his state's racist politicians. Fred Shuttlesworth of Birmingham; William Holmes Borders of Atlanta; Ralph David Abernathy of Montgomery and Atlanta, Kelly Miller Smith of Nashville; and Matthew McCollum of Orangeburg, South Carolina, were only a small part of the hundreds of black preachers and divinity students who repeatedly, sometimes daily, risked their lives in the concerted effort to destroy Jim Crow.

Despite the vital contributions of the black clergy, SNCC stood alone in its unselfish determination to confront the segregationist power structure. By the early summer of 1960, at the suggestion of Rustin, Bob Moses led the development of a voter registration project in Pike County, Alabama. In 1961–62 SNCC joined forces with the NAACP, SCLC and other black groups in Albany, Georgia, to create the Albany Movement for desegregation. Despite the prominent participation of King, Abernathy and other SCLC leaders, the young SNCC workers – James Forman, Norma Collins, Bill Hansen, Charles Sherrod, Cordell Reagon, and many others – distinguished themselves by their willingness to defy the segregation laws, to mobilise poor and working-class blacks in non-violent demonstrations and to go to jail for their principles. It is very difficult, in retrospect, to comprehend the sheer courage of these black teenagers and young adults. Veterans of the Freedom Rides and the bloody Albany campaign, tested repeatedly, freely acknowledged the pre-eminent will to resist that fashioned SNCC members into the 'True Believers' of the struggle. Let two examples illustrate this. On 30 April 1962, Diane Nash Bevel, who had married activist James Bevel the year before, stood before a Mississippi court on charges of contributing to 'juvenile delinquency' – she had taught black teenagers in McComb, Mississippi, techniques needed for non-violent demonstrations. Deliberately, she sat in the 'whites-only' section of the courtroom. The angry judge sentenced the pregnant woman to serve ten days in the local jail for that single act of defiance. Nash responded, 'I believe that if I go to jail now it may help hasten that day when my child and all children will be free – not only on the day of their birth but for all of their lives'.[5] Deep in the heart of Mississippi, Bob Moses helped to create the Council of Federated Organizations (COFO), a coalition of CORE, NAACP and SNCC organisers. Tirelessly, Moses organised voter registration drives in the face of tremendous white resistance. As one black Mississippi resident stated: 'Poor Bob took a lot of beatings, I just couldn't understand what Bob Moses was. Sometimes I think he was Moses in the Bible. He pioneered the way for black people. . . . He had more guts than any one man I've ever known.'[6]

After Albany and the Freedom Rides, the focus of political struggle shifted back towards implementing desegregation in the universities.

Black Mississippi resident James Meredith was refused admission into the segregated University of Mississippi in January 1961. Supported by NAACP attorneys, Meredith managed to overturn the state's segregation restrictions in the federal court of appeals. Supreme Court Justice Hugo L. Black, a native of Alabama, ordered Mississippi governor Ross Barnett and the state courts to allow Meredith to enrol. On 24 September 1962, Barnett declared to the press that any federal officers attempting to assist Meredith would be arrested by state police. The next day, the governor personally blocked Meredith from gaining admission to register in the university. The Kennedy Administration was finally compelled, in the light of this blatant defiance of federal authority, to call 320 federal marshals into Oxford, Mississippi, to gain Meredith's enrolment. On Sunday afternoon, 1 October, the marshals escorted Meredith into a dormitory hall on the campus. Within hours, several thousand racists attacked the federal marshals with shotguns, clubs, broken glass, and home-made bombs. Kennedy had seriously underestimated the brutality of the South, and that night he commanded 1400 troops at Fort Dix and Fort Bragg to disperse the white vigilantes. By dawn, almost 2500 soldiers were stationed in Oxford, but the damage done by the mob was considerable. Two people were killed, 166 marshals and 210 demonstrators were injured, and dozens of automobiles had been destroyed. To ensure the peace, 300 soldiers were stationed at 'Ole Miss' for a year. Meredith was finally allowed to attend the institution. To white Southerners, the 'Battle of Oxford' was a grievous insult and a gross example of federal intervention over the states' traditional rights to segregate 'niggers' from their institutions of higher learning. They blamed King, SNCC, and other so-called 'Communist-inspired' groups for the violence. Northern Democrats and many liberal Republicans were now more repulsed by the South's Massive Resistance, and urged the Kennedy Administration to develop legislation which would force the South to accept desegregation. After the Battle of Oxford, it was clear that Kennedy, who had at first tried to placate both the racists and the desegregationists simultaneously, had to make a decision which side to support.

Meanwhile, the successes achieved by the civil rights forces spawned new types of protest manoeuvres in the North as well as the South, and in turn, generated serious disagreements over strategies and tactics necessary to win desegregation. In the South, CORE locals co-operated closely with SNCC in mounting voter education and registration campaigns. In New Haven, Connecticut, CORE activists led by a 27-year-old worker, Blyden Jackson, staged the first 'sit-outs' – demonstrations wherein blacks in dilapidated public residential units and slums blocked the city's sidewalks in efforts to obtain adequate housing reforms. Seattle, Washington, CORE members picketed a local supermarket in October 1961, and secured employment for five blacks. CORE locals in East St Louis, Illinois, Kansas City, Missouri, Rochester, New York and other cities mobilised blacks to protest against police brutality in their cities. As the focus of CORE shifted towards 'non Southern issues' such as housing and police violence in the North, many members began seriously to question the formation's long-held commitment to Gandhian non-violence. CORE chapters in Cleveland, Ohio and Greensboro, North Carolina, rejected Farmer's protests by supporting a defence committee for Robert Williams. CORE chapters in Hartford, Connecticut, Baltimore, Maryland, New Orleans, Louisiana and at least four other major locals developed close organisational and programmatic links with the Nation of Islam and its fiery spokesperson, Malcolm X. San Francisco CORE held workshops discussing black nationalism in 1962, and many new black recruits of CORE were not sympathetic to the ideal of cultural integration with whites. Partially because of CORE's internal shift in priorities, it soon came under the criticism of the NAACP for being too aggressive and unwilling to compromise with white corporate and political leaders. With some desperation, Farmer admitted at the 1962 CORE convention: 'We no longer are a tight fellowship of a few dedicated advocates of a brilliant new method of social change; we are now a large family spawned by the union of the method-oriented pioneers and the righteously indignant ends-oriented militants'.[7] Black attorney Floyd McKissick was elected national chairman of CORE in 1963, and new CORE leaders Ruth Turner of Cleveland and Harold Brown of San Diego revealed clear sympathies towards a Malcolm X-type militancy and nationalism. The biracial pacifist collective was becoming rapidly more black in constituency and ideology.

   SNCC also began to experience ideological and programmatic growing pains at this juncture. The essence of any social theory evolves from concrete practice. Since SNCC was, admittedly, the real vanguard of the gritty desegregation and voter registration efforts, it was inevitable that the most advanced theoretical positions would emerge from these young people. The idealism of the early years had worn away quickly. By mid-1962, some SCLC leaders in Albany, Georgia, were attempting to moderate SNCC's militant role in the town's desegregation actions. SNCC activists complained about the overwhelming television attention riveted on King, at the expense of local conditions and personalities. King was privately termed 'De Lawd' at this time, a symbolic media figure who actually did little nuts-and-bolts organising at the constant risk of his own life. By 1963, SNCC activists had repeatedly been the targets for murder across the region. SNCC offices were firebombed; SNCC workers were attacked with shotgun blasts, pistols and chains; SNCC organiser Jimmy Travis was attacked by whites armed with machine guns in Greenwood, Mississippi. Southern legislators proclaimed wildly that SNCC was simply a Marxist revolutionary formation, determined to destroy American capitalism and the social institutions of order. Increasingly, Forman urged SNCC leaders to engage in the study of socialist texts, and to learn more about the Cuban revolution and the concurrent African liberation struggles. Rapidly, SNCC lost its initial reluctance to work with avowed Marxists, although few students had ever really read or understood socialist or communist doctrines. In 1963, when King dismissed a key white aide, Jack O'Dell, when the FBI discovered and publicised his previous connections with the Communist Party, many SNCC radicals were outraged. One rising SNCC activist, Stokely Carmichael, charged that King and other Negro moderates must 'stop taking a defensive stand on communism'.[8] Like CORE's militants, many blacks began to question the utility or even the necessity of white participation in their organisation. SNCC's repeated attacks on the milktoast Kennedy Administration embarrassed and humiliated the older and more conservative civil rights leaders. As SNCC matured, it became clear that the students would have to confront their own theoretical and organisational dilemmas at some future point.

III

The dramatic highpoint of the desegregation movement was achieved in 1963. In three difficult years, the Southern struggle had grown from a modest group of black students demonstrating peacefully at one lunchcounter to the largest mass movement for racial reform and civil rights in the twentieth century. Between autumn 1961 and the spring of 1963, 20,000 men, women and children had been arrested. In 1963 alone another 15,000 were imprisoned; 1000 desegregation protests occurred across the region, in more than 100 cities. Above all else, two significant actions during that year stand out – the desegregation campaign in 'America's Johannesburg', Birmingham, Alabama; and the March on Washington, DC.

For decades, Birmingham had represented the citadel of white supremacy. No black resident was ever secure from the wide sweep of white terrorism – institutional and vigilante. White police officers in the city casually picked up black women pedestrians and raped them at gun-point. Throughout the 1950s, black homes and churches were bombed. In April 1959, a black Baptist preacher was kidnapped by the Klan and beaten senseless with tyre chains. Every aspect of cultural, social and economic life in the town was strictly segregated. Birmingham itself 'conjured up all the worst images of southern white urban racism', Vincent Harding notes. 'Unyielding white supremacy, blatant segregation, brutal police, easily organized white mobs, and unresponsive elected officials. . . . Every black person seemed to know someone who had been beaten, bombed, raped, or murdered in Birmingham.'[9] For years, civil rights activists had conceived the plans for attacking Birmingham's Jim Crow laws. In May 1961, Freedom Riders had been threatened and arrested by the city's unrelenting, segregationist police chief, Eugene 'Bull' Conner. Conditions had become even worse with the election of Wallace as the state's governor in 1962. Upon taking his oath of office, the populist-turned-white-supremacist vowed that the Federal government would never dictate racial policies in his state. 'I draw the line in the dust and toss the gauntlet before the feet of tyranny and I say segregation now, segregation tomorrow, segregation forever.'[10] In May 1962, the Reverend Fred Shuttlesworth convinced other SCLC leaders that the time to tackle the most segregated city in the nation had now arrived.

The first organisational tasks in preparing for the demonstrations were given to Wyatt Walker. In January and February, he took careful notes on almost every public building, commercial establishment, and street in the downtown area. Wyatt also recruited 250 persons who were committed to engage in non-violent actions and to go to the city jail. On 3 April 1963, the desegregation campaign began. Sit-ins were held at department stores and restaurants. On 6 April, the Reverend A. D. King and 42 other marchers were arrested for holding a vigil at the town hall. 'Bull' Conner attempted to undercut the actions by closing all public parks and playgrounds. On 10 April, four days before Easter, King, Abernathy and other leaders spoke to a massive church rally. King openly castigated the black preachers who had ignored the demonstrations. 'I'm tired of preachers riding around in big cars, living in fine homes, but not willing to take their part in the fight. If you can't stand up with your people, you are not fit to be a leader!' King urged every black person to stand up for freedom now. 'We are winning the struggle for which we have sacrificed, but we must even be ready to die to be free, if that is what's necessary. Birmingham must put its house in order', King declared. 'It's better to go to jail in dignity than accept segregation in humility.' Abernathy rose to his feet, asking the congregation, 'Who'll volunteer to go to jail with me and Martin. . . ?'[11] Men, women and children surged forward, hands upraised, tears in their eyes, singing and praying. King and Abernathy were arrested on Good Friday; marchers on Easter Sunday were clubbed and taken into custody. On 2 May, Bevel co-ordinated a children's march involving 6000 black youngsters from the ages of 6 to 16. Before national television cameras, Brimingham police let loose vicious police dogs on children as they knelt to pray; 959 children were arrested and jailed. Police used firehoses, dogs and clubs against pregnant women, children, and the elderly. Across the world, humanity was repulsed by the sickening spectacle of American racism, the reality of white democracy.

In April, eight moderate white Birmingham ministers denounced King for what they perceived as his 'impatience' with white segregationists. They went so far as to applaud 'Bull' Conner and his armed thugs for employing 'restraint in maintaining order'. The ministers 'strongly urged our own Negro community to withdraw support from these demonstrations'.[12] King's response was one of the most eloquent essays written in American history, the famous 'Letter from Birmingham Jail'. Writing from his jail cell on 16 April, King observed that the ministers and other white moderates were contributing to segregation by their blind inertia. 'The Negro's greatest stumbling block in the stride toward freedom is not the . . . Ku Klux Klanner, but the white moderate who is more devoted to "order" than to justice . . . who constantly says "I agree with you in the goal you seek, but I can't agree with your methods of direct action"; who paternalistically feels that he can set the timetable for another man's freedom', King declared. The purpose of non-violent action was not

AND
OVERLEAF

to evade or to defy the law. 'One who breaks an unjust law must do it openly, lovingly', King insisted. 'I submit then an individual who breaks a law that conscience tells him is unjust, and willingly accepts the penalty by staying in jail to arouse the conscience of the community over its injustice, is in reality expressing the very highest respect for law.' Perhaps King's most effective criticism was his insistence that the Negro could no longer 'wait' to be freed by benevolent whites:

We have waited for more than 340 years for our constitutional and God-given rights. The nations of Asia and Africa are moving with jetlike speed toward gaining political independence, but we still creep at horse-and-buggy pace toward gaining a cup of coffee at a lunch counter. Perhaps it is easy for those who have never felt the stinging darts of segregation to say, 'Wait.' But when you have seen vicious mobs lynch your mothers and fathers at will and drown your sisters and brothers at whim; when you have seen hate-filled policemen curse, kick and even kill your black brothers and sisters; when you see the vast majority of your twenty million Negro brothers smothering in an airtight cage of poverty in the midst of an affluent society; when you suddenly find your tongue twisted and your speech stammering as you seek to explain to your six-year-old daughter why she can't go to the public amusement park that has just been advertised on television, and see tears welling up in her eyes when she is told that Funtown is closed to colored children, and see ominous clouds of inferiority beginning to form in her little mental sky, and see her begin to distort her personality by an unconscious developing bitterness toward white people; when you have to concoct an answer for a five-year-old son who is asking 'Daddy, why do white people treat colored people so mean?'; when you take a cross-country drive and find it necessary to sleep night after night in the uncomfortable corners of your automobile because no motel will accept you; when you are humiliated day in and day out by nagging signs reading 'white' and 'colored'; when your first name becomes 'nigger', your middle name becomes 'boy' (however old you are) and your last name becomes 'John,' and your wife and mother are never given the respected title 'Mrs.'; when you are harried by day and haunted by night by the fact that you are a Negro, living constantly at tiptoe stance never quite

knowing what to expect next, and are plagued with inner fears and
outer resentments; when you are forever fighting a degenerating
sense of 'nobodiness' – then you will understand why we find it
difficult to wait. There comes a time when the cup of endurance
runs over, and men are no longer willing to be plunged into the
abyss of despair. I hope, sirs, you can understand our legitimate
and unavoidable impatience.[13]

Protests were mounting across the country, demanding that the
Kennedy Administration resolve the battle of Birmingham. A. D.
King's home was bombed, and other bombs exploded in black-owned
buildings in the city. Republican liberal Senator Jacob Javits of New
York and other members of Congress demanded that the Justice
Department intervene in the crisis. 100,000 people marched in San
Francisco and thousands more demonstrated in Detroit to express
solidarity with Birmingham blacks. Tens of thousands of whites who
had up to now stood outside the Civil Rights Movement – teachers,
lawyers, labourers, elected officials, clergy – were recruited into the
cause for justice. Thousands of telegrams were sent to the administration demanding action. Finally, after the brutal beatings and arrests
of black children, the Kennedy Administration went into motion. On
10 May 1963, Assistant Attorney General Burke Marshall, Secretary
of Defense Robert McNamara and Treasury Secretary C. Douglas
Dillon reached an agreement with Birmingham's corporate leaders
and elected officials. The terms included local hiring policies on a
'nondiscriminatory basis' and the immediate release of all black
prisoners. Kennedy warned Wallace that federal troops would be
called in to enforce desegregation and civil order if necessary.

Despite the victory in Birmingham, the racist violence continued
unabated. In Americus, Georgia, local police were using electric
cattle prods and clubs against unarmed citizens; in Plaquemines,
Louisiana, 900 marchers were tear-gassed and clubbed, 400 were
arrested and 150 hospitalised. In June, Mississippi asserted its
rightful place as the most racist state with particular vigour: in Biloxi,
72 blacks were arrested; in Tchula, activist Willie Joe Lovett,
23-years-old, was killed; in Winona, civil rights leader Fannie Lou
Hamer and others were viciously beaten and imprisoned by police.
On the night of 11 June, NAACP state leader Medgar Evers was
executed by racists in front of his Jackson, Mississippi, home.

Kennedy was not unmoved by the carnage and the ordeals of blacks, but the racial crisis alone would not have prompted him to act. Many corporate leaders, always looking at the social costs of doing business in the South, had concluded that desegregation was inevitable; that the Federal government's appropriate role was to ensure the civil order which was essential to business expansion. For both moralistic and economic reasons, then, big business had come to accept the death of Jim Crow, and a number of corporate and financial leaders urged the administration to do the same. On 12 June, Kennedy announced that he would deliver to Congress a strong civil rights bill. Later, promoting its passage, the president defended it 'not merely for reasons of economic efficiency, world diplomacy and domestic tranquility – but above all because it is right'.[14] Kennedy instantly became recognised as a powerful friend of civil rights. In later years, millions of poor and working-class black families framed photos of the late president, alongside those of his brother Robert, and Martin Luther King, and displayed them proudly in their homes. It is critically important to understand Kennedy's motivations for embracing desegregation at this relatively late date. Like Lincoln before him, Kennedy personally felt no great discomfort with racial segregation. In 1956, many Southern delegates to the Democratic national convention favoured his nomination as the party's vice-presidential candidate over that of a rival Southern senator, because of Kennedy's moderate reputation on race and his outspoken anti-communism. The Cold War had again accelerated in the early 1960s: communist forces were winning in Laos and Vietnam; Castro was in power in Havana; a bloody civil war raged in the Congo; and in October 1962, the Cuban Missile Crisis had threatened the total destruction of world civilisation. Kennedy and his advisers, notably Robert Kennedy, had to view Birmingham in a worldwide context, within the greater struggle for hegemony with the Soviet Union over the Third World. The image of battered and bloody black children in the streets of the American South could not help but undermine the US government's image in non-aligned countries. Kennedy's subsequent actions were directly influenced more by cold geopolitical facts than by warm idealism.

As the Birmingham struggle climaxed, another major protest was being planned. Among several leaders, the idea of reviving Randolph's 1941 March on Washington Movement had been discussed. Randolph and Rustin assumed leadership in the planning stages, with the latter doing most of the actual co-ordination. SNCC and a few CORE militants insisted that the march should become a massive civil disobedience demonstration, which would paralyse the nation's capital. But white liberals from labour, religious and political groups would not tolerate this radical approach. The SCLC, the Urban League and the NAACP explained that the demonstration should be planned without any arrests, with the complete co-operation of the federal authorities. This conservative position, backed by Kennedy, eventually became the dominant theme of the march. Instead of a massive, non-violent army of black students and workers – which ironically closely paralleled Randolph's 1941 project – the new march was almost a festive affair, used to promote the Kennedy civil rights bill pending before Congress. 'To orchestrate and guarantee the civility of the new march on Washington, the movement spent tremendous amounts of manpower, energy and money – all of which were diverted from the thrusts of direct action and voter registration in the South and elsewhere.'[15] The result was a biracial audience of 250,000 or more, standing before the Lincoln Memorial, on 28 August 1963. Many movement radicals who attended the gathering agreed with Malcolm X that the event was nothing but a 'farce on Washington'. But for whites and many Negro moderates, the ceremony was the highpoint of their lives.

Televised before a national audience, most of the speakers endeavoured to strike a moderate tone. Shuttlesworth declared: 'We came here because we love our country, because our country needs us and because we need our country'. Randolph, as was his custom, represented black labour. 'We are the advance guard of a massive moral revolution for jobs and freedom', the veteran socialist observed. 'Our white allies know that they cannot be free while we are not.' Roy Wilkins, who was introduced erroneously as 'the acknowledged leader of the civil rights movement', gave vigorous support to the proposed civil rights bill. Whitney M. Young, director of the Urban League, Matthew Ahmann of the Catholic Conference for Interracial Justice, and others gave moderate and unsurprising testimony. Problems surfaced when the contents of John Lewis' speech became known prior to his address. The Catholic Archbishop of Washington, Patrick A. O'Boyle, declared he would leave the podium unless others deleted and rearranged the SNCC leader's presentation. Protesting, but in the end acquiescing, Lewis delivered a 'sanitized' speech which still expressed key elements of his organisation's radical posture. 'We are tired of being beaten by policemen. We are tired of seeing our people locked up in jail over and over again!' Lewis dismissed the Kennedy civil rights bill as 'too little and too late'. King came to the speaker's platform last, and gave what many in the audience declared was a rhetorical 'miracle', his 'I have a Dream' speech. King began by terming the march 'the greatest demonstration of freedom' in American history. He illustrated in resounding oratory his vision of society: a land where freedom rang 'from every mountainside', and where blacks and whites could join hands together to proclaim the words, 'Free at last, free at last; thank God Almighty, we're free at last!' Historians of the movement were struck by the fact that a portion of King's speech was originally delivered in 1956, at the first anniversary ceremonies for the Montgomery Bus Boycott movement. Other parts were derived from political speeches and sermons he had given for over seven years.[16] Militants were bitterly disappointed that King had chosen not to include extensive critical remarks on the recent racist violence in the South, and the failure of most white liberals to respond concretely or adequately to the Negro's economic plight. But before a predominantly white viewing audience in the US, King represented a reasonable and even admirable spokesman for the cause of civil rights. The speech mirrored, in a sense, Booker T. Washington's Atlanta Compromise of September 1895: both were delivered to primarily white audiences; both were self-consciously restrained in their demands; both captured the dominant political trends in white civil society at that point in American racial history. Washington of course championed 'separation of the races', while King called for 'integration' and 'civil rights'. Yet across the gulf of history, the two black men personified a body of public policies which dealt directly with the present and future status of the Negro. Both won the grateful support of their respective Presidential Administrations; both proposed the implementation of their racial policies in the South. King and Washington were catapulted after their respective speeches into international fame.

If the Negro moderates thought that a non-violent celebration would pressure the Congress to adopt the civil rights proposals, they were sadly mistaken. Not a single vote changed in Congress after the march. If anything, the mood among grassroots blacks had swung towards greater defiance. In July 1963, one month before the march, writer Lerone Bennett argued that 'the burning militance of the Birmingham leaders . . . pin-pointed a revolutionary shift in the

attitudes of blacks'. CORE militants in San Francisco declared that
'Birmingham brought a drastic revision in our thinking. You can
nibble away at the surface for a thousand years and not get
anywhere'.[17] CORE chapters across the country began to set firm and
short 'deadlines' for white businesses to hire certain numbers of
blacks, promising to disrupt commercial traffic and to protest
repeatedly unless goals were reached. Many black nationalists
targeted King and other more conservative Negro leaders with
personal and even physical abuse. In Harlem, black separatists
tossed eggs at King after his appearance in a local church. When A.
D. King addressed a Harlem rally of 3000 in May 1963, a section of
the audience jeered: 'We want Malcolm, we want Malcolm!'[18]
Dissatisfied with the mildly reformist policies and practices of the
Negro Old Guard, SNCC leaders increasingly looked overseas for
ideological direction. In December 1963, staff members had a fruitful
discussion with Kenya's socialist Vice President, Oginga Odinga,
when he visited Atlanta. Nine months later eleven SNCC leaders,
including Fannie Lou Hamer, Julian Bond, Ruby Doris Robinson,
John Lewis and James Forman travelled across Africa, and met with
national leaders. In Africa the SNCC delegation met Malcolm X, and
the beginning of an influential relationship was established. Domestically, SNCC moved closer to the organised left. In December 1963,
Lewis urged Congress to abolish HUAC; the following year, SNCC
accepted the legal assistance of the leftist National Lawyers Guild,
over the vigorous objections of NAACP Legal Defense Fund director
Jack Greenberg, a Cold War liberal.[19] Even the SCLC and NAACP
experienced a bewildering sense of 'What Next?' after the March on
Washington. Rustin was disturbed by the 'talk of violence' and
growing sympathy for Malcolm X's nationalism. 'We cannot get our
freedom with guns', Rustin wrote in October 1963. 'You cannot
integrate a school or get a job with a machine gun.' But Rustin
admitted that Kennedy still 'reassures the segregationists' and
privately 'bows to the Dixiecrats and gives them Southern racist
judges'.[20]

Ever-present in the post-march discussions were certain questions:
'once desegregation is legally won, what is the next objective?'; 'what
does freedom actually mean in terms of public policies?'; and 'are
integration and nonviolence the only possible methods to wage the
Second Reconstruction?' Sadly, with the growing exceptions of
SNCC and CORE, the majority of Negro leaders were poorly

equipped theoretically even to grapple with these social and economic contradictions, for at their roots they signified the reality of America's racist and capitalist state. The one black theorist and activist who could have provided the answers had been banished from political discourse. In October 1961, DuBois applied for membership in the Communist Party, and late that year left the US to relocate in Nkrumah's Ghana. He died at the age of 95, hours before the March on Washington. Yet before his final departure, in one of his last public addresses, delivered at Johnson C. Smith College in Charlotte, North Carolina, on 2 April 1960, DuBois predicted the dilemmas which would later confound and confront the civil rights leadership. Long before his critics, DuBois recognised that the struggle for desegregation would be victorious in the end, but that this effort to abolish Jim Crow would not destroy the economic prerogatives of private capital over black lives, which was the basis for all the exploitation and racism which existed in the nation. Further, he warned the sit-in demonstrators not to confuse desegregation as a political goal with cultural assimilation into the white majority. The desegregation struggle in America should not force Negroes ever to forget slavery and 'the whole cultural history of Africans in the world. No! What I have been fighting for . . . is the possibility of black folk and their cultural patterns existing in America without discrimination, and on terms of equality.' Political equality with whites would eventually occur, the black scholar stated, but without an economic programme of socialism, and 'the preservation of African history and culture' among Afro-Americans, a truly biracial democracy was impossible.[21] Few noted or cared for DuBois' remarks; but within five brief years, the words of his predictions would resound throughout the black movement in many ways.

IV

Between 1962 and 1965, Martin Luther King was the acknowledged moral and political leader of millions of Americans, black and white. After the March on Washington, King became one of the three or four most influential figures in the world. His books and articles were read by millions; his speeches were memorised; he was honoured with the 1964 Nobel Peace Prize; he was celebrated by artists and poets of all races and cultures. King's personal achievements and acclaim gave the domestic struggle for biracial democracy an international audience. For the historian, King represents a series of paradoxes, each of which obscures the real meaning of his greatness. Some commentators suggest that without King, the civil rights cause would have faltered, and certain major legislative victories – particularly the Civil Rights Act of 1964 and the Voting Rights Act of 1965 – would not have been won. This idealist interpretation misses the actual relationship between the individual and the dialectical evolution of history. Other social movements throughout human history are often characterised by the singular actions of one prominent figure: Cromwell in the English Civil War; Lenin, during the Russian Revolution of 1917; Mao in China; Robespierre during the French Revolution. But history creates humanity, as well as the conscious choices which are possible for any political leader to select. G. Plekhanov's *The Role of Individual in History* sheds considerable light on this issue. If a social movement for reform or revolution is broad enough, Plekhanov insisted, any series of individuals can arise who can articulate the vision of that movement. 'If the accidental fall of a brick had killed [Robespierre] . . . his place would, of course, have been taken by someone else; and although that other person might have been inferior to him in every respect, events would have nevertheless taken the same course as they did with Robespierre.' A great politician 'sees farther than others and desires things more strongly than others', but he/she cannot overturn the basic direction of struggle.[22] Reconsidering the black movement from 1954 to 1965, King appears 'indispensable' because in retrospect, his great gifts for oratory and his dynamic use of non-violent direct action techniques appear to stand alone. But King did not create the Second Reconstruction; the movement made the young minister its own spokesperson, and could have done the same for others if he had not existed. Had King been killed in Montgomery in 1956, Abernathy was fully equipped to carry out the boycott. Randolph and Wilkins were far better-known; Farmer of CORE was more willing to go to jail and to lead non-violent actions; Shuttlesworth, C. T. Vivian and others would have created an organisation like King's SCLC by the late 1950s; the sit-ins, Freedom Rides, and jail-ins had nothing directly to do with King, and they would have occurred without his input.

King's powerful influence must be explained, therefore, by factors other than his indispensability. First, and probably foremost among his credentials was his identity as a black preacher. Among his contemporaries in the black clergy, King had no peer as an orator.

From small towns in the rural South, to his father's Ebenezer Baptist Church in Atlanta, King delivered sermons with a grace, cadence and power unmatched since the great preachers of the A. M. E. church and other black denominations from the late nineteenth century. Author Louis Lomax describes a typical sermon:

> 'I got my marching shoes!' Martin would shout.
> 'Yes, Lord, me too,' the people answered back.
> 'I woke up this morning with my mind on freedom!'
> 'Preach, doctor, preach.'
> 'I ain't going to let nobody turn me around!'
> 'Let's march, brother; we are with you. . . .'
> 'The struggle is not between black and white!'
> 'No, no,' the people confirmed.
> 'But between good and evil.'
> 'That's it; that's it.'
> 'For God is not dead; I know because I can feel him. . . .'
> 'Deep in my soul!' the people shout completing the line from the Negro spiritual.
>
> Then, arm in arm with the local leader, Martin led the people into the streets to face dogs, tear gas, fire hoses, and, frequently, brutality and additional jailing.[23]

Black novelist James Baldwin described King as a 'great speaker' whose 'secret lies in his intimate knowledge of the people he is addressing', by keeping 'his hearers absolutely tense'. On the church pulpit, King personified their own best hopes, their desire for human equality, their love of God, their will to resist. 'Once he had accepted the place they had prepared for him, their struggle became absolutely indistinguishable from his own, and took over and controlled his life. He suffered with them and, thus, he helped them to suffer.'[24] King appealed to white liberals for other reasons. He had none of Lewis' or Carmichael's fiery political rhetoric; but this allowed him to be judged as a moderate and reasonable counsellor in a time of racial crisis. He lacked Randolph's peerless credentials as a leader of black workers; but this gave the black minister access to corporate directors and many conservatives who still viewed Randolph with some suspicion. King's SCLC had none of the organisational clout or prestige of Wilkins' NAACP; yet this permitted King to be viewed not as a desegregation bureaucrat, but as a moral and spiritual leader.

Writing in 1965, historian August Meier explained that King's 'religious terminology and the manipulation of the Christian symbols of love and nonresistance are responsible for his appeal among whites. To talk in terms of Christianity, love, nonviolence is reassuring to the mentality of white America'. King made white liberals feel guilty every time they saw him lead a non-violent prayer group or march that was assaulted by Southern police, armed with firehoses, dogs and clubs. But King's faith in the essential humanity of even the worst white bigot gave other whites the sense that this black leader valued and respected law and order, tempered with justice. Whites could love King, because King had 'faith that the white man will redeem himself'.[25]

In politics, King tried to strike a balance between protest and accommodation. Inside his own closed coterie of supporters, he listened to the advice of radicals like Bevel and gradualists like Andrew Young. When President Kennedy was assassinated on 22 November 1963, King immediately issued a statement which blamed all American blacks and whites equally, for creating 'a climate where men cannot disagree without being disagreeable, and where they express their disagreement through violence and murder'. King was ready to support Lyndon Johnson as he assumed the presidency, in return for the former segregationist's vigorous endorsement of the Civil Rights bill. Congress passed the legislation on 2 July 1964; King repaid the new president by campaigning for his election throughout that year. In *Why We Can't Wait*, released in July 1964, King praised 'Johnson's emotional and intellectual involvement' in the desegregation campaigns.[26] King urged civil rights leaders to diminish their protest actions during the campaign, in the fear that any black boycotts or jail-ins would undercut Johnson's chances for election. When black urban rebellions erupted in Rochester, Philadelphia, and Harlem – brought about by decades of economic exploitation and Federal government apathy – King took a law-and-order posture. Travelling to New York City's burning ghettoes, even without contacting local black leaders in advance, King insisted that the black underclass should return quietly to their rat-infested slums. 'Lawlessness, looting and violence cannot be condoned whether used by the racist or the reckless of any color', King declared, to the popular acclaim of white politicians and police.[27] Johnson was elected in November over right-wing challenger Barry Goldwater with a massive majority; indeed, had every black voter stayed home, or had voted for Goldwater, Johnson still would have triumphed. Nevertheless, even after the November 1964 elections, King attempted to moderate the activism of the movement in order to maintain the president's support.

King's compromised and contradictory politics were revealed tragically in Selma, Alabama, in 1965. SNCC workers had been organising in that section of black-belt Alabama for two years. One young black man, Jimmy Lee Jackson, was clubbed to death by police officers as he tried to protect his mother. SCLC and SNCC organisers agreed to schedule a march from Selma to Montgomery beginning on 7 March 1965, to protest against the Wallace regime's brutality. On the morning of the march, SNCC leaders were shocked that King was inexplicably absent. Walking across Selma's Pettus Bridge, the 2000 non-violent demonstrators were attacked and brutally beaten by hundreds of state troopers and local police. On 10 March, King agreed to lead a second group of 3000 protestors across the bridge – but secretly made an agreement with Johnson's Attorney General, Nicholas Katzenbach, that the marchers would not confront the Alabama state police again. With King at the head of the march, the demonstrators sang and prayed as they walked over the bridge. As the police barricade approached, King ordered everyone immediately to retreat. In subdued anger, the amazed SNCC leaders and others walked back into Selma, singing 'Ain't Gonna Let Nobody Turn Me 'Round'. Later, after hard bargaining, the march to Montgomery was finally held; but the damage to King's reputation was incalculable. Harding expressed the sense of betrayal which characterised the moment:

When the time came to assert their right to march for freedom, there is every evidence that King backed off. Listening to mediators from President Johnson, he refused to press the movement into so harsh and predictably bloody a confrontation. Many sagging spirits were finally broken with that act of retreat, and the distrust that had been building against King, SCLC, and the Johnson Administration poured out in deep anger and disgust. The powerful, forward thrust of the Southern civil rights struggle had now been finally broken, and that turned out to be the last traditional, major march of the Southern movement.[28]

For five difficult years, King had been the glue which kept the civil rights united front intact. Leaders to his right – Young, Randolph, Wilkins – could accept his activism without personally becoming involved in street demonstrations on a daily basis. He had been a mentor to the left wing of the movement: speaking at SNCC's founding conference, urging teenagers to be arrested for their ideals; writing a powerful fund-raising letter for CORE in 1956, which helped to subsidise its activities; joining CORE's Advisory Committee in 1957, and protecting and aiding Freedom Riders in Montgomery in 1961. Now the myth was shattered, and the politician was something far less than what many True Believers had hoped he was. Robert Allen bitterly denounced King as 'a reluctant accomplice of the white power structure'. King was manipulated by 'the liberal establishment . . . to restrain the threatening rebelliousness of the black masses and the young militants'.[29] Even before Selma, Meier levied the harshest criticisms:

> In a movement in which respect is accorded in direct proportion to the number of times one is arrested, King appears to keep the number of times he goes to jail to a minimum. In a movement in which successful leaders are those who share in the hardships of their followers, in the risks they take, in the beatings they receive, in the length of time they spend in jail, King tends to leave prison for other important engagements, rather than remaining there and suffering with his followers. In a movement in which leadership ordinarily devolves upon persons who mix democratically with their followers, King remains isolated and aloof. In a movement which prides itself on militancy and 'no compromise' with racial discrimination . . . [King] seems amenable to compromises considered by some half a loaf or less, and often appears willing to postpone or avoid a direct confrontation in the streets.[30]

V

Reason and right seemed to triumph. NAACP activist Clarence Mitchell declared that Johnson had 'made a greater contribution to giving a dignified and hopeful status to Negroes in the United States than any President including Lincoln, Roosevelt, and Kennedy'.[31] Johnson committed his Administration to the goal of 'the full assimilation of more than twenty million Negroes into American life'. The Civil Rights Bill of 1964 outlawed Jim Crow in public accommodations of every kind, in every city and state. The Voting Rights Act of 1965, prompted by events at Selma, had even greater scope. By votes of 328 to 74 in the House of Representatives, and 79 to 18 in the Senate, bill H.R. 6400 was signed into law by Johnson on 6 August 1965. 'I pledge we will not delay or we will not hesitate, or will not turn aside until Americans of every race and color and origin in this country have the same rights as all others to share in the progress of democracy', Johnson declared. Federal examiners were sent into the South with the full powers of the government to safeguard the registration and voting of blacks. Within five years, the effects of the Voting Rights Act were apparent to all. Between 1964 and 1969, the percentage of black adults registered to vote in the South soared: Alabama, 19.3 per cent to 61.3 per cent; Georgia, 27.4 per cent to 60.4 per cent; Louisiana, 31.6 per cent to 60.8 per cent; Mississippi, 6.7 per cent to 66.5 per cent.[32] Older blacks, for the first time in their lives, were permitted to cast votes. Black children could shop in department stores, eat at restaurants, and even go to amusement parks which were once off-limits. The left wing of the Civil Rights Movement applauded these legislative achievements, but with a grain of cynicism born from hard experience. 'The Civil Rights Bill was designed to answer three elements at once', Debbie Louis noted. White liberals were pleased with 'the Administration [for] fulfilling its campaign promises'. The black community was placated and its 'explosive' sentiment diffused. Most important of all, the 1964 bill pleased 'the business community whose survival depended on quelling minority unrest and unprofitable white resistance to moderate black demands'.[33]

If anything, the adoption of the 1964 Civil Rights Act increased the institutional, political and vigilante violence against blacks across the South. As Johnson swung the Democratic Party behind the moderate tendency of the desegregation movement, white Southern Democrats abandoned the party by the thousands. An opponent of the Civil Rights Act, Goldwater carried 54.6 per cent of the black belt South's popular votes in 1964, and was the first Republican candidate to receive all the electoral votes of Mississippi, Alabama, Georgia, South Carolina and Louisiana. Dixiecrat Strom Thurmond campaigned for Goldwater, and joined the Republican Party in 1966. The new 'racist-Republicans' won seven additional House seats, elected three Senators and two governors in 1966. Many Southern politicians who remained Democrats shifted to the far right. In Georgia, a racist

Atlanta restaurant owner, Lester Maddox, acquired a widespread following. Maddox was a leader of Georgians Unwilling to Surrender (GUTS) and the White Citizens' Councils. After the Civil Rights Bill was passed, Maddox threatened black would-be patrons with axe handles and physical threats. In 1966, this bizarre yet very American defender of 'God, liberty, free enterprise, and states' rights' was elected governor of Georgia. No one, however, surpassed Wallace of Alabama in crude political ability, fiery demagoguery, or defence of white supremacy. Wallace recognised that the South could not defeat the Federal government's racial policies alone; he knew that many Northern white workers hated and feared blacks, and that this fear could be harnessed into a national political movement. Campaigning against Johnson in the Democratic Party primaries of early 1964, Wallace took his anti-communist, anti-black and quasi-fascist pro-gramme to Northern factories, churches and suburbs. In Indiana, he polled 30 per cent of the Democratic popular vote, 34 per cent in Wisconsin, and 43 per cent in Maryland. Legally barred from running for re-election in Alabama, Wallace proposed that his apolitical wife, Lurleen, be elected governor in his place. On a campaign completely dominated by the racist rhetoric of her husband, Mrs Wallace carried 54 per cent of the Democratic primary vote, and subsequently became governor.[34] The startling success of the Wallaces and Maddoxes created the conditions for racist violence to continue unchecked. During the Mississippi Summer Project of 1964, a joint effort of the NAACP, CORE, SCLC and SNCC to register blacks, there were 6 blacks who were murdered, 1000 arrested, 30 buildings were bombed and three dozen black churches were gutted by fire. Racist attacks still occurred in every Southern city: in Birmingham, blacks at one restaurant were clubbed with baseball bats; in Gransville, Louisiana, the town's leader of the NAACP Youth Council was viciously beaten by white terrorists supervised by the local sheriff; in St. Augustine, Florida, black youths were assaulted by whites with chains and knives. SNCC and CORE activists began to protest that voting rights and desegregated public facilities were not enough. Somehow, the Federal government must halt the racist violence against all blacks.

It was only then that some black activists recognised, at last, the limitations of reform. America's political economy was still pro-foundly racist, and Johnson's legislation had erased only the crudest manifestations of racial suppression. Beyond allowing the Negro the opportunity *not* to be restricted by colour *per se*, Johnson and the Congress would not go. Even as Wallace was becoming a national voice for prejudice, bigotry and modern American fascism, white liberals expressed the view that blacks had no more obstacles to confront. Freedom, for them, was achieved by the Voting Rights Act. Woodward explains their joyful mood:

> American institutions were responding effectively to the most serious domestic problem the country faced. Jim Crow as a legal entity was dead. Congress had fulfilled its role, the courts were vindicated, and the executive furnished inspired leadership. Granted that discrimination and segregation still flourished in spite of the law, nevertheless the means were now at hand to deal with all these problems. . . . With the powerful new laws on the books, with public sentiment behind them, and an Administration thoroughly committed to the cause, a new era of progress was about to dawn.[35]

Virtually none of the black leaders, from left to right, shared this gross misconception. Even Whitney Young of the Urban League, a group distinguished by its conservatism and pro-corporate views, had to offer some dissent. 'I think the white community makes a real mistake in reminding the Negro of the possibility of alienating white people because he pushes for his rights. A Negro mother whose husband is unemployed', Young noted, 'whose children are bitten by rats, who are living in a house without heat, couldn't care less about alienating some white person.'[36]

If the tepid Young could feel hostility towards white liberals, the anger of blacks to his left was tenfold. By the autumn of 1963, as we have seen, many CORE members had begun to re-evaluate their historic commitment to non-violence. In 1964, many blacks were forcing white veterans of CORE to resign their posts as chairs of local chapters. Late that same year, CORE's national membership became, for the first time, predominantly black. Long Island CORE was seized by black nationalists under the direction of militant Lincoln Lynch. In 1965, a black men's caucus was created and led by the egotistical yet charismatic Roy Innis, with the specific political goal of black nationalism. Farmer was increasingly isolated and challenged. In mid-1964, he became fearful that Rustin would be named to replace him. McKissick denounced Farmer for mismanagement and lack of effective leadership. Farmer resigned in January 1966, and was replaced by McKissick. Politically, CORE was increasingly at odds with the Johnson Administration, especially with its policies in Vietnam. Many CORE chapter leaders were among the earliest critics of American involvement in Southeast Asia. McKissick and Farmer co-signed an official condemnation of the war, stating that US money sent to the South Vietnamese regime could be better spent at home to end poverty and institutional racism. CORE had begun to redefine itself, into becoming an all-black formation, although still quite petty bourgeois, which promoted radical reforms and racial pride. Robert Allen described this metamorphosis from biracial pacifism to black militancy in CORE as an attempt 'to respond to and organize the new militancy which had infected certain parts of the black middle classes, as a result of the rebellions initiated by the black masses'.[37]

SNCC was again at the vanguard of change. White liberals watched with horror and dismay as an assertive black nationalist trend became more pronounced in the group. The most articulate voice for nationalism was young Stokely Carmichael. Once a proponent of Rustin's form of gradualist socialism, Carmichael became a SNCC worker on a full-time basis after graduating from Howard University in 1964. Widely praised as a natural organiser of rural workers and farmers, Carmichael registered black voters in Mississippi. From the beginning, however, he could not accept the religious and non-violent tenets of many SNCC activists. Jailed repeatedly with his co-workers, he refused to participate in the prayers with others in his cell. During organising efforts in Lowndes County, Alabama, in 1965, Carmichael usually carried a loaded pistol for protection, and advised his friends to do the same. Carmichael and others organised a militant, all-black political formation, the Lowndes County Freedom Organization – better known in the state as the Black Panther Party – to oppose the Wallacites electorally. Earlier than CORE, SNCC also publicly denounced Johnson's war policies. Bob Moses spoke at an anti-war rally of 25,000 in Washington, DC on 17 April 1965. Other SNCC leaders, notably Bond, urged the organisation to emphasise the issue. By July 1965, SNCC members produced their first uncompromising statement of the war, declaring that blacks should not 'fight in Vietnam for the white man's freedom, until all the Negro people are free in Mississippi'.[38]

In the process of social transformation, there are always bitter seeds of defeat hidden within the fruit of victory. Jim Crow was legally finished, yet black workers and sharecroppers were still the victims of bombings, lynchings and rapes. Thousands had been imprisoned, and their jailers were still at large; Wallace was now a dangerous national figure to be reckoned with; white liberals were demanding that the Negro 'quiet down' and 'accept' the gains that he/she had gained. Black Southerners had the electoral franchise; but what of economic security, housing, childcare, medical care, and the right to live without fear? So much had been won, but the greatest expectations of the black poor and working class had not yet been achieved. The 'echoes from Paul Robeson and W. E. B. DuBois were sounding in Mississippi', writes Harding. 'Every movement forward had been purchased at great cost. Bleeding ulcers, nervous breakdowns, mysterious, incurable ailments took their toll on young lives.' Yet what of freedom? Was this too simply an illusion? 'Every time they smashed away some obstacle to black freedom and equality, another larger, newly perceived hindrance loomed before them, challenging the last ounce of their strength and their spirit.'[39] The idealistic teenagers of 1960 had become the steely veterans of racial reform. If white liberals blocked proposals for gaining a decent material life for the masses of poor blacks, then they would have to leave our organisations. If Johnson persisted in sending off young black men to die in an Asian war, his Administration would have to be toppled. If non-violence could not win the white racists to biracial democracy and justice, then their brutal terror would be met, blow for blow. If equality was impossible within the political economy of American capitalism, that system which perpetuated black exploitation would have to be overturned. No more compromises; no more betrayals by Negro moderates. Rebellion would supplant reform.

5. Black Power, 1965–1970

We are living in an era of revolution, and the revolt of the American Negro is part of the rebellion against the oppression and colonialism which has characterized this era. . . . It is incorrect to classify the revolt of the Negro as simply a racial conflict of black against white, or as a purely American problem. Rather, we are today seeing a global rebellion of the oppressed against the oppressor, the exploited against the exploiter.

Malcolm X, 1965

If a man hasn't found something he will die for, he isn't fit to live.

Martin Luther King

I

Walter Rodney, the noted Guyanese historian and political theorist, once observed that the slave revolts in his native land 'had taught the lesson that slavery as a form of control over labour was proving uneconomical and unstable'.[1] The same can be said for the US black non-violent uprisings of the early 1960s as they related to the Jim Crow system of American caste and class oppression. Racial segregation had become an international embarrassment for the Kennedy and Johnson Administrations. Every world headline for George Wallace, and every citation of a fresh atrocity against blacks in the South destroyed the credibility of the US as a nation committed to democracy and human equality. Domestically, racial unrest was costly to the private sector. Eastern US capital and the multinational corporations had no direct historic commitment to the maintenance of rigid caste divisions within the American working class. They viewed the mild reforms proposed by Wilkins, Young and Randolph with no great anxiety. If desegregation could provide the necessary civil order to maintain private capital accumulation, why not ratify Federal legislation to that effect? Racism itself – the systemic exploitation of black labour power and the political and cultural hegemony of capital's interests over black labour – would still remain intact. The fragile black middle strata could be absorbed into marginal levels of affluence in both the private sector and the government. This price was modest compared to the greater costs of permitting racial conflagration to continue as it had for five years and more. The rightist tendency of the desegregationist forces were amenable to this proposal. Dedicated anti-communists themselves, their goal had never been to overturn the political economy of capitalism. As integrationists, they simply desired an 'equal opportunity' to compete within society and the labour force, without the debilitating restrictions of caste. They were opposed to the notions of black nationalists that blacks should concentrate their own numbers into a power bloc which would demand structural changes in the racist/capitalist order. Their dream of 'freedom' was as American as Horatio Alger: social acceptance and upward mobility within the very centres of corporate power. Black radicals in SNCC had come to repudiate this dream; black nationalists had never shared it. As the civil rights united front gradually came unstuck, the only original voice which articulated an alternative vision for black Americans was that of Malcolm X.

It is difficult for historians to capture the vibrant essence of Malcolm X, his earthy and human character, his position as a revolutionary teacher for a generation of young militants, his total love for the dispossessed. Part of his greatness as a social figure was derived from his sordid urban origins. As we have seen, Malcolm rose from being a pimp, drug dealer and ghetto hustler into the most forceful proponent of nationalism since Garvey. His rhetoric, more so than even King's, was almost hypnotic upon black audiences. As the chief spokesperson for the Nation of Islam, he preached a militant message which changed the lives of thousands of poor and oppressed blacks. In any typical sermon, Malcolm might speak these words:

> My beautiful, black brothers and sisters! Look at your skins! We're all black to the white man, but we're a thousand and one different colors. Turn around, look at each other! . . . During slavery it was a rare one of our black grandmothers who escaped the white rapist

slavemaster. That rapist slavemaster who emasculated the black man with threats, with fear until even today the black man lives with fear of the white man in his heart!

Think of it – think of that black slave man filled with fear and dread, hearing the screams of his wife, his mother, his daughter being taken – in the barn, the kitchen, in the bushes! . . . And you were too filled with *fear* of the rapist to do anything about it! . . .

Every white man in America, when he looks into a black man's eyes, should fall to his knees and say 'I'm sorry, I'm sorry – my kind has committed history's greatest crime against your kind; will you give me the chance to atone?' But do you brothers and sisters expect any white man to do that? *No*, you *know* better! . . .

Every time you see a white man, think about the devil you're seeing! Think of how it was on *your* slave foreparents' bloody, sweaty backs that he built this empire that's today the richest of all nations – where his evil and his greed cause him to be hated around the world![2]

As a devout organiser for the Nation of Islam, Malcolm had served in Detroit, Boston and Philadelphia before leading the powerful Temple Number Seven of Harlem. Word of his sermons brought in hundreds of 'Southern migrant people' who in Malcolm's words 'would go anywhere to hear what they called "good preaching" '. After hours on the speaking platform, Malcolm 'would become so choked up sometimes I would walk in the streets until late into the night. Sometimes I would speak to no one for hours, thinking to myself about what the white man had done to our poor people here in America'.[3] As Malcolm began to become better known outside the Nation of Islam, he became the object of bitter attacks from the media and many Negro leaders. His teachings were described in newspapers as 'fascist', 'violent', 'racist', 'anti-Christian', and surprisingly, even 'Communist-inspired'. When white interviewers asked Malcolm, 'why do you teach black supremacy, and hate?', Malcolm's response was 'to pour on pure fire in return': 'For the white man to ask the black man if he hates him is just like the rapist asking the raped, or the wolf asking the sheep, "Do you hate me?" The white man is in no moral position to accuse anyone else of hate!'[4] Even as a follower of Elijah Muhammad, Malcolm insisted at every opportunity that he opposed racial segregation 'even more militantly' than the leaders of the NAACP and other integrationists. For the Muslims, segregation was a system which was 'forced upon inferiors by superiors'. Complete racial separation, however, would be a means for blacks to stop 'begging' the system 'for jobs, food, clothing and housing'.[5]

In 1962 and 1963, Malcolm's personal prominence began to create tensions and organisational rivalries within the Nation of Islam. Malcolm began to speak out less on religious issues, and increasingly asserted himself on contemporary political questions. The Muslim newspaper he had founded, *Muhammad Speaks*, was ordered to print less about Malcolm. Muhammad's tight authoritarianism prohibited Malcolm and other more activist-oriented ministers from becoming involved in black political struggles. Finally, two events forced Malcolm to divorce himself from the Nation entirely. On 3 July 1963, two former secretaries of Muhammad filed paternity suits against him claiming that the 67-year-old patriarch had fathered their four children. Any other Muslim member or leader would have been promptly expelled for the crime of adultery, yet Muhammad maintained his high post, even after admitting that the charges were true. Malcolm interviewed the women, and learned that Muhammad had described him privately as a 'dangerous' threat to his own position. When President Kennedy was assassinated, Malcolm commented to the press that his death was a case of 'the chickens coming home to roost . . . that the hate in white men had not stopped with the killing of defenseless black people, but that hate, allowed to spread unchecked, finally had struck down this country's Chief of State'.[6] Muhammad used this statement as a pretext to neutralise his chief spokesperson. Malcolm was ordered into 'silence' for ninety days, not allowed to teach in his own mosque, nor to speak with the media. Returning to New York, Malcolm was shattered to discover that Muhammad might have authorised several Muslims to assassinate him. By March 1964, it was apparent that the Nation of Islam had no desire to reinstate Malcolm under any conditions of submission. Malcolm left the Nation, and announced the creation of a new organisation on 8 March 1964, the Muslim Mosque, Inc. Malcolm informed the press that he was now 'prepared to cooperate in local civil rights actions in the South and elsewhere and shall do so because every campaign for specific objectives can only heighten the political consciousness of the Negroes and intensify their identification against white society'.[7]

In his last hectic year of life, Malcolm was attempting to develop a revolutionary ideology and programme appropriate to the conditions confronting black Americans. In this search, Malcolm's greatest obstacle was his own earlier public image. 'I was trying to turn a corner, into a new regard by the public, especially Negroes', he stated in his autobiography. 'I was no less angry than I had been, but at the same time the true brotherhood I had seen' in a 1964 journey to the Middle East and Africa 'had influenced me to recognize that anger can blind human vision'.[8] Renamed El-Hajj-Malik El-Shabazz after his visit to Mecca, Malcolm adopted Sunni Islam as his personal faith, but carefully separated his religious tenets from the political work in which he was engaged. In the summer of 1964, Malcolm and his growing cadre of followers formed the Organisation for Afro-American Unity (OAAU), a militant black nationalist force based primarily in New York City. During these months, Malcolm restructured many of his older ideas into a clearly uncompromising programme which was both anti-racist and anti-capitalist. Like DuBois before him, Malcolm and the OAAU planned to submit a list of human rights violations and acts of genocide against US blacks to the United Nations. He criticised blacks for endorsing Johnson's 1964 Presidential candidacy, predicting with grim accuracy that Johnson would stop far short of providing a meaningful economic and social programme which benefited minorities. Criticising the Negro middle strata's commitment to private enterprise, Malcolm declared, 'you can't have capitalism without racism. And if you find [anti-racists] usually they're socialists or their political philosophy is socialism'.[9] The actual programme of the OAAU was reformist rather than revolutionary. Their programme included the following: the election of independent black candidates for public office, voter registration drives, rent strikes to promote better housing conditions for blacks, the building of all-black community schools, the creation of cultural centres, and initiating black committees for community and neighbourhood self-defence. At one point, Malcolm even suggested that his older apocalyptic vision of a race war was no longer viable. 'America is the first country . . . that can actually have a blood-less revolution.' Evoking some of the ideas of Henry Lee Moon, Malcolm stated, 'the Negro holds the balance of power, and if the Negro in this country were given what the Constitution says he is supposed to have, the added power of the Negro in this country would sweep all of the racists and the segregationists out of office. It would change the entire political structure of the country'.[10]

Malcolm's base of supporters cut deeply into the Civil Rights Movement. Robert Gore, the assistant community relations director of CORE, attended a debate between Malcolm and Bayard Rustin in 1962, with the intention of rooting 'with Bayard all the way'. Gore left the debate 'applauding more for Malcolm X'. Half-ashamed, he wrote that Malcolm's eloquence was so moving that 'it did my heart a world of good to sit back and listen to [Malcolm X] list the sins of the white man'.[11] By late 1963, Malcolm was having a direct impact upon many CORE chapters. While Farmer futilely attacked Malcolm, declaring that 'we cannot leave the ghetto to the rabid nationalists', other local leaders in the organisation championed his ideas.[12] In April 1964, Malcolm urged activists to start 'rifle clubs' to defend the black community against police brutality and white vigilante violence. In a similar vein, Cleveland CORE activist Lewis Robinson initiated a proposal for creating a gun club. Malcolm's impact upon SNCC was even greater. White activist Howard Zinn urged SNCC members to repudiate revolutionary black nationalism. 'Friendships, and love affairs, have crossed race lines in SNCC', Zinn wrote in early 1964. 'Recent calls by Malcolm X and others for Negroes to use self-defense, and even retaliation, against acts of violence by whites', must not be condoned.[13] Later that year, however, Hamer and SNCC's 'Freedom Singers' attended an OAAU meeting in Harlem. In early February 1965, Malcolm was asked by SNCC to speak to black students and workers in Selma, Alabama. Malcolm's electrifying speech gave the radical nationalist tendency within SNCC another boost. Even John Lewis, now increasingly at odds with more radical SNCC members, commented that Malcolm 'more than any single personality' was able to 'articulate the aspirations, bitterness, and frustrations of the Negro people'.[14]

On 21 February 1965, Malcolm was assassinated by gunmen as he rose to address a black Harlem audience. For over a year, he had been followed by the spectre of death: in a Cairo visit, he was severely poisoned; on 14 February 1965, his home was fire-bombed. There is now substantial documentation indicating that Malcolm's assassination may have involved the FBI and other agencies of the Federal government.[15] From the moment of his death, however, both the Nation of Islam and most of the mainstream civil rights leaders attempted to eradicate Malcolm's political influence among young blacks. Muhammad cyncially attributed Malcolm's death to his advocacy of violence. 'He seems to have taken weapons as his god. Therefore we couldn't tolerate a man like that. He preached war. We preach peace.' Muhammad moved rapidly to isolate pro-Malcolm opponents and to win over key dissidents, including one of his own sons, the Islamic scholar Wallace D. Muhammad, who had briefly sided with Malcom. Wilfred X and Philbert X, Malcolm's brothers, who had also become leading Muslim ministers, defended Muhammad. For very different reasons, some integrationist leaders quickly seized the opportunity to join the Nation's attacks on Malcolm. A prominent journalist and black appointee in the Johnson Administration, Carl Rowan, described him as 'an ex-convict, ex-dope peddler who became a racial fanatic . . . a Negro who preached segregation and race hatred'. The most vitriolic yet articulate assaults on Malcolm came from Rustin. 'Now that he is dead, we must resist the temptation to idealize Malcolm X, to elevate charisma to greatness', Rustin noted in March 1965. 'Malcolm is not a hero of the movement, he is a tragic victim of the ghetto.' Rustin insisted that Malcolm was a political failure; that 'having blown the trumpet, he could summon, even at the very end, only a handful of followers'; that Malcolm's 'central error' was his dedication 'to the preservation of the ghetto, which he thought could either be transformed from within or transplanted to a happier environment'. Rustin argued, 'the movement we build . . . must be dedicated to [the ghetto's] destruction. White America, not the Negro people, will determine Malcolm's role in history'.[16]

These sad attempts at blunting Malcolm's influence were ineffectual. In death, the dynamic black activist carried a greater effect upon the mood of black Americans and other non-whites than anyone in a generation. Newspapers across the Third World hailed Malcolm as 'the militant and most popular of Afro-American anti-segregationist leaders'. Black psychologist Kenneth Clark praised Malcolm for trying 'to find a place in the fight for civil rights'; author James Baldwin termed Malcolm's death 'a major setback for the Negro movement'. Widely quoted and long remembered were the remarks of black actor Ossie Davis at Malcolm's funeral:

Many will ask what Harlem finds to honor in this stormy, controversial and bold young captain – and we will smile. They will say that he is of hate – a fanatic, a racist. . . . And we will answer. . . . Did you ever talk to Brother Malcolm? Did you ever touch him, or have him smile at you? Did you ever really listen to him? Did he ever do a mean thing? Was he ever himself associated with violence or any public disturbance? For if you did you would know him . . . Malcolm was our manhood, our living, black manhood! This was his meaning to his people. And, in honoring him, we honor the best in ourselves. And we will know him then for what he was and is – a Prince – our own black shining Prince! – who didn't hesitate to die, because he loved us so.

Dead at the age of 39, Malcolm quickly became the fountainhead of the modern renaissance of black nationalism in the late 1960s. His autobiography and published speeches were widely read; even millions of white radicals grew to respect and honour Malcolm's legacy. Black nationalist groups with very divergent political and economic programmes all referred to Malcolm as their theoretical touchstone. Even among his bitterest opponents, Malcolm evoked a kind of grudging respect. Prophetically, Wilkins said of him, 'Master spell-binder that he was, Malcolm X in death cast a spell more far-flung and more disturbing than any he cast in life'.[17]

II

Even before the assassination of Malcolm, many social critics sensed that non-violent direct action, a tactic of protest used effectively in the South, would have little appeal in the Northern ghetto. Far more likely were a series of urban social upheavals which could not be controlled or channelled by the civil rights leadership. In 1963, James Baldwin predicted that race riots would soon 'spread to every metropolitan center in the nation which has a significant Negro population'.[18] In the spring and summer months of 1964, 1965, 1966, 1967 and 1968, massive black rebellions swept across almost every major US city in the Northeast, Middle West and California. In Watts and Compton, the black districts of Los Angeles, black men and women took to the streets, attacking and burning white-owned property and institutions. The Watts rebellion left $40 million in private property damage and 34 persons killed. Federal authorities ordered 15,000 state police and National Guardsmen into Detroit to quell that city's uprising of 1967. In Detroit 43 residents were killed; almost 2000 were injured; 2700 white-owned ghetto businesses were broken into, and 50 per cent of these were gutted by fire or completely destroyed; fourteen square miles of Detroit's inner city were torched; 5000 black persons were left without homes. Combining the total weight of socio-economic destruction, the ghetto rebellions from 1964 to 1972 led to 250 deaths, 10,000 serious injuries, and 60,000 arrests, at a cost of police, troops, other coercive measures taken by the state and losses to business amounting to billions of dollars.

Sociologists and politicians alike were at a loss to explain the furore of these 'twentieth century slave revolts'. They tacitly had assumed that Federal measures toward desegregation would lead to a lessening of racial tensions. Now they had to confront their own theoretical inadequacies. A few white liberals, reluctant as always to accept harsh realities, attempted to explain away the revolts, claiming that most blacks were satisfied with gradual, liberal reforms, and opposed the violence in their communities. Many others defined the rebellions as quasi-anarchistic 'riots', which were grounded in an urban youth subculture of social deviance. Herbert J. Gans, a consultant to the National Advisory Commission on Civil Disorders, claimed: 'No one knows exactly what sets off the spiraling process [of urban rebellion]. However, most of the rebellious . . . takes on the mood of a carnival. This is not because the participants are callous, but because they are happy at the sudden chance to exact revenge against those who have long exploited and harassed them. The rebellion becomes a community event.'[19] Closer to the mark was black sociologist Kenneth Clark, author of *Dark Ghetto*, who suggested: 'Human beings who are forced to live under ghetto conditions and whose daily experience tells them that almost nowhere in society are they respected and granted the ordinary dignity and courtesy accorded to others, will, as a matter of course, begin to doubt their own worth'. The act of rebellion, the collective venting of long-held hostilities, was in a social and psychological sense a rejection of blacks' 'pernicious self- and group-hatred' imposed by the white society.[20] Another important yet overlooked factor in understanding these rebellions was the growth of unfulfilled 'rising expectations' among many blacks. In some respects, the 1960s brought an unprecedented improvement in the material, day-to-day conditions for the black working class. From 1964 to 1969, the median black family income in the US increased from $5921 to $8074. The ratio between the median family incomes between blacks and whites narrowed from 54 per cent to 61 per cent. The percentage of black families below the US poverty level declined from 48.1 per cent in 1959 to 27.9 per cent in 1969. Unemployment rates for non-white married males with families dropped from 7.2 per cent in 1962, 4.3 per cent in 1965, to a low 2.5 per cent in 1969. But even these modest advances in jobs, civil rights, and other areas did not keep pace with the expectations of freedom which had awakened the black masses during the decade. Non-white youth unemployment actually increased in these years, from 24.4 per cent in 1960 to 29.1 per cent in 1970. The quality of black urban life – poor housing, rat infestation, crime, high infant mortality rates, disease, poor public education – continued to deteriorate.

Against this volatile background of black urban rebellion, the Civil Rights Movement could not exist as it had in previous years. On 5 June 1966, the first black student to attend the University of Mississippi, James Meredith, began a march from Memphis to Jackson as an individualist act to assert all blacks' rights to move across the South unmolested. Within hours, Meredith was the victim of a shotgun attack. Promptly flying to Memphis, King, McKissick and Carmichael agreed to complete Meredith's symbolic march to Jackson. From the beginning, dissension filled the ranks. Charles Evers, the brother of the martyred NAACP leader, complained, 'I don't see how walking up and down a hot highway helps: I'm for walking house to house and fence to fence to get Negroes registered'.[21] King was having an increasingly difficult time trying to keep SNCC's black nationalists in check. Carmichael pressured King to accept the request of the Deacons of Defense, a militant, Southern black organisation, to provide paramilitary protection during the protest. As the march progressed, SNCC activist Willie Ricks began to promote the slogan, 'Black Power'. As a political expression, Black Power was nothing new: novelist Richard Wright and politician Adam Clayton Powell had used it before, as well as others. But combined with Ricks' infectious contempt for Mississippi's white authorities, and in the context of the Meredith March, the slogan captured the mood of the majority of CORE and SNCC activists and most rural blacks as well. On 16 June, Carmichael and several others were arrested and held for six hours in Greenwood, Mississippi. After his release, Carmichael informed a rally of supporters: 'This is the twenty-seventh time I have been arrested. I ain't going to jail no more. What we gonna start saying now is "black power". ' Ricks perceptively picked up the phrase, demanding, 'What do you want?' Blacks from the rural community and SNCC activists alike chanted,

'Black Power!' Later, King desperately tried to keep others from using the phrase, describing it as 'an unfortunate choice of words'. It was too late.[22] McKissick now sided firmly with Carmichael, explaining that 'Black Power is not Black supremacy; it is a united Black Voice reflecting racial pride in the tradition of our heterogeneous nation. Black Power does not mean the exclusion of White Americans from the Negro Revolution; it means the inclusion of all men in a common moral and political struggle.'[23] Within two weeks, 'black power' sparked a national debate, dividing old friends, and bringing to an abrupt halt the last vestiges of unity between the left and right wings of the desegregation movement.

Never had the Old Guard integrationists moved so swiftly, even in battling the forces of racism. At the July 1966 NAACP convention, Wilkins led the assault. 'No matter how endlessly they try to explain it, the term "black power" means anti-white power', he declared. 'It is a reverse Mississippi, reverse Hitler, a reverse Ku Klux Klan.' Black Power was a 'quick, uncritical and highly emotional' slogan that would culminate in 'black death'.[24] Whitney Young warned that the Urban League would denounce ties with SNCC, CORE, or any group that 'formally adopted black power' or attached issues of 'domestic civil rights with the Vietnam conflict'. Johnson and Vice President Hubert H. Humphrey also condemned Black Power, as did the rising leader of the Democratic Party's liberal wing, New York Senator Robert Kennedy.[25] After decades of pursuing the goal of black independent political power, NAACP leader Henry Lee Moon was repelled to confront his own logic. Black Power is a 'naive expression, at worst diabolical, in the sense that at worst it's designed to create chaos', Moon stated defensively. The most articulate attack came from the Old Guard's most authoritative intellectual, Bayard Rustin. The former radical declared that Black Powerites had no real social programme or coherent political philosophy; like Garveyism, it depended on simplistic 'slogan' politics; and that it was 'utopian and reactionary – the former for the by now obvious reason that one-tenth of the population cannot accomplish much by itself, the latter because [it] would remove Negroes from the main area of political struggle. . . .' National media painted Carmichael, McKissick and other defenders of Black Power as 'racist demagogues' who were 'inching dangerously toward a philosophy of black separatism'.[26] King also had little choice except to denounce Black Power, but in doing so, he strived to maintain some personal link with the young people who had once idealised him. In his last book, *Where Do We Go From Here: Chaos or Community?*, King admitted that there were 'positive aspects of Black Power, which are compatible with what we have sought to do in the civil rights movement. . . .' On balance, however, Black Power's 'negative values prevent it from having the substance and program to become the basic strategy for the civil rights movement. Beneath all the satisfaction of a gratifying slogan, Black Power is a nihilistic philosophy born out of the conviction that the Negro can't win.'[27]

In the movement's militant wing, Black Power simply completed the evolution from integrationist to black nationalist ideologies which had begun three years before. Setting the tone for CORE, McKissick announced, '1966 shall be remembered as the year we left our imposed status of Negroes and became *Black Men* . . . when black men realized their full worth in society – their dignity and their beauty – and their power'. CORE's 1966 convention was an inversion of the NAACP conference. Speaking at a CORE plenary session, Carmichael stated, 'We don't need white liberals. . . . We have to make integration irrelevant'. Harlem leader Roy Innis pushed through a successful resolution which stated officially that CORE no longer favoured integration. CORE proclaimed that non-violent direct action was 'a dying philosophy', and whites were told that they were no longer welcome in the formation.[28] As a result of the convention's actions, almost all white liberal patronage of CORE ceased. Several locals with white members vehemently opposed Black Power, and left the organisation by the autumn of 1966. In two years, McKissick was replaced by the more militant nationalist, Innis. Inside SNCC, most white veterans had left, or were soon to resign. Lewis and SNCC's former field secretary Charles Sherrod quit the group in 1966. In public image, SNCC became more violent and revolutionary. When a Carmichael appearance at Vanderbilt University accidentally coincided with an urban rebellion in which 94 persons were jailed, Tennessee legislators demanded that Carmichael be deported from the US. Radical nationalists even attacked the much respected Fannie Lou Hamer for not accepting the necessity to expel whites, charging that she was 'no longer relevant' to the cause of black liberation. SNCC activities in Houston were involved in a May 1967 campus demonstration in which two police and one student were shot and 481 were jailed. On 7 February 1968 former SNCC leader Cleveland Sellers organised a student demonstration at South

Carolina State College which later culminated in a white police riot, leaving 3 students killed and 33 others wounded.

By 1967 and early 1968, Black Power had become the dominant ideological concept among a majority of black youth, and significant portions of the black working class and middle strata. But 'Black Power' itself still remained as elusive and imprecise as it had been when Ricks chanted the phrase on a rural Mississippi highway. What was Black Power? Most radical blacks disagreed among themselves. In the 1967 book *Black Power*, co-authors Carmichael and political scientist Charles V. Hamilton declared that the concept was 'a political framework and ideology which represents the last reasonable opportunity for this society to work out its racial problems short of prolonged destructive guerrilla warfare'. Black Power would permit blacks to 'exercise control over our lives, politically, economically and psychically. We will also contribute to the development of a viable larger society . . . there is nothing unilateral about the movement to free black people.'[29] One militant CORE leader from Brooklyn, Robert Carson, related Black Power to a socialist transformation of the US. 'I believe that capitalism has to be destroyed if black people are to be free', Carson told CORE's 1968 convention in Columbus, Ohio. 'We don't want anything to do with the white power structure as it is now.'[30] SNCC staff member Julius Lester wrote that Black Power was 'only another manifestation of what is transpiring in Latin America, Asia, and Africa. People are reclaiming their lives on those three continents and blacks in America are reclaiming theirs. These liberation movements are not saying give us a share; they are saying we want it all!'[31] Further to the right, Julian Bond described Black Power as simply 'a natural extension of the work of the civil rights movement. . . . From the courtroom to the streets in favor of integrated facilities; from the streets on backwoods roads in quest of the right to vote; from the ballot box to the meat of politics, the organization of voters into self-interest units'.[32] Perhaps the most radical interpretation of Black Power was made by black socialist theorist James Boggs, a former Detroit autoworker. The US was a 'fascist' state with a 'master majority race', Boggs wrote in early 1967. Black Power was first the 'scientific' recognition that 'there is no historical basis for the promise, constantly made to blacks by American radicals, that the white workers will join with them against the capitalist enemy'. As a political ideology, it represented the new revolutionary social force of the black population concentrated in the black belt of the South and in the urban ghettoes of the North – a revolutionary social force which must struggle not only against the capitalists but against the workers and middle classes who benefit by and support the system which has oppressed and exploited blacks. To expect the Black Power struggle to embrace white workers inside the black struggle is in fact to expect the revolution to welcome the enemy into its camp.

Other black radicals, in the Communist Party and elsewhere, tended to view Black Power as an anti-capitalist slogan.[33]

These lofty theoretical constructs had no direct impact upon Afro-American reality. For as the black left sought to reconstruct itself, after the harsh vacuum imposed by years of McCarthysim and Cold War Liberalism, Black Power quickly became the cornerstone of conservative forces. The first major Black Power Conference was held in Newark, New Jersey, in July 1967, and was organised by a black Republican, Nathan Wright. The conference was housed in a plush, white-owned hotel, and a stiff registration fee ($25) held down the number of black poor peoples' activists and working-class progressives who wished to attend. The conference attracted 1300 mostly middle-class black professionals, and concluded with a statement to the effect that Black Power connoted getting a 'fair share' of American capitalism. The subsequent Black Power Conference, held in Philadelphia in June 1968, was formally co-sponsored by a white corporation, Clairol Company. Clairol's president spoke before the black gathering and gave a hearty endorsement for Black Power. The phrase in his words meant black 'ownership of apartments, ownership of homes, ownership of businesses, as well as equitable treatment for all people'. In short, Black Power was Black Capitalism. Quickly perceiving this, Richard Nixon, who was running again for the presidency in 1968, took an aggressive pro-Black Power posture. As Nixon defined the term in a Milwaukee, Wisconsin, speech on 28 March 1968, Black Power was 'the power that people should have over their own destinies, the power to affect their own communities, the power that comes from participation in the political and economic processes of society'. Nixon spelled out his thesis at greater length in a subsequent address:

. . . Much of the black militant talk these days is actually in terms far closer to the doctrines of free enterprise than to those of the welfarist thirties – terms of 'pride', 'ownership', 'private enterprise', 'capital', 'self-assurance', 'self-respect'. . . . What most of the militants are asking is not separation, but to be included in – not as supplicants, but as owners, as entrepreneurs – to have a share of the wealth and a piece of the action. And this is precisely what the Federal central target of the new approach ought to be. It ought to be oriented toward more black ownership, for from this can flow the rest – black pride, black jobs, black opportunity and yes, black power . . .[34]

Nixon's endorsement of Black Power as Black Capitalism was applauded by major corporations and the financial sector's chief organ, the *Wall Street Journal*. It was also supported and praised by McKissick and Innis.

The only major social theorist who understood the fundamentally pro-capitalist thrust of many Black Powerites by 1967 was Harold Cruse. Cruse drafted an essay 'Behind the Black Power Slogan', which was prepared for a US Socialist Scholars' Conference. In his characteristically abrasive style, Cruse argued with socialists that Black Power had absolutely nothing to do with revolutionary demands or Marxism:

> *Black Power is nothing but the economic and political philosophy of Booker T. Washington given a 1960's militant shot in the arm and brought up to date.* The curious fact about it is that the very last people to admit that Black Power is militant Booker T-ism are the Black Power theorists themselves. . . . The Black Power ideology is *not* at all revolutionary in terms of its economic and political ambitions; it is, in fact, a *social reformist* ideology. It is not meant to be a criticism of the Black Power movement to call it 'reformist'; there is nothing wrong or detrimental about social reforms. But we must not fail to call reformism what it in fact is. The Black Power theorists who believe their slogan is in fact a revolutionary slogan are mistaken. . . . What *does* have a revolutionary implication about Black Power is the 'defensive violence' upheld and practiced by its ultra-extremist-nationalist-urban guerrilla wing, which is a *revolutionary anarchist* tendency. Thus we have a unique American form of black revolutionary anarchism with a social reform economic and political 'program.'

Cruse

Cruse also dismissed the socialists' now-popular interpretation of Malcolm as becoming a revolutionary 'internationalist socialist' in the months before his assassination. Tracing his theoretical roots from the traditional black nationalism of Garvey, and then back into the political accommodationism of Washington, Cruse argued that Malcolm 'was headed toward what became the Black Power position – which is *not* a revolutionary position. None of Malcolm's views on economics, politics, and self-defense was original with him. Malcolm X remained a militant black nationalist until the moment he died.'[35]

Thus, from its origins, Black Power was not a coherent ideology, and never developed a unitary programme which was commonly supported by a majority of its proponents. As the radical theoreticians and conservatives laid claims to the mantle of Malcolm, the notion of Black Power was transmitted to all strata of black society as a contradictory set of dogmas, platitudes, political beliefs, and cultural activities. Cruse noted with biting cynicism, 'many of the rebellious urban youth think Black Power means "Get the cops!" "Burn, baby, burn!" "Down with Whitey!" or "Let's get the loot!" '[36] Debbie Louis explained that Black Power's popularity was a product of its inherent ambiguity. In the late 1960s, 'the black community stood as a conglomeration of often contradictory interests and directions, dubiously tied together by a common mood which combined centuries of anger with new hope, increasing desperation with new confidence'. Black Power was diluted and expressed popularly in divergent ways: 'black people were addressing each other as "brother" when they passed in the streets; "soul food" restaurants became a matter of community pride; "black history" the all-consuming topic, Malcolm X the authoritative source. Even seven-year-old black children seemed to know a phrase or two of Swahili. Was this black power?'[37]

III

Black Power was not the only issue which divided black America in the mid- and late 1960s. Concurrent with the domestic unrest over the present and future position of the Negro was a growing public debate over the government's involvement in Southeast Asia. During the Cold War, the Eisenhower Administration assisted in the establishment of a corrupt, pro-US dictatorship in South Vietnam. Under Kennedy, the number of US military advisers increased steadily. In

January 1965, 25,000 US troops were stationed in Vietnam, and were actively fighting both communist North Vietnamese regulars and the popular organisation of the South's workers and peasants, the National Liberation Front. In 1966, US forces in the country increased to 184,000; by January 1969, 536,000 US troops were stationed in Vietnam. For black Americans, the war had a direct impact upon every community.

In the two decades after World War II, the number of blacks in all services almost tripled, from 107,000 in 1949 to 303,000 in 1967. Even after the desegregation of the armed services, blacks were poorly represented in the officers' ranks, and grossly over-represented among enlisted personnel. For example, in 1967, in the Marine Corps, 9.6 per cent of all enlisted men were black, while only 0.7 per cent were officers; in the army, 13.5 per cent of all enlisted personnel were black, and only 3.4 per cent of the army's officers were black. Afro-Americans comprised one out of every seven US soldiers stationed in Vietnam, and because blacks tended to be placed in 'combat units' more often than middle-class whites, they also bore unfairly higher risks of being killed and wounded. From January to November 1966, 22.4 per cent of all army casualties were black. Black leaders in the NAACP and Urban League viewed the Vietnam War as a tremendous opportunity to ingratiate themselves with the Johnson Administration. In one polemic against Black Power, drafted in November 1966, and signed by Rustin, Wilkins, Young, A.M.E. Church Bishop Carey A. Gibbs, Dorothy Height (leader of the National Council of Negro Women), and others, they reminded white Americans that most blacks eschewed domestic violence in favour of fighting abroad to protect US interests. 'For every Negro who tosses a Molotov cocktail, there are a thousand fighting and dying on the battlefields of Vietnam', they stated.[38] To their black critics, they warned that Vietnam had nothing to do with domestic politics and civil rights. Both the NAACP and the Urban League concluded that the mounting black casualty totals from Southeast Asia were irrelevant to the struggle to win racial reforms at home.

Malcolm X understood that the Old Guard's position was both politically stupid and morally bankrupt. Even before 3000 black troops had been stationed in Vietnam, he analysed the issue and had condemned both the Johnson Administration and the Negro élite. Malcolm argued that the French had not been able to defeat the Vietnamese nationalists, and that the US would also have to admit failure within a few years. The war itself 'shows the real ignorance of those who control the American power structure . . . [their] ignorance and blindness'.[39] SNCC was the first civil rights group to denounce the Vietnam War in uncompromising terms. In a press release of 6 January 1966, SNCC declared that the US government 'has been deceptive in its claims of concern for the freedom of the Vietnamese people'. The Johnson Administration was 'pursuing an aggressive policy in violation of international law. We maintain that our country's cry of "preserve freedom in the world" is a hypocritical mask behind which it squashed liberation movements which are not bound and refuse to be bound by the expedience of the United States cold war policy'.[40] The SNCC statement was bitterly attacked by Wilkins. Clifford Alexander, one of Johnson's chief black assistants, began to organise black US Representatives and others to blunt the effect of the statement. But SNCC continued its attack on Johnson's Vietnam policies. When SNCC decided to demonstrate in front of the White House during the wedding of Johnson's daughter, in symbolic protest against the Vietnam War, Wilkins, King, Randolph and Young pleaded with the group to cancel the action. SNCC activists challenged black youth to oppose the war. At Baltimore's Morgan State University, Carmichael insisted, 'the war in Vietnam should interest you not only personally, but also because it is very political for black people'. Black students were urged to resist the draft. 'Either you go to the Leavenworth Federal penitentiary in Kansas or you become a killer. I will choose to suffer', Carmichael stated. 'I will go to jail. To hell with this country.'[41]

Black progressives in electoral politics began to speak in opposition to the war. Julian Bond, elected to the Georgia State House of Representatives, defended the right of 'the Vietnamese peasants who . . . have expressed a real desire to govern themselves'. The 'gunboat diplomacy of the past' had little place in contemporary world affairs.[42] The most articulate opponent of the US war effort, black or white, was US Representative Ronald V. Dellums. From the floor of Congress, Dellums declared:

I consider our involvement in Indochina illegal, immoral, and insane. We are in a war which is the greatest human and economic drain on American resources in modern times – a war disproportionately waged on the backs of blacks and browns and reds and yellows and poor and working class whites, a war resulting in an untold number of deaths of the Vietnamese people, a war that is justified only by the notion that we, as a nation, must save face . . . the only way this nation can save face with respect to our involvement in Indochina is to stand up and admit to the world we made a tragic mistake in Southeast Asia and then to get out of Vietnam. . . . Millions of people in the country are no longer willing to engage in such folly and be cannon fodder, and go across the water to spill their blood on foreign soil in a cause many of them do not even understand.[43]

Black activists and intellectuals, who were part of the Black Power movement, had grave reservations about participating in anti-war organisations dominated by white liberals and leftists. But almost all of them, including CORE's proponents of Black Capitalism, had little to say in favour of black participation in the war effort. In April 1968, SNCC activist John Wilson organised a national anti-war conference in New York City which brought together hundreds of black nationalists and community militants. Baldwin lent his considerable talents as a polemicist to the anti-war cause. 'Long, long before the Americans decided to liberate the Southeast Asians, they decided to liberate me: my ancestors carried these scars to the grave, and so will I', Baldwin wrote. 'A racist society can't but fight a racist war – this is the bitter truth. The assumptions acted on at home are also acted on abroad, and every American Negro knows this, for he, after the American Indian, was the first "Viet Cong" victim.' Black literary critic Addison Gayle, Jr., praised the 'large number of black men [who] would prefer to die fighting tyranny, oppression, hunger and disease in the black ghettoes of America than to die in the jungles of Vietnam'. Black poets were also among the most effective critics of America's war. S. E. Anderson's 'Junglegrave' was written as an ode to the black soldiers overseas:

> Send me no flowers, for they will die
> before they leave America
> Send me home, no matter how far strewn
> I am across this rice-filled land
> Send me home, man, send me home
> even if I am headless or faceless
> Keep my casket open and my grave uncovered . . .
> Vietnam: land of yellow and black genocide

Send the President my flowers cremated and
scented with the odors
Of my brothers' napalmed flesh and my
sisters' bombed out skulls
Send me no flowers . . .

Robert Hayden's 'Words in the Mourning Time' evoked echoes of
DuBois' yearnings for peace a generation before:

Vietnam bloodclotted name in my consciousness/
recurring and recurring/ like the obsessive thought
many midnights/ now of my own dying
Vietnam and I think of the villages/
mistakenly burning the schoolrooms
devouring/ their children and I think
of those who/ were my students/
brutalized killing/ wasted by horror/
in ultimate loneliness/ dying/
Vietnam Vietnam.[44]

During the bitter national debate on Vietnam, all public leaders
within black America were forced to choose sides. As a dedicated
pacifist, King could not look upon the conflict benignly without
taking some kind of public stand against the war. At the annual SCLC
executive board meeting held in Baltimore on 1–2 April 1965, King
expressed the need to criticise the Johnson Administration's policies
in Southeast Asia. His old colleagues, fearful that King's support for
the anti-war movement would hurt the SCLC financially and
politically, voted to allow him to do so only as a private person,
without organisational endorsement. Rustin, who still maintained
close ties with King, tried to pressure the SCLC leader into a position
of neutrality on Vietnam. On 10 September 1965, Rustin, King, and
SCLC aides Andrew Young and Bernard Lee met with United
Nation's Ambassador Arthur Goldberg. Goldberg convinced King,
for the moment, that the Johnson Administration had every
intention of bringing the conflict to a peaceful resolution. For several
months, King watched patiently as the number of US troops
increased. Finally in January 1966, King published a strong attack on
the Vietnam War. 'Some of my friends of both races and others who
do not consider themselves my friends have expressed disapproval

because I have been voicing concern over the war in Vietnam', King stated. But as a Christian, he had no choice except to 'declare that war is wrong'. Black leaders could not become blind to the rest of the world's issues, while engaged solely in problems of domestic race relations. 'The Negro must not allow himself to become a victim of the self-serving philosophy of those who manufacture war that the survival of the world is the white man's business alone.'[45] The negative response to King's statement was swift. SCLC leaders in Chattanooga, Tennessee, severed relations with the organisation in protest. Whitney Young replied that blacks were not interested in the issue. King lobbied hard among his allies in SCLC to back his position on Vietnam, and in the spring of 1966 the organisation's executive board came out officially against the war.

The SCLC's primary national focus shifted to Chicago in 1966, in an effort to gain jobs and housing desegregation in a major Northern city. Chicago's political machine, led by the city's tough and unscrupulous mayor Richard Daley, was more than a match for the SCLC. Unlike the Southern segregationists, Daley had the full support of the Johnson Administration and the Democratic Party. The meagre anti-racist concessions which King and other top aides, notably Jesse Jackson, James Bevel, and Andrew Young, were able to extract from the 'Northern segregationists' did not justify the financial and personnel expenditures of the long and hard campaign. Increasingly, King's attention was drawn to the Vietnam issue, and also to the necessity for black Americans to devise a more radical strategy for domestic reforms. 'For years I labored with the idea of reforming the existing institutions of the society, a little change here, a little change there. Now I feel quite differently', King admitted in 1966.[46] Quietly, King was beginning to articulate a democratic socialist vision for American society: the nationalisation of basic industries; massive federal expenditures to revive central cities and to provide jobs for ghetto residents; a guaranteed income for every adult American. King had concluded, like Malcolm X, that America's political economy of capitalism had to be transformed, that the Civil Rights Movement's old goals of voter education, registration, and desegregated public facilities were only a beginning step down the long road towards biracial democracy. And like DuBois, King recognised the correlation between his democratic socialist ideals and the peace issue. Massive US military spending and the bloody war effort in Vietnam meant that the nation as a whole had less revenue to attack domestic poverty, illiteracy, and unemployment. These new ideas forced King to conclude that the Vietnam conflict had to end immediately. On 4 April 1967, speaking at New York City's Riverside Church, King announced: 'It would be very inconsistent for me to teach and preach nonviolence in this situation and then applaud violence when thousands and thousands of people, both adults and children, are being maimed and mutilated and many killed in this war'.[47] Eleven days later, in New York City's Central Park, King led a rally of 125,000 in protest against the war.

Just as the Truman Administration had sponsored a 'political assassination' of DuBois' influence during the 1950s, another Democratic president was now ready and quite willing to take steps towards reducing King's reputation. Johnson's black epigones did whatever they could to destroy the image and popularity of King. Ralph Bunche urged King either to cease his attacks on the Johnson Administration, or to relinquish his role as a civil rights leader. Rustin, who was appointed director of the A. Philip Randolph Institute, vilified King's stance on the war. NAACP and Urban League officials privately and publicly attacked King and defended Johnson. Black Republican Edward Brooke, elected to the Senate from Massachusetts on an anti-war platform, swung behind the Vietnam War in 1967 and joined the anti-King chorus. Carl Rowan drafted a vicious, brutal essay against King which appeared in *Reader's Digest* magazine. King's response was identical with that of DuBois – he moved even further to the left. Defiantly, King announced an SCLC-sponsored campaign against poverty, the Poor Peoples' March, which would bring thousands of the unemployed and the oppressed of all races into Washington, DC in April 1968. Their demands for legislative action would include a federal guaranteed incomes policy. On 23 February 1968, the one-hundredth anniversary of the birth of DuBois, King gave the keynote address honouring him in New York City. 'So many would like to ignore the fact that DuBois was a Communist in his last years', King noted. In an obvious reference to Vietnam, King added, 'Our irrational, obsessive anti-Communism has led us into too many quagmires'.[48] When black Memphis sanitation workers voted to strike on 12 February, to protest against low wages and the accidental deaths of two black garbage men twelve days before, they asked the SCLC for help. King and his closest associates – Abernathy, Young, Jackson, Bevel – arrived in the Southern city to help mobilise popular support for the strike. The pacifist minister who once struggled for desegregated buses, was now, thirteen years after Montgomery, organising militant black urban workers, building a national poor peoples' march, and defying a president. He had come a long way; so had his vision for reconstructing America.

Speaking before a black audience in Memphis on 3 April, King was prediciting that their struggle would succeed. Then, abruptly and rather strangely, he began to talk about himself in the past tense:

> I don't know what will happen now. But it really doesn't matter to me now. Because I've been to the mountaintop. I won't mind. Like anybody, I would like to live a long life. Longevity has its place. But I'm not concerned about that now. I just want to do God's will. And He's allowed me to go up to the mountain. And I've looked over, and I've seen the promised land. . . . I may not get there with you, but I want you to know tonight that we as a people will get to the promised land. So I'm happy tonight. I'm not worried about anything. I'm not fearing any man. 'Mine eyes have seen the glory of the coming of the Lord.'[49]

King's assistants were bewildered and even a little angry with him. What was the meaning of the speech? Perhaps King sensed something that no-one else could possibly know. At 6:08 p.m., that next day, he was assassinated by a white man, James Earl Ray, in Memphis. Strangely, the police who had been guarding King were absent at the time of his death. Blacks across the country, even the militant nationalists, felt a grievous loss to the cause for racial freedom. White anti-war activists had lost their most effective and prominent representative; poor people and the black working class had lost a major spokesperson. More than anyone else in the period 1945–82, King would come closest to bringing together a biracial coalition demanding peace, civil rights, and basic structural changes within the capitalist order. King's assassination meant that any linkages between these vital reform movements would be much more difficult to achieve. And in the light of subsequent Congressional testimony and historical research on his death, King's unfinished search for more radical reforms in America may have been the central reason he was killed.

IV

King's assassination was only one more indication to black nationalists that white capitalist America had no intention of resolving racial
conflicts 'nonviolently'. By 1968, the black nationalist renaissance
had begun to inspire a tremendous outpouring of literary criticism,
poetry, music and art, all of which served to reinforce Black Power
and the uneven nationalist movement, in politics. In their myriad
voices, the new black aestheticians played a critical role in forging a
popular nationalist consciousness. Post-Harlem Renaissance poets
Dudley Randall, Margaret Walker and Gwendolyn Brooks, all of
whom were over 50-years-old, acted informally as patrons and
inspirations for the younger artists. Hoyt W. Fuller, editor of the *Black
World*, used his magazine to introduce to black America a growing list
of poets and playwrights: Etheridge Knight, author of *Poems From
Prison* (1968); Naomi Madgett, author of *Star by Star* (1965); Carolyn
M. Rodgers, whose poems appeared in *Paper Soul* (1968); and *Songs of
a Blackbird* (1970); Mari Evans, author of *Where Is All the Music?*
(1967); and *I Am A Black Woman* (1970); Sonia Sanchez, author of
Homecoming (1969) and *We are a BaddDDD people* (1970); Don L. Lee,
founder of the Institute of Positive Education in Chicago, Third
World Press, and author of *Black Pride* (1968); *Think Black* (1969),
Don't Cry, Scream (1969), and *We Walk the Way of the New World* (1970);
and essayist June Jordan, whose collected poems appeared in *Some
Changes* (1970). Perhaps the two most popular black poets of the
period were LeRoi Jones (Imamu Amiri Baraka) and Nikki
Giovanni. Born in 1934, Jones was first part of the 'beat generation' of
essayists and critics in America's version of the Left Bank, Greenwich
Village, New York. In the mid-1960s he became actively involved as a
nationalist in Harlem and nearby Newark, New Jersey. Changing his
name, renouncing his white wife and liberal associates, Baraka
established Spirit House, a centre for the black arts and culture in
Newark. Baraka won acclaim as a prolific nationalist writer: *Home:
Social Essays* (1966); *Black Music* (1970); *Raise, Race, Rays, Race* (1971);
It's Nation Time (1970); Kawaida Studies: *The New Nationalism* (1972);
Afrikan Revolution (1973). His political poetry and plays were recited
and performed by thousands of young blacks in secondary schools
and colleges across the country. Ten years Baraka's junior,
Giovanni's emergence was especially meteoric. In her popular poetry

collection *Black Feeling, Black Talk, Black Judgement* (1970), Giovanni
spoke uncompromisingly of the necessity for violence:

> Nigger
> Can you Kill
> Can you Kill
> Can a nigger kill
> Can a nigger kill a honkie . . .
> Can you shoot straight and
> Fire for good measure
> Can you splatter their brains in the street
> Can you kill them
> Can you lure them to bed to kill them
> We kill in Viet Nam for them . . .
> Can we learn to kill WHITE for BLACK
> Learn to kill niggers
> Learn to be Black men.[50]

Integration was a bogus illusion; the liberation of 'the black nation'
would not be achieved via the ballotbox:

> . . . this second reconstruction is being aborted as was the first . . .
> if we vote this season we ought to seek to make it effective
> the barrel of a gun is the best voting machine
> your best protest vote is a dead honkie. . . .[51]

The rejection of integration as a social and cultural ideal sparked
the development of a new interest in Africa. The writings of
Martinique's revolutionary social theorist Frantz Fanon, a psychiatrist who took part in the Algerian revolution of the 1950s, were
popularly read by black Americans. Books by African socialists and
leaders such as Tanzania's Julius Nyerere, Ghana's Kwame
Nkrumah, and Guiné-Bissau theorist Amilcar Cabral became an
integral part of the Afro-American revolutionary nationalists' lexi-
con. It is not altogether clear that black Americans adopted the
insights of African and Caribbean revolutionaries in constructive and
appropriate ways. West coast nationalist Maulana Ron Karenga
developed a black cultural catechism, the 'nguzo saba', and a black
holiday, 'Kwanzaa', which employed the Swahili language and
cultural imagery of Tanzanian traditional society. Karenga argued

that black revolution was not a class struggle, but a battle to change 'racist minds' and the patterns of black culture. 'The international issue is racism, not economics', he suggested in 1967. 'Race rules out economics because whites are racists, not just capitalists.'[52] Yet Nyerere's *Ujamaa: Essays on Socialism*, make the point that 'socialism and racialism are incompatible. The man or woman who hates "Jews", or "Asians", or "Europeans", or even "West Europeans" and Americans is not a socialist', Nyerere argued. 'He is denying the equality and brotherhood of man. Those who stand for the interests of the workers and peasants, anywhere in the world, are our friends.'[53] Carmichael declared that Fanon was one of his 'patron saints', and after the summer rebellions of 1967, one radical editor declared that 'every brother on a rooftop can quote Fanon'. Militant nationalists praised Fanon's advocacy of revolutionary violence, and his polemical thrusts aimed at the Negro petty bourgeoisie in colonial Africa. But what did Fanon think about the Afro-American struggle? 'The test cases of civil liberty whereby both whites and blacks in America try to drive back racial discrimination have very little in common in their principles and objectives' with African liberation efforts. For Fanon, the struggle to destroy white oppression was not in essence a racial dialectic, but an anti-racist movement that welcomed the participation of committed whites. In *Black Skin, White Masks* (1952), Fanon's most 'nationalist-oriented' work, he explained that his ultimate vision for the US was the liberation of all exploited people: 'I can already see a white man and a black man hand in hand'.[54] The question here is not much that of intellectual dishonesty, but a failure of many Black Powerites to relate their eclectic versions of nationalism to the actual material needs and aspirations of the black working class and the poor. Addison Gayle characterised many of these dogmatic black separatists as 'black fascists' in 1970:

> The Professional Nationalist [has] a 'more militant than thou' attitude. He has read Fanon – although he does not understand him . . . and quotes Malcolm verbatim. This superficial machinery is designed to prove his militancy; yet, in effect, it allows him to serve as a liaison between the black community uptown and the [white] Man downtown. . . . The [black] fascist is not interested in persuading men to accept his point of view through reason and logic – since his point of view differs little from The Man's. Instead, he hopes to establish a totalitarian apparatus wherein all proposals

will be subject to his authority. . . . If the fascists are allowed to take over a movement begun by sincere and honest people, then we will have not Black Power but Black Fascism, differing in no respect from the white fascism against which Blacks have fought and died throughout our history in this country.[55]

Nationalists of every kind, from the nihilistic 'cultural nationalists' or 'black fascists' which Gayle described, to the socialist-oriented nationalists on the left, to Black Capitalists, rapidly created institutions and groups which influenced electoral politics. In Michigan, many nationalists were involved in the Freedom Now Party, which in 1964 placed 39 black independent candidates on the ballot. In 1968, two black independents were presidential candidates, former prisoner and black revolutionary writer Eldridge Cleaver and social critic Dick Gregory. Cleaver, endorsed as the Peace and Freedom Party candidate, received 195,135 votes nationally, mostly from black revolutionary nationalists and white leftists. In a campaign marked more by political satire than actual political content, Gregory totalled 148,622 votes. At municipal levels, many black nationalists simply endorsed black middle-class candidates who ran independently from traditional, white-controlled business and political interests. Within the Democratic Party, middle-class Black Powerites supported the nominations of the Reverend Channing Phillips of Washington, DC for the president and Julian Bond for vice president at the Chicago national convention in August 1968. In the South, nationalists and integrationists alike supported several independent electoral efforts, including the black National Democratic Party of Alabama and Georgia's Party of Christian Democracy, both formed in 1968.

The most provocative challenge to white liberal politics was generated by the Black Panther Party, founded in Oakland, California, in October 1966, by two black college students, Huey P. Newton and Bobby Seale. Using the name of SNCC's formation from Lowndes County, Alabama, Newton and Seale developed a political cadre of militant young blacks. Their political philosophy, despite their revolutionary rhetoric, was basically that of radical reform. In their original 'Ten Point Program', the Black Panthers demanded from the American state the following reforms:

1. We want freedom. We want power to determine the destiny of our black community.

2. We want full employment for our people.
3. We want an end to the robbery by the white man of our black community.
4. We want decent housing, fit shelter of human beings.
5. We want education for our people that exposes the true nature of this decadent American society. We want education that teaches us our true history and our role in the present day society.
6. We want all black men to be exempt from military service.
7. We want an immediate end to *police brutality* and *murder* of black people.
8. We want freedom for all black men held in federal, state, county, and city prisons and jails.
9. We want all black people when brought to trial to be tried in court by a jury of their peer group or people from their black communities, as defined by the Constitution of the United States.
10. We want land, bread, housing, education, clothing, justice and peace.[56]

The Panthers recruited from the black working-class and poverty-stricken districts of East Oakland, California, organising armed patrols to defend the black community against police attacks. Newton, who had considerable knowledge of state and local laws, monitored police arrests of black inner city citizens, armed with a shotgun to ensure his own protection. In late 1967 the Panthers initiated a free breakfast programme for black children, and offered free health services to ghetto residents. Many white critics viewed the Black Panthers as a dangerous ultraleftist group and a threat to social order. But the Panthers pointedly affirmed their commitment to the American tradition of social change by quoting slaveholder Thomas Jefferson, the author of the Declaration of Independence, in their own programme:

Governments are instituted among men, deriving their just powers from the consent of the governed, [but] whenever any form of government becomes destructive . . . it is the right of people to alter or abolish it, and to institute new government, laying its foundations on such principles and organizing its powers in such form as to them shall seem most likely to effect their safety and happiness.

Unlike many nationalists, the Black Panthers quickly established organisational and programmatic relations with radical whites, and sought to lead a progressive coalition of Third World and white groups to battle the 'Establishment'.[57]

By the late 1960s, the Black Panthers had become the most influential revolutionary nationalist organisation in the US. Eldridge Cleaver joined the Panthers as their Minister of Information, and soon began to attract his own left tendency within the formation, oriented around his questionable thesis of 'lumpenproletarian revolution'. Cleaver married SNCC activist Kathleen Neal, who soon became the organisation's communication secretary. By early 1968, other SNCC veterans had become Panthers. Bob Brown, a close ally and friend of Carmichael, became director of the Chicago branch of the Black Panther Party; SNCC leader Chico Neblett served as the Panther's 'Field Marshal' for the western states of the US; Forman briefly assisted the Panther's organisational efforts, and in February 1968, Carmichael was named the party's Prime Minister. By 1969, Carmichael and his successor as head of SNCC, Hubert 'Rap' Brown, had broken with the Black Panthers because of Newton's and Cleaver's close ties with white leftists and the biracial Peace and Freedom Party. Other cultural nationalists viewed the Black Panther Party's emphasis on class struggle with great suspicion. Karenga's cultural nationalist formation, called US, bitterly opposed the Black Panthers' actions in California. Nationally, however, the Panthers succeeded in organising chapters in several dozen states, and had at least 5000 members by the end of 1968.

The black nationalist upsurgence was viewed by the American government with considerable alarm. Remarkably few black nationalists and Black Powerites had advocated violence against white-owned property, the subversion of authority, or the seizure of state power. Most Black Power spokespersons came from upwardly mobile working-class or middle-class backgrounds, were trained at universities, and had been groomed for ultimate assimilation into the existing system. Forman was an economics and management major at Chicago's Roosevelt University, president of his student body, and had done graduate work in African affairs at Boston University in the 1950s; Bevel was a ministerial student in Nashville's American Baptist Theological Seminary; Rap Brown was a student at Southern University; SNCC's Ralph Featherstone was an elementary school-teacher; Carmichael and Baraka were graduates of Howard University; Giovanni, Lester, Nash and Barry were trained at Fisk University; Karenga was the first black student body president at his junior college in Los Angeles, and was at work on a master's degree in politics at the University of California; Newton was the principal student leader at Oakland's Merrit College, and would later work towards a PhD degree. Only one small fraction of the major proponents of Black Power had the gritty background of Malcolm X, whose actual ordeal as part of the ghetto underworld served as a crucible for his ultimate political trajectory. But federal and state authorities, after years of inaction or, at times, active co-operation with racists and white supremacists, could not listen to the rhetoric of blacks with anything except severe trepidation. Black Power defined as Black Capitalism seemed harmless enough. But black nationalism, either in its most radical tendency as expressed by the Black Panthers, or in its more inchoate and chauvinistic manifestation as cultural nationalism, was seen as a direct threat to the survival of the republic. It was not enough to buttress the Old Guard integrationists, for they had lost much of their respectability in the eyes of millions of blacks. A more effective means to thwart black nationalism was to employ illegal and covert methods of repression against its proponents.

SNCC was the first radical black group targeted by the Federal Bureau of Investigation (FBI) and the US Justice Department for surveillance, disruption, and suppression. In late 1960, FBI agents began to monitor SNCC meetings. Johnson's Attorney General, Nicholas Katzenbach, gave approval for the FBI to wiretap all SNCC leaders' telephones in 1965. In August 1967, FBI Director J. Edgar Hoover ordered the extensive infiltration and disruption of SNCC, as well as other Black Power-oriented formations, such as the Militant Revolutionary Action Movements, the Deacons of Defense, and CORE. Hoover also included for federal scrutiny and repression non-revolutionary nationalist groups, such as the SCLC and the Nation of Islam. FBI agents spread the rumour that Carmichael was an agent for the CIA, creating severe rifts between SNCC activists. FBI agents were sent to monitor Carmichael and Brown wherever they went, seeking to elicit evidence to imprison them. Brown was charged with inciting a race riot in Maryland, and was eventually sentenced to five years in a federal penitentiary for carrying a rifle across state lines while under criminal indictment. Featherstone and SNCC activist Ché Payne were murdered on 9 March 1970, when a bomb exploded in their automobile in Bel Air, Maryland. Sellers was indicted for organising black students in South Carolina and for resisting the draft. Newton was shot in a 1967 confrontation in which one white police officer was killed, and was sentenced to prison for three years. Cleaver was forced to flee the US in late 1968 for violating parole restrictions, and went into exile. Seale was tried with several white radicals for inciting a riot in Chicago, and in the courtroom the judge ordered that he be bound and gagged. Local police and federal marshals raided Black Panther offices across the country. By July 1969, the Panthers had been targeted by 233 separate actions under the FBI's COINTELPRO, or Counter Intelligence Program. In 1969 alone, 27 Black Panthers were killed by the police, and 749 were jailed or arrested. Whenever possible, the FBI provoked violence between cultural and revolutionary nationalists. In 1969, the FBI was directly or indirectly responsible for engineering several murders, shootings and bombing attacks between US and the Black Panther Party. In Hoover's words, any illegal acts of suppression were justified, because the Panthers were 'the greatest threat to the internal security of the country'. The federal authorities would resort to political assassinations and any other gross violations of civil liberties to 'prevent a coalition of militant black nationalist groups' and to 'prevent the rise of a messiah' who could lead the black masses.[58]

The possibility for greater political repression increased with the presidential election of 1968. The three major candidates did not inspire enthusiastic support among many blacks or progressive whites: George Wallace, running as an independent on a platform of 'law-and-order' and racial bigotry; Democrat Hubert Humphrey, a Cold War liberal who had defended the Vietnam War during his undistinguished tenure as Johnson's vice president; and Republican nominee Richard Nixon. The assassination of Robert Kennedy in June 1968 left liberal Democrats bickering with unpopular Johnson's handpicked successor, Humphrey, and Wallace was able to mount a major effort, winning sizeable shares of the white working-class vote across the country. Blacks overwhelmingly supported Humphrey in the end, but by a margin of only one-half million votes out of 73.2 million cast, Nixon emerged as the winner with only 43.4 per cent of the popular vote. Nixon sought to placate the black middle class by appointing Farmer to his administration as assistant secretary of Health, Education and Welfare, and by continuing his advocacy of Black Capitalism. Towards progressives in the black movement, however, Nixon was absolutely ruthless. Nixon's vice president, former Maryland governor Spiro T. Agnew, was well known for his orders for police to 'shoot-to-kill' black urban rebels in Baltimore; for his statement that Rap Brown should be arrested – 'pick him up soon, put him away and throw away the key'; and for his blatant racism – 'when you've seen one ghetto, you've seen them all'.[59] Nixon's Attorney General, John Mitchell, co-operated with Hoover and the FBI to exterminate the Black Panthers and other militant Black organisations. Nixon made it perfectly clear to the NAACP and other Negro moderate groups that he had no intention of pursuing desegregation goals. Within one year after taking office, Leon E. Panetta, the director of civil rights for the Department of Health, Education and Welfare, resigned to protest against Nixon's reinstatement of Jim Crow directives. In the spring of 1970, 125 staff members in the Office of Civil Rights sent an open letter to Nixon, declaring 'bitter disappointment' over Panetta's departure and criticising the president's lack of 'strong moral leadership that we feel is now essential to avoid a reversal of the nation's long-standing commitment to equal opportunity'. For openly expressing views favourable to desegregation, Nixon's US Commissioner of Education, James A. Allen, was fired in 1970.[60]

The forces of racial inequality had won a major victory with the election of Richard Nixon. Yet the Black Power movement had not been checked. As the Black Panther Party was being destroyed as a national organisation by the FBI, other lesser known black activist groups were arising from community centres and colleges across the country. As the militant defenders of Black Power were silenced – either through imprisonment, exile, or assassination – newer, younger voices were still being heard. The integrationist Old Guard had been temporarily forced into retreat, buffeted by the massive popularity of black nationalism and under attack by the racist policies of the Nixon Administration. The number of black elected officials in the US had climbed from 100 in 1964 to 1400 in 1970; many of these men and women were also sympathetic to one or more variants of the Black Power trend. Thus, after the assassinations of Malcolm and Martin, the modern black movement for biracial democracy had been crippled, to be sure, but it was by no means destroyed. Yet the absence of a widely shared theory and strategy for black liberation was still missing; the political goal of black equality was still murky and ill-defined; the opportunism and accommodation of many black militants and political leaders still raised unresolved questions for future struggles; and the programmatic relationship between democracy and racial justice, socialism and peace that DuBois and King had strived to attain was becoming ever more distant.

6. Black Rebellion: Zenith and Decline, 1970–1976

It is the worst thing that can happen to the leader of an extreme party when he is forced to seize power in an epoch which is not yet ripe for the rule of a class which he represents, and for the carrying-out of the measures which this class demands. What he *can* do does not depend upon his will, but upon the level of the conflict between the classes and of the development of the material conditions of existence. . . . What he *can* do contradicts all his previous positions, his principles and the immediate interest of his party; and what he *should* do cannot be done. He is, in a word, forced to represent, not his party, not his class, but that class for whose rule the time is ripe.

Freiderich Engels

Hurl me into the next existence the descent into hell won't turn me. I'll crawl back to dog his trail forever. They won't defeat my revenge, never, never. I'm part of a righteous people who anger slowly, but rage undamned. We'll gather at his door in such number that the rumbling of our feet will make the earth tremble.

George Jackson

The idea that Black people can have unity is the most dangerous idea we've ever let loose.

Bayard Rustin

I

Most historians fail to observe that the massive efforts waged for desegregation and, to a lesser extent, for Black Power, were basically black workers' movements. Black workers had comprised the great majority of those who had sacrificed during the local battles to uproot Jim Crow. They had been arrested, attacked by police with dogs and firehoses, intimidated, fired from their jobs, and even killed. King's gradual recognition that the civil rights campaigns needed to address the necessity of social guarantees for jobs, housing and health care pushed the movement clearly towards the premises of democratic socialism – the politics of much of the working class in other advanced capitalist nations. Gradually, the impetus towards racial reform which black workers pressed against the larger society began to be manifested within organised labour itself. By 1968, over two and a half million blacks were members of the AFL–CIO and the UAW. Most unions had abandoned their anti-black restrictions on membership, and a few of the more liberal unions had actively supported the desegregation actions in the South. Yet Randolph's original goals of creating an effective and powerful presence for blacks inside the House of Labor were not realised. Patterns of racist discrimination still existed, and black workers tended to occupy the most dangerous, lower-paid jobs inside the unions. Within the steelworkers' union, for example, not a single black leader served as an officer in its 30 districts, and less than 100 black employees were hired among the union's staff members. Less than 2 per cent of the members of the carpenters' union and the largest construction union were black. Only 0.3 per cent of the steel-metal workers were black in 1968. Even after the passage of the Civil Rights Act, segregated locals were still affiliated with the AFL–CIO: the all-white Brotherhood of Railway Clerks, Sulphite and Paper Mill Workers, United Papermakers and Paperworkers, International Association of Machinists, and the American Federation of Musicians. Thus, the struggle for biracial democracy and equality was still blocked by racist resistance and a deliberate policy of white supremacy fostered by most American trade union leaders.

Impatient with decades of AFL–CIO apathy and inaction, black workers influenced by the Black Power trend began to fight union racism through the creation of their own unions. In 1967, Detroit workers formed the Trades Union Local 124 to manoeuvre around white racists in that industrial city's union bureaucracy. Black nationalists and young workers at Ford Motor Company's major automobile plant in Mahwah, New Jersey, established the militant United Black Brothers, that same year. In 1968, Boston black labourers formed the United Community Construction Workers of Boston; black steelworkers in Maryland created the Shipyard Workers for Job Equality to fight the racist practices of both the unions and the steel corporation where they were employed. Civil rights activists continued for a time the policy of relating desegregation efforts to the broader labour movement. In September 1968, Ralph Abernathy, Andrew Young and Hosea Williams were jailed for leading an action of black sanitation workers in Atlanta. The most militant black labour tendency to emerge out of the Black Power period, however, centred in Detroit. In September 1967, a group of revolutionary black nationalists and independent black Marxists launched a militant black workers' newspaper, *Inner City Voice*. The key activists behind the effort – Marxist attorney Ken Cockrel, theorist Mike Hamlin, General Baker, John Watson, and John Williams – soon developed extensive organisational ties with rank-and-file black autoworkers and Detroit's growing black working class. In the spring of 1968, these radical black workers and intellectuals created the Dodge Revolutionary Union Movement (DRUM), in response to Baker's expulsion from the Dodge Main automobile plant, along with six other workers. DRUM attacked the management's use of plant 'speed-ups', racist hiring policies, the lack of adequate medical facilities in the factory, unequal pay between black and white labourers, and other long-standing grievances. DRUM co-ordinated pickets and 'wildcat strikes' against Dodge, and criticised the UAW's leadership for bowing to capital's interests over those of all workers. Within a year, other black revolutionary labour organisations developed along DRUM's model: the Ford Revolutionary Union Movement (FRUM); the Eldron Avenue Revolutionary Union Movement (ELRUM); the Harvester Revolutionary Union Movement in Chicago (HARUM); the Black Panther Caucus of Fremont, California; the General Motors Revolutionary Union Movement (GRUM), and many others. In 1969, many of these militant formations coalesced into the League of Revolutionary Black Workers, which was co-ordinated by Hamlin, Baker and Cockrel. For a time, former SNCC leader James Forman aided the process, participating in the formation of the Black Workers' Congress.

The UAW's response to the black radicals was twofold: first, it attempted to characterise DRUM as anti-working class and fanatical; second, it tried to split off older black workers from independent movements through a combination of paternalistic measures and co-optation. UAW Secretary-Treasurer Emil Mazey attacked DRUM in March 1969, as 'a handful of fanatics . . . black fascists whose actions are an attempt to destroy this union'. Mazey declared that the 'black peril' of Black Power was worse than the infamous 'red peril' of earlier years.[1] A. Philip Randolph was also instrumental in AFL–CIO efforts to quiet the black militants. Throughout the 1960s, he had begun to move even further to the right politically, and he halted his criticisms of the labour bureaucracy. In December 1965, Randolph announced proudly at the AFL–CIO convention in San Francisco that racial bias was no longer a major problem within organised labour. The following year, he resigned his position as president of the Negro American Labor Council, and counselled his old colleagues to cease their stinging condemnations of white union officials. Randolph's demise as a representative of black labour militancy was quickly followed, if not directly encouraged, by that of Rustin. At the September 1972 convention of the International Association of Machinists, Rustin declared that blacks themselves were the major reason for labour's record of blatant discrimination. 'I want to say to our trade union Black brothers, nobody got anything because he was colored', Rustin stated. 'That is a lot of bull. . . . Stop griping always that nobody has problems but you black people.' The point must be made, however, that the Machinists whom Rustin had praised so vigorously had maintained for 60 years a mandatory policy excluding black membership.[2]

Rustin's and Randolph's accommodation to racism and betrayal of the black working class did not go unanswered. In September 1972, a progressive conference of 1200 black workers was held in Chicago, co-ordinated by five black national spokespersons of labour: Cleveland Robinson of the Distributive Workers Union; William Lucy of the American Federation of State, County, and Municipal Employees; William Simons of the American Federation of Teachers; Charles Hayes, vice president of the Amalgamated Meatcutters and Butcher Workmen; and Nelson Jack Edwards, vice president of the UAW. The new organisation formed at the conference, the Coalition of Black Trade Unionists, aggressively attacked the racism of the Nixon Administration and proposed meaningful social democratic reforms akin to those expressed by King shortly before his assassination. A statement of these five black unionists, made at the Coalition's second convention in May 1973, expressed the view that:

A free and progressive trade union movement should and must reflect greater participation of black trade unionists at every level of its decision-making process. As black trade unionists, we have an important role to fulfill, if the goals of the overall labor movement are to be achieved on behalf of all workers. . . . Today, blacks occupy key positions in the political machinery of the labor movement and hold the critical balance of political power in this nation . . . it is our challenge to make the labor movement more relevant to the needs and aspirations of black and poor workers. The CBTU will insist that black union officials become full partners in the leadership and decision-making of the American labor movement.[3]

Despite growing black opposition from the rank-and-file to top officials, many unions continued to fight attempts to bring racial equality and justice within their ranks. Black workers in the International Longshoreman's Association (ILA) protested to white union officials against a systemic pattern of segregated locals and racist job referral policies with no avail. Using Title Seven of the Civil Rights Act, black ILA members in Philadelphia, Baltimore, and Galveston–Port Arthur, Texas, successfully sued their union in the federal court in the early 1970s. Although ILA lawyers explained that their segregated locals were 'separate but equal', the federal courts ruled that 'the segregated unions . . . by their very nature deny equal employment opportunities'.[4] When the Johnson Administration established 'Project Build', an apprenticeship programme funded by the Department of Labor with the goal of increasing the number of blacks in the construction crafts unions, white unionists devised elaborate methods to circumvent the law. After ten years, only 25 per cent of the minority workers had completed the programme; those who did finish usually found themselves assigned by unions to tasks as lowly-paid labourers. Black graduates of the apprenticeship programme of the Operating Engineers Union in Philadelphia, who were also excluded from full union membership and jobs commensurate with their training, filed suit against the union in August 1970. During their legal battle, white engineers physically assaulted black apprentice graduates at work sites and in their union hall. Ruling against the racism of the Operating Engineers Union, federal judge A. Leon Higginbotham, Jr., declared:

Here we have a tragic situation where Black men going to the union hall looking for work are attacked by large numbers of white operating engineers without any justification. . . . By the laws and the Constitution of the United States the defendant union is not permitted to be a divisive and coercive force to retard Blacks from also seeking an open society with the usual rights of other men. . . . It is now too late in the corridors of history for a court to sanction defendant-labor union's attempt to turn back the swelling tides of equal racial justice which the federal law demands.[5]

White union opposition to racial equality continued to fester, much to the trade union movement's own detriment. A number of unions, especially the American Federation of Teachers–AFL–CIO, led by racist social democrat Al Shanker, fought to oppose the enstatement of 'affirmative action' policies designed to increase the percentages of racial minorities and women within the labour force. At local levels, many white trade unionists were prominent participants in protests to halt the desegregation of public schools. In Boston, for example, a former leader of the Sheet Metal Workers' Union, James Kelley, became affiliated with a white racist paramilitary group which terrorised black poor and working-class families. In electoral politics, the backlash of white workers against black equality was translated into support for anti-working-class conservatives. In Southern cities with large white working-class populations in 1968, Wallace polled 33 per cent of the popular vote in Little Rock, Arkansas; 23 per cent in Greensboro, North Carolina; 36 per cent in Jacksonville, Florida; and 38 per cent in Nashville, Tennessee. In the Democratic Party primaries of 1972, working-class whites gave Wallace victories in Florida, Michigan, and Maryland. Nixon and Agnew also made direct appeals to the conservatism and racism of white trade unionists, and reaped similar gains. The AFL–CIO was part of this conservative strategy, and did little to halt the trend to the right. When the Democrats nominated a social democrat who opposed the Vietnam War, Senator George McGovern, as their presidential candidate against Nixon in 1972, Meany and other labour leaders declared their 'neutrality' in the contest. As a result, at least two-thirds of white working-class voters supported the anti-labour candidate Nixon, whereas 85 per cent or more black voters cast ballots for McGovern's losing effort.

The bitter irony of labour's racist and pro-corporate positions was that they crippled the overall trade union movement; they alienated minorities and women from taking part in unionisation efforts; and they diminished the ability of the working class to affect meaningful federal and state legislation which would benefit all of labour. The fruits of these practices and policies meant a decline in labour's ability to organise American working people. Union membership as a percentage of the labour force, for instance, dropped from 36 per cent in 1960 to 20.9 per cent in 1980. From 1973 to 1978, unions actually lost over three-fourths of all certified workplace elections. During the Nixon and Ford Administrations the absence of a unified, strong union movement was directly responsible for federal inaction to reduce unemployment rates. From 1969 to 1975, joblessness for married males increased from 1.4 per cent to 4.8 per cent for whites, and from 2.5 per cent to 8.3 per cent for non-whites. Overall unemployment rates during these years jumped from 3.1 per cent to 7.8 per cent for whites, and 6.4 per cent to 13.9 per cent for non-whites. Beyond all other factors, racism undermined the political strength of labour, and concurrently made the blacks' struggle for desegregation and biracial democracy much more difficult.

II

In electoral politics, Black Power was translated into a growing voting bloc which blacks exercised in several specific ways. Between 1964 and 1972, the number of black Americans of voting age increased from 10.3 million to 13.5 million. The Voting Rights Act of 1965, combined with the registration campaigns of SNCC, CORE and the NAACP, dramatically increased the numbers of black potential voters. Thus the number of black elected officials continued to climb at an unprecedented rate. In March 1969, there were 994 black men and 131 black women who held offices across the country. By May 1975, this figure had more than tripled, to 2969 black men and 530 black women. In the latter year, there were 18 blacks in Congress; 281 serving as state legislators or executives; 135 mayors of cities, towns, or municipalities; 305 county executives; 387 judges and elected law enforcement officers; 939 elected to city or county boards of education; and another 1438 elected to other positions of municipal government. The Southern states contained slightly more than half of these new politicians: 82 of the 135 black mayors were in the South; 1702 of the 3069 county, municipal, educational, and law enforcement officers and judges were Southerners. This growing list of black officials represented, to be sure, a victory for proponents of civil rights. Yet within that victory resided certain ambiguities. Many of these men and women were nominally members of some desegregationist organisation, such as the NAACP, CORE, or locally-based groups. Perhaps a majority of them, however, had no prior experience as activists within desegregation campaigns. Most tended to come from the black middle class – doctors, lawyers, entrepreneurs, college professors – and not directly from the black working class or poor. This is not to suggest that the new black élites did not retain empathy for the conditions and plight of black labour; yet their ideological outlook and basic political practices tended to align them more with other parvenu élites than with the black working class. Part of the reason for this is reflected in the class and educational composition of the national black electorate. Among the black poor, where levels of education tend to be much lower than among the black élite, voting participation levels are also much lower. In the presidential election of 1972, for example, only 35.9 per cent of black adults with educational levels below 5 years actually voted. For black high school graduates, the voting rate was 46.9 per cent; blacks with 1 to 3 years of college education, 63.5 per cent; black college graduates, 80.3 per cent. Thus the relative weight of the black middle classes and blacks with advanced education was, within the 'electoral marketplace', almost twice that of lower income, poorly educated black workers. The result of this bias towards the élite was reflected in the types of black candidates who were invariably elected to office.

Most civil rights leaders and black nationalists agreed that any major electoral victories registered by blacks would occur in major cities. In 1972, there were 89 US cities which had populations exceeding 50,000, in which 20 per cent or more of the total population was black. Combined, the total adult population of these cities was 23.7 million, of which 6.7 million, or 28.3 per cent, were blacks. In larger cities, blacks were represented in even greater numbers. In 1972, there were ten major US cities with total populations of half a million or more in which blacks comprised over 31 per cent of the voters. These included Baltimore, with 273,000 black potential voters, 43.7 per cent of the electorate; Detroit, 423,000 black voters, and 39.4 per cent; New Orleans, 164,000 black voters, and 39.7 per cent; Atlanta, 168,000 black voters, and 47.3 per cent; and St. Louis, 159,000 black voters, and 35.9 per cent. Yet in 1972 none of these five major cities above had black mayors. In most metropolitan centres, old and well-entrenched political machines, established in the late 1800s and early 1900s by white ethnics tied to the Democratic Party, systemically kept blacks from achieving elective offices at the local level. During the early 1970s, urban blacks recognised that the efforts towards desegregating the rural South had to be channelled into the cities. In Newark, New Jersey, where blacks totalled 54.2 per cent of the city's total population, only one-third of the members of the city council were black. Memphis blacks held only 3 out of 13 city council posts in 1972. New Orleans blacks did not have a single city council position that year. Black Atlantans held only 2 of 9 city council chairs. In Oakland, California, a city with a black voting age population of almost 30 per cent, only 1 out of 8 council members was black. Despite the black gains in Congressional representation since the 1960s, here too there was a pattern of relative powerlessness. In the 92nd Congress, for example, 12 congressional districts had black populations between 38.2 per cent and 49.8 per cent, yet only one of these seats was held by a black person, Dellums of California. In a few instances, such as Mississippi's arch-racist Thomas G. Abernathy, whose House district held a 46.2 per cent black population, the US Representatives from these districts were adamantly opposed to civil rights legislation. It was clear to all blacks, therefore, that Black Power could only become relevant to the material interests of blacks if and when their newly won electoral power was transferred into a greater share of public offices.

In Congress, black representatives began to devise a national strategy to boost the number of black elected officials (BEOs). In 1969, Representative Charles Diggs of Detroit initiated the Democratic Select Committee, a council of all nine black Congressmen, to lobby against the Nixon Administration's initiatives against black and poor people. Within a year, former CORE activist William Clay, elected as Representative from St. Louis in 1968, began to push his colleagues towards a more formal organisation. In 1971, after the election of three more black Representatives – Dellums of Oakland, California, George Collins of Chicago, and Parren Mitchell of Baltimore – the Congressional Black Caucus (CBC) was formed. During 1971 and 1972, CBC attempted to represent a 'united voice for Black America' in the Congress, and to an extent, across the nation.[6] CBC staff members supported local races of black candidates; lobbied for progressive reforms in job training, healthcare, welfare and social service programmes; and attempted to fashion a national strategy to increase black political power from local to federal levels. The black nationalists at this point began a period of tactical co-operation with many CBC members, particularly Diggs, who was vice chairperson of the House Committee on African Relations, and Dellums, who was at the time the only avowed socialist in the Congress. Baraka began to discuss with them the idea of developing an all-black 'pre-party formation' which could be used both as a means to mobilise black voters and as a structure which would force the Democratic Party's white leadership to become more compliant with blacks' interests. In short order, Detroit Representative John Conyers and Percy Sutton, Malcolm X's former lawyer and a major political leader in New York City, promulgated the suggestion. A meeting was called by Richard Hatcher, newly-elected mayor of Gary, Indiana, to determine a firm strategy. The North-lake, Illinois, conference of 24–25 September 1971, co-ordinated by Hatcher, was probably the only instance between 1965 and 1983 when representatives of virtually every major tendency of the black movement sat down together in the same room. At Northlake were Julian Bond; CBC members Walter Fauntroy of Washington, DC, Augustus Hawkins of California, and Conyers; the new leader of the Urban League, Vernon Jordan; Roy Innis of CORE; Atlanta attorney Maynard Jackson; SCLC representative Andrew Young; Percy Sutton, recently elected as Manhattan Borough president; and Baraka. These diverse and often feuding representatives of both integrationist and nationalist tendencies came to terms by accepting Baraka's plans for holding a major black independent political convention in early 1972.

The result of Northlake was the Gary Convention of 10–11 March 1972, the largest black political convention in US history. About 3000 official delegates were in attendance, representing revolutionary nationalist, cultural nationalist, moderate integrationist, and Black Capitalist tendencies. In all, about 12,000 persons attended the proceedings, which were co-chaired by an intriguing troika: Baraka, Hatcher, and Diggs. Almost every faction of the black movement was there: Jesse Jackson, the SCLC leader who had recently launched his own Operation PUSH (People United to Save Humanity), Martin's widow, Coretta Scott King, and Dorothy Height, during one moment of Black Power frenzy were heard to shout the black nationalists' slogan – 'Nationtime! Nationtime! Nationtime!' The convention established a political formation, the National Black Political Assembly, which would help elect black mayors, Congressional Representatives, and other officials, as well as mobilise poor and working-class blacks at neighbourhood levels around key issues of concern. What was particularly important about Gary was the political tone of black nationalism which filled the convention hall, and affected the policies and even the rhetoric of all BEOs and diehard integrationists. Among the Old Guard, only some NAACP leaders refused to take part in the convention. Indeed, Wilkins bitterly attacked the policy statements of the Gary meeting *before* the convention was actually held. No one at Gary really cared. For the moment, the nationalists were in control of the black movement, a fact of political life that many CBC members and black mayors like Hatcher astutely recognised. The National Black Political Assembly was a marriage of convenience between the aspiring and somewhat radicalised black petty bourgeoisie and the black nationalist movement. Gary represented, in retrospect, the zenith not only of black nationalism, but of the entire black movement during the Second Reconstruction. The collective vision of the convention represented a desire to seize electoral control of America's major cities, to move the black masses from the politics of desegregation to the politics of real empowerment, ultimately to create their own independent black political party.[7]

What almost no nationalists and only a very few BEOs recognised *before* manoeuvring for political power were the many structural crises which confronted America's major cities. A decade before Black Power assumed an electoral form in the campaigns to win public offices for blacks, urban metropolitan centres were faced with a series of fiscal problems which white mayors and city councils had left unresolved. Millions of white upper-to-middle-class families had fled the central cities; of the 212 US towns with populations exceeding 50,000, 60 had declined in total population between 1950–60. Historian Carl Degler notes: 'Between 1952 and 1959 expenditures by local governments rose almost twice as fast as the gross national product'. One consequence of these expenditures was that 'the public debt of localities rose 40 times as fast in the 1950s as did the federal debt. In 1960 alone, expenditures by local governments exceeded their total income by $18 billion'. By the era of Black Power, most cities were in the Kafkaesque situation of 'spending more on interest payments than they were on the fire department'.[8] Thus the BEOs were faced with the task of providing immediate and tangible benefits to their black and liberal white constituencies, while the governmental terrain upon which they operated had become quicksand. Political scientists William E. Nelson, Jr., and Philip J. Meranto listed some of the 'most vexing problems adversely affecting the leadership capabilities' of the new black mayors and local officials during this period:

(1) A declining tax base spawned by reliance on the property tax and the dispersal of large sectors of the white community – both citizens and business – into surrounding suburbs;

(2) the influx into central cities of high-cost citizens – especially poor blacks – in desperate need of governmental assistance for survival;

(3) racial conflict generated by competition between blacks and whites for dwindling job opportunities and access to decent schools, homes, and recreational facilities in the central cities;

(4) the emergence of a city bureaucracy protected by civil service . . . ;

(5) decentralisation of power from strong party organisations over which the mayor exercised control to a plethora of governmental agencies and competing interest groups over which he had little effective control;

(6) the impact on the social, economic, and political life of cities of policies made by corporate élites in private sanctuaries beyond the effective scrutiny and influence of any public official, including mayors;

(7) insensitivity to central city needs by important state and national officials.[9]

With relatively few exceptions, the black mayors and councillors were caught in an unenviable position, between black constituents with high expectations, a massive fiscal debt, a deteriorating industrial and commercial base, and an alienated and fearful white constituency. Cleveland, Ohio, while only one example, displayed many of the problems in all such cities. By 1967, Cleveland's black population had reached 36 per cent of the city's total. In the city bureaucracy, all of the lowest-paying jobs (transit workers, parks and recreation employees, and sanitation workers) were held disproportionately by blacks, while the highest-paying positions (police, administrators, firemen) were held almost exclusively by whites.

Whites had for a generation fled the inner city – from 1930 to 1960, almost 300,000 whites had left Cleveland, and they were replaced by an addition of 204,000 blacks. Economically, conditions for blacks were every bit as bad as they had been in some Southern, segregated towns. In 1965, black unemployment reached 8.9 per cent vs. 2.4 per cent among whites. Well-established trade unions continued to practise policies of Jim Crow. In 1966, for example, of Cleveland's 1482 plumbers, only 3 were black; out of 1786 members of the local ironworkers' union, none were black. Thousands of Afro-American families lived in rat-infested, dilapidated, and overcrowded housing. In this environment, Ohio state legislator Carl B. Stokes was elected mayor in November 1967, defeating a white Republican opponent by a margin of 1679 votes. Stokes' election was clearly along racial lines: 95 per cent of the black wards supported Stokes, while 78.5 per cent of the white wards favoured his conservative opponent. Stokes' slender victory was the result of a massive black voter turnout, 79.7 per cent of all registered voters, and because one-fifth of all white voters decided to support him.

Almost the day after Stokes' election as mayor, he ran into a series of difficulties. Two important Stokes allies, his former campaign manager and the city's acting mayor, both resigned from his administration after less than six months, claiming that the mayor was unwilling to listen to their suggestions for municipal reform. Stokes' appointment of Benjamin O. Davis, Jr., a black former general, as director of public safety backfired. A political conservative, Davis publicly pursued the police suppression of local black nationalists; he failed 'to aggressively pursue whites who regularly attacked blacks in white neighborhoods'; and he openly sided with racist white policemen by demanding the right for officers to use ' "dum-dum" bullets (soft-core bullets that expand on impact)'. Davis was forced to resign by 1970, but not before notifying the press that Stokes gave 'continued support and comfort . . . to the enemies of law enforcement'. Stokes' administration was plagued by almost endless scandals: one of his black aides was forced to leave when the press publicised her part-ownership of an illegal liquor establishment; his public relations assistant resigned when the media learned of his questionable financial dealings; two other top Stokes appointees resigned in a 'civil service scandal'. Scandals of this type are a recurring theme of US big-city politics, but under the administration of a black mayor, these events became major racial crises. By 1969, relations between Stokes and white city employees had reached rock-bottom. At one point, during a racial disturbance, white police and firemen refused to answer dispatches and emergency calls. Requests for police services at fires or shootings were responded to by epithets such as, 'Let Mayor Stokes go piss on it'; 'Let 'em burn the damn place down'; 'To hell with the mayor'.[10] Local white supporters of George Wallace initiated a political move legally to separate the city's black districts from the rest of Cleveland. Stokes tried to resolve his political problems by soliciting large sums of federal aid for the city. In 1968, he received a $12 million federal grant for much-needed urban renewal. From 1968–70, Stokes' 'Cleveland Now' fund-raising effort collected $177 million for new jobs, improved health care delivery services, and public housing. Despite these fiscal successes, Stokes' relations with the white working class and even with many black voters continued to deteriorate. A transit workers' strike in 1970 crippled downtown businesses, as thousands of employees were unable to get to their jobs. A long sanitation workers' strike left Cleveland's inner city beneath tons of uncollected garbage. By 1971, the black community was thoroughly disoriented and frustrated with Stokes' inability to provide solutions to their festering socio-economic problems. Stokes did not seek re-election, and a conservative white Republican, Ralph Perk, was elected mayor over two rival black candidates. Stokes resigned from politics altogether, and since 1971 Cleveland to date has not had another black mayor. After Perk's election, white Republicans dismissed most of the 270 black administrators that Stokes had elevated into the city's bureaucracy. Leading black Democrats, including Stokes' brother, Congressman Louis Stokes, feuded with each other to control what was left of the crumbling black political power base in Cleveland. Disillusioned, many blacks ceased voting at all, and between 1971 and 1975, total black registration dropped from 127,000 to 102,000 in the city. Black voter turnouts in general elections plummeted from 81.7 per cent in 1967 to only 47.7 per cent in 1979. Great expectations had been overtaken by great apathy and an omnipresent sense of failure. The experience in Cleveland and the collapse of independent black politics would be mirrored in other major cities in the 1980s.

III

Even before the flawed electoral strategies of black nationalists and the emerging black élite had been tested nationally, the Nixon Administration set about the task of systematically destroying the still powerful radical wing of the Black Power Movement. Politically, this was accomplished through several means. It was clear that many white Americans had to be prepared ideologically to accept the massive violation of civil liberties, the denial of human rights, and the illegal executions which were necessary to blunt the rhetoric and reality of black militancy. By the late 1960s, Nixon and his conservative supporters, in both the Republican and Democratic parties, employed the rhetorical slogan, 'law-and-order' in their campaigns for office in order to instil reactionary anxieties among whites. They pointed out to nervous voters that the number of murders in the US had doubled between 1965 and 1975. Reported incidents of rape per 100,000 jumped from 12 to 26, and aggravated assaults from 111 to 227, during the decade. They insisted that black urban unrest and the militancy of the more nationalistic Black Power groups was somehow connected with the breakdown in civil obedience and social peace. The conservative politicians did not usually add the fact, however, that most violent crimes committed were not black-against-white, but were intra-racial; that black male homicide rates were between 600 to 800 per cent higher than for white males. The political propaganda to increase the length of jail sentences, to silence militant blacks, produced a popular white political reaction. By 1972, 74 per cent of all Americans believed that the US criminal justice system 'was not dealing harshly enough with criminals'.[11] By 1978, this figure had reached 90 per cent. Thus Nixon and other political reactionaries developed a popular mandate for expanding the activities of COINTELPRO, and for unleashing the Department of Justice, the FBI and state law enforcement agencies to eradicate the most militant tendencies of the black movement, all in the name of 'law-and-order'.

The arrests and executions of Black Panthers continued under Nixon, with the FBI in close co-operation with local law enforcement agencies. On 4 December 1969, Chicago leaders Mark Clark and Fred Hampton were murdered by police in a raid on the Black Panthers' headquarters. A federal grand jury ruled in May 1970, that 'the police fired eighty-three shots into the apartment while only one shot was fired toward the police'. The grand jury implied strongly that the police raid was used as a pretext to assassinate the black revolutionaries.[12] FBI directives to nine field offices in January 1970, ordered officials to 'counteract any favorable support in publicity to the Black Panther Party' by placing anti-Panther propaganda in the media. In Los Angeles and San Francisco, the FBI drafted 'editorials' and 'news articles' for local television stations and newspapers which attacked the organisation.[13] In August 1971, FBI agents and local police arrested two Black Panthers in Omaha, Nebraska, David Rice and Ed Poindexter, on charges of killing a local policeman. In subsequent investigations by Amnesty International and other human rights agencies, it was revealed that the FBI had collected over 2000 pages of information on the Omaha chapter of the Black Panthers, and that the actual murderer of the police officer was a former drug addict who was soon released by authorities, and who subsequently 'disappeared'. Both Rice and Poindexter were convicted, however, and still remain in federal penitentiaries. Other black activists having no connection with the Black Panthers were similarly harassed, arrested and imprisoned. On 18 August 1971, FBI agents and 36 policemen armed with shotguns, machine guns and an armoured car raided the headquarters of a black nationalist organisation, the Republic of New Afrika (RNA), in Jackson, Mississippi. RNA leader Imari Obadele (Richard Henry) and ten others were arrested on charges of murder, assault, and 'treason against the state of Mississippi!' Nine other RNA members were arrested on questionable charges such as 'spitting and talking back to an officer'. Three weeks later, 65 Detroit police raided that city's RNA headquarters and arrested group members at gunpoint. An FBI internal memo, dated 8 September 1971, reveals that the Federal government wanted to imprison Obadele at all costs: 'If Obadele can be kept off the streets, it may prevent further problems involving the RNA inasmuch as he completely dominates this organisation and all members act under his instructions'. In September 1973, Obadele and six other RNA leaders were 'found guilty of conspiracy to assault federal officers, assault, and the use of firearms to commit a felony'. Obadele was given a sentence of twelve years.[14]

Most instances of blatant injustice against black activists received little or no media attention. Three cases, however, ultimately became major international issues. The Reverend Benjamin Chavis, civil rights organiser for the United Church of Christ, led two non-violent demonstrations in Wilmington, North Carolina, in pursuit of quality education for black children in the city. In March 1972, Chavis, eight black student leaders and one progressive white woman were arrested for burning a local grocery store. A jury of ten whites (some of whom admitted to membership in the Ku Klux Klan) and two elderly, intimidated blacks gave sentences to the 'Wilmington Ten' which totalled 282 years. In order to ensure their convictions, the FBI and the Alcohol, Tobacco and Firearms (ATF) division of the US Treasury Department secretly paid three witnesses, two convicted criminals and a 15-year-old boy, to testify against Chavis. From prison, Chavis wrote a stirring appeal to the 1977 Belgrade Conference on the Helsinki Accords guaranteeing the protection of human rights:

> From a torturous prison cell in the state of North Carolina I make to the world community . . . an urgent public appeal for human rights. As one of many victims, I shall not keep silent.
> . . . I wish in no manner to embarrass or criticize my country unduly. I love my country. It is because I love my country that I decry publicly the domestic exploitation, persecution and imprisonment of innocent citizens for political, economic and racist motives. No doubt I will face reprisals and retaliatory punishment for daring to write and speak these truths which are self-evident but I take the risk, accepting what may come with courage. In the United States the present reality for millions of Black Americans, Native American Indians, Puerto Ricans, Chicanos, Asian Americans and other oppressed national minorities is that violations of fundamental human rights and freedoms are commonplace. . . . We are the victims of racism and monopoly economic exploitation. And yes, we are the victims of governmental repression.[15]

Two other prominent victims of political repression were Angela Davis and George Jackson. In June 1969, Davis was dismissed from her position as philosophy professor at the University of California-Los Angeles by the order of California's ultra-conservative governor, Ronald Reagan, for her membership of the US Communist Party. In August 1970, FBI agents charged her with involvement in a California shootout which led to several deaths, including one judge and a member of the Black Panthers, 17-year-old Jonathan Jackson. Davis immediately went 'underground', and was arrested in New York City after FBI officials named her as one of the country's 'ten most wanted criminals'.[16] Jailed at first in the same prison which once housed Claudia Jones, she was constantly harassed and supervised.

On 4 June 1972, after a massive international campaign had been waged, a California jury declared her innocent of all charges. The older brother of Jonathan Jackson, George Jackson, had been sentenced at the age of 18 to serve a term of 'one year-to-life' for stealing $70 from a store. Annually denied parole, Jackson was determined not to be dehumanised by his prison environment. By 1970, thousands of black and white prisoners in every federal penitentiary knew of his legendary regimen: 1000 finger-tip push-up exercises each day; authoring two major works of political theory and dozens of essays; being named national 'Field Marshal' of the Black Panther Party while behind bars. Prison officials determined to break Jackson, placed in solitary confinement for years, segregated him from other prisoners, and attempted to bribe convicts to kill him. Jackson's public following grew alarmingly after the publication of his book *Soledad Brother*. On 21 August 1971, Jackson was executed by guards in San Quentin prison. Officials justified Jackson's death with an unbelievable story: that Jackson's attorney smuggled a 32-ounce, 8-inch long pistol to him inside the prison during an interview, and that Jackson hid the gun 'in his medium-sized Afro [hair], before he was searched in the nude, then walked approximately 100 yards with a guard before the pistol was detected'. During the unrest after Jackson's death, 26 San Quentin prisoners were 'stripped, beaten and tortured and forced to lie naked in the [prison's] outside yard for seven hours'.[17] Blacks were shocked and outraged that the 29-year-old Black Panther had been murdered. The East Palo Alto, California, city council immediately passed a resolution, stating:

> It is utterly incredible that a prisoner in isolation in a maximum security facility could acquire and conceal possession of a gun as has been claimed by authorities. . . . We do hereby affirm our disgust and dismay at this atrocious act of genocide. We demand, full, complete, and fair investigation of George Jackson's murder and a redress of grievances including the conviction and execution of all parties to this cowardly and criminal act.[18]

Protests against Jackson's death assumed many forms, both outside and inside the nation's prisons. One black underground formation, the George Jackson Assault Squad, killed a California police officer with a shotgun blast on 30 August 1971, in an act of vengeance. Radical whites sympathetic with Jackson bombed police buildings in three California cities. One group set fire to the Bank of America's downtown offices in San Francisco. Prisoners in the Attica, New York, penitentiary staged a one-day fast on 27 August in tribute to Jackson. Prison officials retaliated by tightening restrictions. On 9 September, Attica's 1300 inmates – black, Puerto Rican and white – seized control of the state facility, demanding 'that all inmates be given adequate food, water, and shelter'. Other demands included 'complete amnesty from physical, mental, and legal reprisals'; 'true religious freedom' inside prisons; 'an effective drug treatment program for all inmates who request it'; the modernisation of 'the inmate education system which would include a Spanish language library and a criminal law library'; and the 'end of all censorship of newspapers, magazines, and letters'. In short, Attica prisoners wanted to be treated like human beings. New York Governor Nelson Rockefeller consulted with Nixon and state law enforcement officials, and decided to retake the prison. Hundreds of armed National Guardsmen, local and state police, and Attica prison guards attacked, killing 29 prisoners and 10 guards who had been held hostage. Unarmed prisoners stood before the police unafraid: 'Go ahead and shoot, you pig bastards!' one victim cried aloud before his death. Screaming, the police surged forward, yelling and shooting wildly, indiscriminately. One prisoner who survived the attack had a rifle pointed at his head by a police officer who shouted: 'Get on your feet you dirty, black nigger bastard! I'll kill all you niggers!' Recapturing the prison, troopers wrote racist obscenities along walls: 'black blood will flow freely; Angela Davis sucks Troopers dicks; the Black Panthers are pussys; die, Jackson, die; All Blacks are Niggers'. Attica's convicts 'didn't believe they'd come in with guns and grenades', one surviving prisoner wrote in the *Black Scholar*. In a situation in which a bloody massacre could have been prevented through reasonable negotiations, US officials deliberately chose to employ the harshest methods possible to restore 'law-and-order'. On 21 December 1973, 60 of Attica's leaders were tried for 'murder, kidnapping, and other assorted felonies'.[19]

After the Attica uprising, white American politicians seized on the incident as an excuse to create even more repressive conditions. Annual government expenditures for prisons grew to exceed $4.6 billion in 1977, and local government expenditures for police forces more than doubled, reaching $8.8 billion. Between 1970 and 1975, the prison population in some states increased 100 per cent. Over half a million mentally ill persons were arrested and jailed every year; about half of the US prison population was black, and half were under the age of 29. Prison conditions became so miserable, with chronic overcrowding, that a few federal judges even ruled in state cases that imprisonment under inhumane situations constituted 'cruel and unusual punishment'. The consequences of the deterioration of prison life in the 1970s were not only greater unrest, but other manifestations of suffering. In 1973, the suicide rate for the US penal population was 600 per cent higher than that of the general population. Less than 10 per cent of all prisoners were involved in vocational education programmes, which would aid them in becoming productive citizens once released. Young black male prisoners were often the victims of homosexual gang rape. Black women prisoners, particularly in municipal and county jails, were habitually raped by guards and law enforcement officers. One notorious instance of sexual abuse occurred in Beaufort County, North Carolina, in which a black garment factory worker, Joan Little, was raped by her guard. On 27 August 1974, Little struggled in her cell with her rapist jailer, managed to kill him, and fled the jail. Surrendering herself on 3 September 1974, she was promptly charged with murder. After an extensive trial and litigation, Little was declared not guilty by reason of self-defence. Despite this solitary yet important victory for civil rights, thousands of 'Joan Littles', the rape victims of police and penal authorities, remained unheard and unknown.

Given Nixon's massive electoral mandate of November 1972, it is entirely possible that even greater criminal acts against black nationalists, Marxists, community organisers, elected officials, and ministers would have transpired during his second term of office. What undermined the construction of an American majority for the right, at least temporarily, was the Watergate scandal. On 18 June 1972, five men directed by a former FBI agent were arrested while burgling the Democratic National Committee headquarters at the Watergate Hotel in Washington, DC. A Senate special investigating committee learned that Attorney General John Mitchell not only

had sanctioned the break-in but also revealed that the administration had taken punitive action against its political opponents, had ordered unwarranted Internal Revenue Service audits of their tax returns, had tapped the telephones of government officials and

newspaper reporters without court approval, and had hired agents
to break into a psychiatrist's office and ransack his files in an effort
to embarrass Daniel Ellsberg, a critic of the Vietnam War who
had consulted the doctor professionally.

Vice President Agnew was forced to resign in disgrace when a court
ruled that he had accepted corporate bribes. Nixon took the offensive,
claiming arrogantly in one press conference, 'I am *not* a crook'. Yet in
April 1974, the public learned that the president had paid in 1971–72
only $800 in taxes on an annual salary exceeding $200,000 and that he
owed the government $432,000 in taxes. Gradually, as the admini-
stration fought desperately to restore public confidence, Nixon's
ability to pursue aggressive domestic and foreign policies diminished.
On 28 March 1973, the last US troops were withdrawn from
Vietnam. In two years, North Vietnamese troops would enter Saigon
as liberators. At home, COINTELPRO, officially ending operations
in 1971, began to place the FBI and other federal agencies on the
defensive. Liberal Democratic Senator Frank Church, chairperson of
the Senate Select Committee to Study Governmental Operations
with respect to Intelligence Activities, later exposed a sickening
pattern of illegal surveillance acts which victimised blacks with
absolutely no credentials in the black liberation movement. Roy
Wilkins, actress Eartha Kitt, heavyweight boxing champion
Muhammad Ali; retired boxer Joe Louis; and actors Ossie Davis and
Harry Belafonte.

Nixon's grandiose plan to unite 'the likeminded, the forgotten
Americans, the good, decent, taxpaying, law abiding people' against
blacks, Latinos and liberals came crashing to an end with his
resignation on 9 August 1974. Nixon was replaced by the former
House Republican minority leader, Gerald R. Ford, a political
functionary possessing all the charisma, it was said, of a sleepy clam.
The significance of Watergate was not lost upon black nationalists
and progressives. Political theorist William Strickland, a leader of a
progressive black research centre, the Institute of the Black World,
suggested in December 1973, 'Watergate is no mere accident of
history':

It is the natural consequence of a government faced with the
problem of trying to preserve the façade of democracy before its
citizens while waging imperialist war abroad, plundering the

public treasury at home, and supporting reaction wherever it can be found. To maintain the myth of American righteousness, the government has no other recourse except to lie. Indeed, lying becomes the central political behavior of the state . . . white politics seems to prefer the known evil to the possible unknown good. In the face of the greatest mass of criminal evidence ever assembled against a political figure, white politics and white people sit doe-like, almost hypnotically subservient to Big Brother.[21]

The wheels of governmental repression did not grind entirely to a halt in the mid-1970s, however, and the massive damage accomplished in Nixon's five and a half years of rule against the black freedom movement would never be undone. The possibility of a conservative restoration, and the effective end of the Second Reconstruction, was set during the Nixon years. But this would not be fully realised until the election of 1980.

IV

For historian Vincent Harding, and many black scholars and activists, the Gary Convention and the founding of the National Black Political Assembly represented the culmination of the entire legacy of black struggles, from the Montgomery bus boycott and the Greensboro sit-ins, to Malcolm X and the Black Power rebellions. 'When we all gathered at Gary, many persons instinctively seemed to sense something of the powerful meaning of the last words of the preamble to the convention's declaration: "We stand on the edge of history. We cannot turn back".' The delegates may have wondered: 'Is this what Malcolm and Martin had seen and felt before us? Was this the vision that so troubled each of them in the last churning months of their lives?' In the weeks following the convention, Harding recognised that for many, this illuminating vision of black liberation, the powerful responsibility to make new history, was too weighty to bear. 'Instead, in response to the most fundamental challenging calls of the convention's black agenda, many persons turned back to politics-as-usual, turned aside to the demands of self-interest, or wandered off into unclear, necessarily solitary ways, searching for their own best responses to the new time.'[22] The CBC was the first significant force, although not the last, to back away from the mandate of Gary. Two controversial resolutions passed at Gary caused the greatest concern.

Delegates declared themselves, first, in favour of black-controlled community schools, and in opposition to federal court-ordered busing for school desegregation purposes. Second, the convention called for the political right to self-determination for all peoples of colour, including the Palestinians. Mindful of US Jewish organisational support for civil rights legislation, the CBC promptly declared 'its friendship with the State of Israel', stating, 'we vigorously oppose the efforts of any group that would seek to weaken or undermine Israel's right to exist'.[23] This statement immediately alienated many nationalists, who were politically sympathetic with the Palestine Liberation Organisation, and who opposed the obvious military and economic linkages between Israel and the racist regime of *apartheid* South Africa. Shirley Chisholm, who had already begun a campaign for the Democratic Party's presidential nomination, viewed Gary as a 'personal rebuff to her'. By May 1972, most CBC members had aligned themselves behind a white Democratic candidate. Representatives Clay and Fauntroy, along with Jesse Jackson, touted the merits of McGovern, while Charles Evers and Stokes' protégé Arnold Pinckney backed Humphrey. A few Black Powerites, notably McKissick, endorsed Nixon's re-election in 1972. Soon after the election, most of the black Democrats were firmly back into the fold. By the second major convention of the National Black Political Assembly, which was held in Little Rock, Arkansas, in 1974, only newly elected Atlanta mayor Maynard Jackson, Hatcher, and a paltry collection of BEOs were in attendance. Despite the election of Youngstown, Ohio, black nationalist leader Ronald Daniels to the chairman's spot, replacing Diggs, many observers felt that the Assembly was at a dead end. Cynical as always, Harold Cruse denounced the Little Rock gathering of 2000 activists as 'a betrayal of the Black militant potential built up during the struggles of the Sixties. It was a political retreat from the field of political battle on which the enemy itself was floundering with its flanks openly exposed to further ambush.'[24]

At this time, the nationalists perpetuated a series of theoretical debates and organisational ruptures which effectively broke their short hegemony over the black movement as a whole. After Nixon's espousal of Black Power as Black Capitalism, most progressive nationalists and cultural nationalists ceased to use the term. Instead, they championed the politics of 'Pan-Africanism', an eclectic political theory which called for the liberation of all peoples of African descent across the black diaspora, and within the continent. From the outset, Pan-Africanism retained all of the ambiguities and contradictions which Black Power had come to symbolise. In 1971, political theorist Ladun Anise warned activists,

> Pan-Africanism has always been an ideology of progressively enlarging levels of consciousness, meanings, interpretations, and socio-political goals which can be understood only in relation to the differing configurations of problems within changing historical periods. It is an inclusive and open-minded ideology that means different things to the same people at different periods and, in the same period different things to different people.[25]

In 1972–73, the popularity of Pan-Africanism among broad segments of the black population was manifested in the activities of the nationalists' African Liberation Support Committee (ALSC). The ALSC was instrumental in sponsoring a series of popular mass demonstrations in the US which expressed support for African independence from colonial and *apartheid* rule, called the 'African Liberation Day' (ALD). At the ALD in Washington, DC, held in May 1972, 20,000 black youngsters, workers and activists crowded around 'Patrice Lumumba Square' – what nationalists called the grounds surrounding the Washington Monument. Speakers at the ALD included poet Don L. Lee (Haki Madhubuti), Baraka, and CBC members Fauntroy and Diggs, who was particularly resplendent in his purple dashiki. In 1973, ALSC raised $40,000 for African nationalists engaged in armed struggle, and the ALD marches nationally attracted over 100,000 people. Dissent surfaced in late 1973, however, when ALSC's chief organiser Owusu Sadaukai (Howard Fuller) began to reevaluate his opposition to Marxist ideology, and shifted to the left. At a national ALSC meeting in Frogmore, South Carolina, Sadaukai and his supporters declared themselves as favouring Marxism-Leninism, and defined Pan-Africanism as the struggle against both 'racism and imperialism'. Subsequently, the various forces which had successfully established ALD as a major political event were splintered over the issue of Marxism.[26]

The 'Great Debate' between black independent Marxist-Leninists and the narrow cultural nationalists from 1973–76 was a kind of replay of the Black Panthers–US battle of the late 1960s. Nationalist college students in the Students Organized for Black Unity (SOBU) adopted a Leninist position, and renamed their formation Youth Organized for Black Unity (YOBU), to reflect a more class-conscious mentality. Fisk University professor Abd-al Hakimu Ibn Alkalimat (Gerald McWorter), one of the founders of the Institute of the Black World, had been among the most dogmatically narrow nationalists. By the early 1970s, Alkalimat had become a Leninist, establishing a Marxist institute, 'Peoples College', in Nashville, and was decisive in moving many former cultural nationalists to the left.[27] Baraka underwent a similar metamorphosis. Founding the Congress of Afrikan People (CAP) in 1970, Baraka and his cultural nationalist supporters exercised a major role in the nationalists' hegemony over the BEOs. Influenced by Sadaukai's movement to the left, and Karenga's incorporation of certain Marxian concepts into his own formation, Baraka revised his political posture accordingly. By late 1974, CAP had become Marxist-Leninist in all but name, and Baraka's allies inside the National Black Political Assembly became increasingly at odds with Daniels and other nationalists. Cultural nationalists attacked Baraka, Alkalimat, Sadaukai and others for 'selling out' to the white man. Haki Madhubuti expressed their somewhat metaphysical view in September 1974:

The ideology of white supremacy precedes the economic structure of capitalism and imperialism, the latter of which are falsely stated as the cause of racism. To believe that the white boy mis-used and manipulated us for centuries up until today for purely economic reasons is racist and void of any historical reality. . . . Chinese are for Chinese first (Yellow Power), Europeans are for Europeans first (White Power), and Afrikans should be for Afrikans first (Black Power). . . . The Capitalist West convincingly uses anti-communism as an ideological weapon to protect themselves and the Communist East uses anti-imperialism and anti-capitalism as ideological weapons to protect themselves. As far as we are concerned communism and capitalism are the left and right arms in the same white body. And *the highest stage of white supremacy is imperialism whether it's communist or capitalist.*[28]

The struggle between the competing tendencies of black nationalism became increasingly fratricidal. Organisations collapsed beneath the weight of polemics; old friends turned against each other;

marriages were broken over which African liberation organisation one chose to support; individuals lost their jobs inside Black Studies Departments at universities, depending upon where they stood politically on the Leninist-cultural nationalist debate. Each side put forward its own theoreticians in the confrontation. Shawna Maglan-bayan's *Garney, Lumumba, Malcolm: Black Nationalist Separatists* declared that all communists, 'whether they go under the pseudonyms of trotskyism, castroism or marxist-leninism, have consistently sought to sap the life-blood from Black political thinking and sidetrack the struggle of Black mankind by undermining and sabotaging every Black Nationalist-Separatist effort'. Chairman of Howard University's political science department and a leading theorist for the National Black Political Assembly, Ronald Walters, argued that 'imperialism is not the highest stage of capitalism as some would have us believe, but is the highest stage of white culture and development: therefore, Black people in the world are oppressed not because we are workers but because we are Black'.[29] Some narrow nationalists even suggested that their former co-workers were being paid by Moscow or Peking; that the new black Marxist-Leninists had turned 'traitor' in order to receive sexual favours from their white female 'comrades'. Black Marxists such as Mark Smith retorted that Madhubuti and others suffered from an 'idealist' perspective, that they viewed the black working class with complete contempt, and that their bogus interpretation of Pan-Africanism was pro-imperialist and profoundly 'petty bourgeois'. Smith argued, 'the right-wing nationalists' standard line of attack' against Marxism was just what 'the State Department and the imperialists wanted to hear'.[30] A few intellectuals tried to salvage the nationalists' unity by articulating a synthesis of the two positions. Hoyt Fuller, editor of *Black World* magazine, argued forcefully in July 1974:

. . . there is no disputing that class conflict is integral to the (Black) struggle. Nor is the persistence of Marxist analysis, in itself, such a negative thing to Blacks with a sense of history and some balance in their world view. It seems that where Marxism has the power to terrorize is in those Black enclaves which are wedded to the proposition that 'the American way' is the best of all possible approaches to 'the good life.'. . . There is no certainty of a *solid* middle ground as refuge between the Marxists and those middle-class Black strivers whose selfishness and short-sightedness serves the Marxists' purposes. . . . What I deplore most, I think, is the [Marxists'] absence of originality in their new intellectual and theoretical stances. What I miss most in what they now are saying is organic thought, ideas which have grown naturally from the struggle they, themselves, have waged and which are directly applicable to the situation they have tried against such odds and with so little support to change for the better.

With some sadness, Fuller declared, 'We have come to another fork in the road . . . the NAACPs and the PUSHs may seem to have it all their way. . . .'[31]

It would not be fair to say that the Old Guard had trounced the Pan-Africanists, black Marxists and nationalists; rather, it was the black militants who defeated themselves. Theoretically obtuse and organisationally fractious, nationalist groups took turns in purging various tendencies out of their respective formations. After mapping out a detailed strategy, Daniels and a former ally of Baraka's, Mtangulizi Sanyika (Haywood Henry), managed to neutralise Baraka within the Assembly at a particularly bitter brawl in Dayton, Ohio, in late 1975. ALD shrank significantly, down to 7000 participants in Washington, DC in 1974, and less than 4000 two years later. The number of Black Studies departments dropped roughly by half between 1971 and 1976, as feuding scholars and preoccupied polemicists tended to take some blacks' attention away from white-sponsored reductions in minority staff and faculties, and other administrative attacks against blacks on white campuses. Tragically, the rhetoric of many black radicals had less to do with Marxism than with a crude economic determinism and a simplistic adaptation of the ideas of Mao Tse Tung to the terrain of black America. Many black activists who *claimed* to be Marxists had never actually read Marx, and if they had, they had left undigested the rich corpus of modern socialist theory which concretely relates Marx to the unique conditions of social transformation under late capitalism – Antonio Gramsci, Walter Rodney, Amilcar Cabral, Louis Althusser, Nicos Poulantzas. Most cultural nationalists articulated a political praxis that was at best incoherent, profoundly ethnocentric and ideologically inert. Despite powerful sociological evidence from a variety of sources providing beyond any reasonable doubt the centrality of class and the emergence of a conservative black élite, the narrow nationalists preferred to damn material reality, and embrace sterile cultural mutterings and blind dogmas to the death. The Old Guard simply watched their critics bludgeon themselves into political oblivion. In March 1976, the National Black Political Assembly could barely muster 1000 participants at its third national convention in Cincinnati, Ohio. Dellums and Bond rejected the convention's 1976 draft to initiate an independent black presidential candidacy, and by 1977 the Assembly had less than 300 members nationally. The vision of Gary was gone.

V

The inchoate black rebellion of 1965–75 also inspired and, to a profound degree, initiated similar revolts among other American people of colour. In New York City, Puerto Rican workers had joined with progressive whites and blacks in a series of successful labour union efforts. An outstanding example of multiracial co-operation was in the militant Drug and Hospital Employees Local 1199. The union's activities won the support of King, Malcolm X, and Randolph, and brought a number of Puerto Rican rank-and-file organisers into positions of local political leadership. More decisive, however, was the emergence of militant nationalist formations which called for the independence of Puerto Rico from the US. In the early 1960s, the Movement for Puerto Rican Independence (MPI) arose from a political fraction within the moderate Puerto Rican Independence Party. MPI shared many of the characteristics of the later SNCC and the Black Panther Party, with its commitment to street demonstrations, its opposition to the Vietnam War, and its ideological efforts to combine socialism with their own aggressive nationalist programme. At the end of the decade, the Puerto Rican Socialist Party (PSP) developed from the MPI, as an even more doctrinaire Marxist formation. At its height in the early to mid-1970s, PSP 'made some inroads in the labor movement, succeeding in organizing a labor federation independent of the AFL–CIO', radical sociologist Stanley Aronowitz observes. 'In the United States PSP established a branch which, although primarily dedicated to the independence movement, also participated in anti-war and other political protests and became for a time an important force on the American left, particularly on the East Coast and in the Midwest.'[32]

The political unrest among Indians was channelled largely outside traditional trade unionism and Marxist-Leninist politics. More reformist and conservative Indian leaders maintained their political support for the Association on American Indian Affairs, the National Congress of American Indians, and the Indian Rights Association. Young nationalist militants increasingly viewed such groups as black radicals saw the Urban League and the NAACP – as irrelevant social anachronisms which often did more harm than good. Indian activists frequently noted that their people held potential economic and political power which had not been co-ordinated collectively by conservative tribal leaders. On their meagre land holdings still maintained as Indian reservations, Native Americans controlled about 3 per cent of all US oil and gas reserves, 15 per cent of all coal, 55 per cent of the US supply of uranium, and about 11 per cent of all uranium reserves in the world. Yet economic development programmes promoted by private US firms and the federal government usually stripped these mineral and natural resources from the reservations, still leaving the Indian people in a state of perpetual penury. US courts generally refused to grant civil justice to Indians' land claims, and local and state courts and law enforcement officials often treated Indians as aliens. No effective social programmes for housing, education and health care were maintained for urban Indians. As late as 1966, less than 2000 Indians were in college or graduate school, out of a population of 710,000. Over one-half of all Indians could not read or write in English, and infant mortality among Indians still remained the highest in the country.[33]

The clearest manifestation of a renaissance in Indian nationalism first occurred in 1969, when advocates of 'Red Power' took control of Alcatraz Island, a former prison set in San Francisco Bay. Maintaining the island for one and a half years, the militants announced to the media that the island was the property of Indian people. This symbolic act of resistance was repeated elsewhere. In 1971 Indian activists in New York City defaced a statue of George Washington, to bring greater public attention to the genocidal policies of the American government. Indian militants in Minneapolis–St. Paul, Minnesota, led by Chippewa Indian organiser Dennis Banks, launched the American Indian Movement (AIM) in 1968. Like the Black Panther Party in Oakland, AIM's first goal was to address police brutality against non-whites in their city. Patrolling Minneapolis and St. Paul streets after dark, Banks and AIM activists stopped police officers from harassing individual Indians, and promptly publicised incidences of police violence. AIM's direct intervention was responsible for reducing the number of weekend arrests of Indians from 200 down to nearly zero. From 1969 to 1972, AIM's programme expanded to include a variety of public welfare and political training projects. Pressuring a major Minneapolis employer, Honeywell corporation, AIM increased the number of Indian workers at that firm by 450 persons. AIM pressured city officials in Minneapolis to establish a centre for Indian culture, and after seven years of political effort, a $1.9 million public institute was opened. Creating their own housing corporation, AIM leaders initiated the construction of homes for Indians in Minneapolis. Funded by the federal government's Housing and Urban Development Department, AIM used a $4.3 million grant to build 241 homes. In Minnesota's public school systems, Indian militants fought to change the educational curriculum to reflect a more multicultural perspective. When local school boards ignored AIM's demands, the organisation initiated urban Indian schools in Minneapolis, St. Paul, and later in Rapid City, South Dakota. Challenging the racism of the penal system, AIM backed an Indian candidate's successful election to the Minneapolis State Parole Board in 1972.

AIM's constructive successes in educational, economic and social welfare work among Indians brought the group into close political scrutiny by the FBI and local law enforcement agencies. Unlike more traditional Indian public interest organisations, AIM developed a vision of American society without oppression, a critique of the status quo which drew consciously both from their own resistance leaders of the nineteenth century, and from Malcolm X and Martin Luther King. In a 1976 interview, Dennis Banks observed that AIM was founded because of the 'many deaths in this country of Native Americans', but added that a broad coalition of poor people and workers of different nationalities and races was essential in order to change American society:

When Martin Luther King was standing we should have stood with him no matter what his beliefs because we know objectively he was also asking for social change in this country. . . . We have been divided. Indian people are being killed and we are the only ones fighting for Indian people. Blacks are being killed and only blacks are fighting for blacks. Poor whites are fighting for change in the poor white section. Asians and Chicanos are the same way. I think that inspired AIM to stand up finally and say look, we have got to pull it together, and that is where we are at right now, trying to bring non-Indians and the Indians together and bring about massive change in this society.[34]

Confrontation between AIM and federal authorities broke out into open warfare in early 1973. The Pine Ridge Sioux Oglala Civil Rights Organization asked AIM to assist them in removing the accommodationist Tribal Council in their South Dakota reservation. Many of the Minnesota leaders of AIM had been originally from the Pine Ridge reservation, and they quickly joined forces with older, more experienced Indian elders who had been resisting federal authorities for three and four decades. When the Indian nationalists took control of the site, federal authorities and army personnel laid siege on Wounded Knee, South Dakota from 27 February to 8 May 1973. During the siege, Indians across the nation were inspired to new levels of resistance. Dozens of militant organisers journeyed to Wounded Knee, and almost every civic club, political association, and cultural group run by Native American people became involved in the controversy. Two local Indian militants, Pedro Bissonette and Buddy LaMonte, were killed by federal officers, but a peaceful settlement was finally reached. Federal authorities under the Nixon Administration were determined at last to uproot and to destroy AIM and to use the Pine Ridge reservation as a graphic example for other Indian nationalist organisations and leaders of what legal repression might hold for their own formations. Pine Ridge became an 'occupied zone'; local Indians who participated in the Wounded Knee takeover were tried, imprisoned and assassinated. When two FBI agents at Pine Ridge were assassinated in 1975, Indian leader Leonard Peltier was legally framed for the murders and was ordered to serve a life sentence in a federal prison. Indian conservatives stuffed ballot boxes to keep AIM leader Russell Means from winning the Tribal Council's Chairmanship in the Pine Ridge elections held in 1974. In three years, Indian 'goon squads', local white police officers and the FBI were responsible for the execution or disappearance of over 300 Indian women and men in Pine Ridge and across the country. In 1976 the FBI declared that AIM had replaced the Black Panther Party and other black nationalists formations as the 'number one terrorist organization in the United States'.[35] Dennis Banks was charged by federal authorities with 'rioting while armed with intent to kill' in the aftermath of a courtroom disturbance in South Dakota.[36] An all-white jury promptly convicted Banks. Believing with some justification that the FBI or penal authorities planned his assassination, Banks fled to California. The FBI initiated a massive nationwide manhunt, and finally captured the nationalist leader in California in early 1976.

As in its bloody suppression of the Black Panthers, the FBI was absolutely ruthless in its treatment of AIM activists. AIM leader Annie Mae Aquash disappeared and was found dead on the Pine Ridge reservation. FBI officials claimed that Aquash's death was due to exposure. Finally, an independent coroner was allowed to view her remains at the repeated insistence of her family. Aquash had been brutally shot in the brain, and her hands had been chopped off. AIM organiser Byron DeSersa was assassinated in South Dakota. Russell Means and John Thomas were wounded. Local leader Raymond Yellow Thunder was murdered in Nebraska, which led Indian organisations across that state and in South Dakota to form a civil rights coalition which demanded an investigation. But even in the midst of repression, Indian advocates of Red Power fought back. In June 1974, thousands of AIM supporters and members created the International Treaty Council at the Standing Rock Sioux reservation. Indians called for the intervention of the United Nations and other 'international forces necessary to obtain the recognition of our treaties'. The new Council expressed political solidarity with all Third World struggles for emancipation, giving special note of the 'colonized Puerto Rican People in their struggle for Independence from the same United States of America'.[37] One year later, Navajo factory workers and AIM activists expropriated an electronics firm on the Navajo reservation, which had exploited Indians with low wages and benefits. In 1976 Navajo refinery labourers and AIM took control of an oil refinery on the Navajo reservation. Dozens of Indian groups became more involved in militant union confrontation with corporations and industries which had traditionally underpaid Native Americans. The National Congress of American Indians became affiliated with the internationalist World Council of Indigenous Peoples, established in Canada in 1975. Other progressive resources for Indians which formed included the Indian Law Resource Center and the pan-Indian publication *Akwesasne Notes*. From February to August 1978, Indian activists staged the 'Longest Walk' protest across the US to demonstrate against discriminatory laws. AIM survived the Nixon–Ford Administrations' repression, and the nationalist spirit among the Indian people continued to rise.

The recent history of the Chicano *movimiento* provides even more parallels with the rise and fall of black nationalism. Before 1960, there were almost five million Chicanos in the US. Although hundreds of thousands still provided cheap labour for the ranches, vegetable and fruit farms of California, Texas, and other Southwestern states, many Mexican-American families flocked to urban areas in search of higher pay and a decent standard of living. San Diego, Los Angeles, Denver, Phoenix, Tucson, Albuquerque, El Paso, and San Antonio acquired large Chicano working- and middle-class populations. Smaller Chicano neighbourhoods could be found in Chicago, Kansas City, and even New York. By 1950, two-thirds of all Chicanos lived in urban areas. In 1960, about four out of five Mexican-Americans were urban dwellers. Like blacks, Chicanos occupied the lowest level of industrial and commercial employment, and tended to be confined to manual and semi-skilled blue-collar and service jobs. In the South-western states in 1960, the median family income of a Chicano family was $4164, only 64.4 per cent that of white median family income in the region. In 1970, national Chicano median family income was still only $6002. Over a half of all rural Chicano families were judged by federal authorities to exist below the poverty line, a much higher rate than that among rural whites and about the same level as that of rural blacks. Almost one out of three urban Mexican-American families were poor. The new stresses of urban life impacted upon the social and cultural traditions of Chicano households. By 1970, one out of six Mexican-American families was a single-parent home. Youth gangs became prevalent in the lower income barrios of Los Angeles and San Diego. Of all Chicanos, 85 per cent had been born inside the US, but according to US Census records, 72 per cent claimed Spanish as their principal language. Separated by culture, language, and socio-economic status, whites in the Southwest continued to view Chicanos as having only a 'temporary or tentative' position within American political society. Anti-Mexican stereotypes and racist language were often tolerated within local political campaigns. In one five-year period during the 1950s, almost four million Mexican-Americans were seized and expelled from the country.[38]

In central California, a traditional vehicle for Chicano working-class opposition emerged in the early 1960s – the National Farm Workers Association of Cesar Chavez. Born in 1927 in Arizona,

Chavez began to work as a migrant worker at the age of ten. In 1952 he became active in the Community Service Organization of California and gained experience registering thousands of Chicanos to vote. Ten years later he joined the National Farm Workers Association, and began the tedious and often dangerous process of organising rural Mexican-American farm labourers. The objective material conditions which California plantation life imposed upon poor Chicanos was literally only a step above slavery. Most workers lived in 'barracks-like labor camps', and were forced to accept 'polluted drinking water, no toilet facilities, inadequate sanitation and health care, infestation by insects and rodents, and overcrowding'. The typical hourly wage in 1969 was $1.33 and 'due to the seasonal nature of the work, average annual wages were about $1,000'.[39] White farmowners and businessmen routinely fired and harassed Chavez's supporters and organisers from the fields. When Filipino farmworkers began a 1965 strike against California grape-growers, Chavez quickly followed suit. For almost five years, Chavez conducted a massive nation-wide boycott of all grapes from California produced by non-unionised labourers. Civil rights organisations, black nationalists, feminist organisations, organised labour and many church groups honoured the grape boycott. Despite extraordinary pressure by the agricultural corporations, the union finally forced management to acquiesce to its demands. Chicanos and people of colour across the nation were thrilled by the farmworkers' triumph. Chavez himself 'emerged as a passionately charismatic leader, a spokesman for the Mexican-American's desire to reclaim his manhood, and a religious leader with the mystic qualities of a Gandhi'.[40] Forming his labourers into the United Farm Workers (UFW) of America AFL–CIO, Chavez used his new political leverage in other struggles. In 1973, farmers signed a union contract with the Teamsters, a powerful US union with strong links to organised crime, rather than with the UFW. A second field boycott was waged successfully until 1975, when the state government was forced to intervene. In spite of intimidation by the Teamsters, over two-thirds of all labour elections in 1976 determining the official representatives of the workers were won by the UFW. Chavez's influence grew within both the California and the national Democratic Party, as the UFW pursued national policies which addressed the economic and social needs of low-income whites and all national minorities.

The emergence of Cesar Chavez as a national labour and civil rights leader in the late 1960s marked the simultaneous rise of hundreds of Chicano political activists across the nation. A 1967 survey of five Southwestern states indicated that of the 603 members of state legislatures '48 were Mexican-American: the New Mexico legislature having the greatest number – 33; and Texas having 10. New Mexico was also represented in the United States Congress by a Mexican-American [senator]'.[41] In Colorado, the Crusade for Justice was formed among Denver Chicanos by Rudolfo 'Corky' Gonzales. Gonzales developed a political philosophy which paralleled that of Imamu Baraka in the early 1970s, or of Frantz Fanon a decade before, an uneven mixture of fiery nationalism and socialism. Chicano scholar Richard A. Garcia describes Gonzales' approach to politics:

> Gonzales's socialism was somewhat similar to Malcolm X's social-ism: it emanated more from experience and emotions than from philosophy and reason. Gonzales's world view posited a society divided into two diametrically opposed categories: Chicanos and Anglos. For him the political and social struggle was always basically bipolar. The Chicano struggle was for equality and freedom, but it was not . . . within the United States, but in the mythical Chicano nation of Aztlán. On occasions, for Gonzales, the myth blurred the reality. His basic goal was separation, not integration, and he fought a nationalist, not a workers', struggle. Gonzales's 'nationalist heart' was always in conflict with his 'socialist head'; he could not fully accept a fusion of socialism and nationalism.[42]

Perhaps the most articulate young proponent of Chicano nationalism was Reies Lopez Tijerina of New Mexico. Tijerina acquired a rural and poor peoples' following in the northern part of his state by campaigning for the return of all lands stolen by the Anglo settlers to their rightful owners, the Chicano peasantry and workers. Despite his militant language and provocative style, Tijerina was probably the most politically moderate of the new generation of leaders. Finally, the most complex and pragmatic activist was from Texas, José Angel Gutierrez. As leader of the Texas La Raza Unida Party, Gutierrez came to national attention by delivering a militant speech termed 'Death to the Anglos' at a 1968 south Texas Chicano rally. Gutierrez built an electoral bloc of Chicano voters, and with some marginal degree of national support provided by the Trotskyist Socialist

Workers Party and Chicano leftists, effectively challenged the state's Democratic Party from the left. Unlike Gonzales, however, Gutierrez was always a practical politician whose goals for the Chicano *movimiento* were a cultural pluralist society within the context of the US, and a greater share of economic and political power for the Chicano people.[43]

By the early 1970s, Chicano activism reached virtually every level of civil and political society in the Southwestern US. Youth created the Brown Berets in California and Texas, patterned largely after the Black Panther Party cadre. In Texas, the Mexican-American Youth Organization emerged and created ties with Gonzalez's Crusade for Justice. Nationalist-oriented Chicano entrepreneurs joined the *movimiento*, calling for Brown Capitalism and the creation of federal programmes which would promote capital formation among their own petty bourgeois strata. Chicano university students initiated MECHA (Movimiento Estudiantil Chicano de Aztlán). In Los Angeles, Marxist-Leninists within the Chicano community created the Center for Autonomous Social Action–General Brotherhood of Workers (CASA–HGT), which championed a Cuban-style socialist agenda.

This unprecedented social ferment impacted the more reformist Chicano associations, exactly as SNCC, the National Plack Political Assembly, and the League of Revolutionary Black Workers had influenced the black political mainstream. LULAC was forced to assume a more activist orientation, and began to develop strategies to become involved in state and national politics. Chicano members of the Texas Democratic Party effectively pointed to their left at La Raza Unida, and gradually won substantial concessions from entrenched party conservatives who feared the spectre of Gutierrez and the threat of Chicano political hegemony in that state. Despite the multiplicity of organisations and programmes which were inspired by 'el espiritú de La Raza', political observers concurred that there were four dominant activists who maintained a regional or national presence among Chicano nationalists: Chavez, Gutierrez, Gonzales, and Tijerina. 'By 1972 these four chieftains had sectioned off the Southwest and, like the rebels of the Mexican Revolution, each distrusted, envied, and skirmished programmatically with the others', notes Garcia. 'Each chieftain had his own personal ideological interpretation of nationalism'.[44]

The 1972 El Paso, Texas, convention of the Raza Unida Party was, in critical respects, similar to the Gary Black Political Convention as a highpoint for Chicano nationalism. Delegates at the convention voted to adopt the nationalistic and socialist programme of Gonzales, but elected Gutierrez to serve as party chairman. Bitterly disappointed, Gonzales returned to Denver, 'beaten and hounded by left-leaning lieutenants'. Local police officers stepped up their harassment of the Crusade's activities, and within several years his group fell into a narrow chauvinistic posture, turning 'ideologically inward [and] politically and organizationally powerless'.[45] Angered by his repudiation, Tijerina rejected the Raza Unida and any efforts to build an independent Chicano political party. Chavez left the convention with a firm commitment to build a Chicano presence in the left wing of the national Democratic Party, and by the late 1970s he exercised a major influence on the policies of the rather eccentric liberal Democratic governor of California, Edmund Brown, Jr. Gutierrez continued to exercise some influence in Texas politics, winning a country judgeship and electing his supporters to local office. But his political style and Machiavellian outlook bothered even his most dedicated followers. After cultivating a cosy relationship with white and Chicano Trotskyists, for example, he personally ordered the delegates from the Socialist Workers Party to be thrown out of the El Paso convention. After the Trotskyists ran a Chicano activist, Pedro Camejo, as their symbolic candidate for President in 1976, Gutierrez warmed toward them again. Taking advantage of the situation, LULAC and other liberal political and cultural groups were able to recover their losses, and recruited thousands of young militants who had become casualties of the fractious battles between various Chicano nationalist formations. One testament to the collapse of La Raza was represented by the July 1977 conference of 'Mexican American Democrats' in El Paso. Of the 400 delegates, a majority were middle-class urban liberals, a smaller number of Chicano rural farmers and political conservatives, and some leaders from La Raza Unida Party. The expressed goal of the convention was 'to organize Mexican Americans in Texas under a single political banner' – in short, within the populist and liberal flank of the Democratic Party.[46] Neither the Chicano nor the black movements had collapsed without a trace, yet both had become part of a broader, non-socialist reform impulse which sought incremental change within the system. As the fringe elements of both nationalist movements fought each other, lurching deeper into theoretical confusion and cultural mysticism, the main-

stream was able to incorporate the very valid social criticisms of the
nationalists into a more realistic and limited series of socio-economic
and political goals.

VI

For black and Chicano nationalists, the period of their respective
ideological and cultural hegemony had come to an unceremonious
end. Splintered, confused, weary of polemical debate, most had
returned to their original neighbourhoods, far from the national
stage, leaving their reformist counterparts firmly in place to dictate
the national minority agenda. As the presidential campaign of 1976
proceeded, both Chicano and Afro-American civil rights leaders
prepared to build a solid base of support for whoever the Democratic
Party decided to select as its nominee. In the state primaries, an
obscure, one-term governor of Georgia began to emerge as the
front-runner, James E. (Jimmy) Carter. Bond was the first black
leader to denounce Carter on the basis of principle. He observed that
in Carter's primary electoral victory of 1970 in Georgia he polled less
than 10 per cent of the blacks' votes; that Carter's 'running mate' that
year was none other than Lester Maddox, the notorious bigot; that
Carter did not believe in 'traditionally liberal principles and
humanistic values'; and that the former governor was a 'liar', prone to
'chameleon-like rhetoric'.[47] Other black leaders, sensing Carter's
momentum, ignored the Southerner's contradictory background and
campaigned vigorously for him. Some of the first to wear 'Carter-
for-President' buttons were the cultural nationalists, such as Nikki
Giovanni. The black mayors, notably Maynard Jackson of Atlanta
and Coleman Young of Detroit, were early Carter proponents.
Martin's family, including Coretta Scott King and the Reverend
Martin Luther King, Sr. campaigned for Carter. Carter's greatest
supporter in the black community, and indeed his most valuable ally,
was former King aide Andrew Young, then a two-term US
Representative from Atlanta. After Carter's nomination, the Old
Guard went to work to bring the black electorate to the polls. The
NAACP and other groups initiated 'Operation Big Vote', a campaign
to register blacks in 36 major cities. Black supporters of Carter,
especially Young, Mrs King, former SNCC leader John Lewis, and
Georgia state senator Ben Brown, travelled and spoke extensively for
the Georgian. In November 1976, Carter defeated the incumbent

president, Gerald Ford, by 40.3 million v. 38.5 million votes. Carter's electoral college victory was, however, much closer, 297 to 241 votes. As in 1960, blacks proved to be the decisive margin of victory for the Democratic candidate. In one industrial state, Ohio, out of 4 million votes cast, Carter carried the state by a slender margin of 7600 votes: Ohio's blacks had cast roughly 280,000 ballots for Carter. In Mississippi, Carter polled an 11,500 vote edge over Ford; 59 per cent of all whites had voted for Ford, but over 90 per cent of the state's 187,000 black voters endorsed Carter. States where the black vote was decisive included Pennsylvania, Alabama, Texas, New York, and seven others. The Carter victory left BEOs and many black political scientists in rapture. Eddie N. Williams, President of the Joint Center of Political Studies in Washington, DC, announced proudly that Carter's narrow victory had made 'blacks full partners in the nation's policy making franchise'. The new president should 'start by integrating' civil rights leaders and BEOs into the upper hierarchy of the state's 'apparatus'.[48] Without hesitation, the president-elect notified the press that Young would become the new United Nations ambassador for the US, and a full member of Carter's presidential cabinet. Seemingly, a new phase in American race relations had begun, the Second Reconstruction would be renewed.

Many observers viewed Young's appointment as a dramatic vindication of the struggles and sacrifices of King and the entire Civil Rights Movement. Black mayors supported Carter with nervous anticipation, hoping that fresh federal funds would be poured into the major cities for economic development, to restore public schools, health delivery systems and necessary social services. Black desegregation activists such as John Lewis and Louisiana attorney Weldon Rougeau were appointed to power posts in the federal bureaucracy. Yet there were present, even then, troubling indications that Carter's election would not produce meaningful reforms. During Carter's primary campaign in Pennsylvania, he treated black local leaders with a kind of cautious contempt, what political scientist Chuck Stone described as 'a veiled warning of retributive hostility'.[49] Before the general election, Carter refused to attend national conferences held by the CBC, the black National Association of Media Women, and the National Negro Business League. There was also a larger question to consider. In the four years after the Gary convention, BEOs broke off all organisational ties with black nationalists, and along with the integrationist Old Guard, had reaffirmed their commitment to a bourgeois democratic road towards black freedom. King had died fighting a Democratic president; his protégés now rushed to embrace a Democratic president from a Deep South state, whose own credentials as a proponent of civil rights prior to 1970 were non-existent. King was killed mobilising sanitation workers in Memphis and anti-war demonstrators in the streets; his followers had joined with Martin's bitterest black opponents on the right in accepting posts in the new administration. The Civil Rights Movement was flushed with victory, yet in retrospect, it was a victory in defeat. COINTELPRO and the fratricidal struggles between leftists and dogmatic separatists had reduced the nationalist movement to a whimpering, self-flagellating set of marginal sects. The League of Revolutionary Black Workers, DRUM, the Black Workers' Congress and other revolutionary black labour organisations had disappeared. Nationally, black workers and the poor felt more powerless to elicit meaningful social change within the system, and large numbers simply stopped voting. The percentage of the black voting age population who actually voted declined from 57.6 per cent in 1968, 52.1 per cent in 1972, down to 49 per cent in 1976. The black movement for biracial democracy had left the lunchcounters and the streets and had moved squarely into the corridors of electoral politics – a process wherein, not coincidentally, millions of blacks became 'depoliticised'. Could freedom be won in concert with a former segregationist, and within the mechanics of the racist/capitalist state? Retreating from the vision of Gary, most black leaders were now determined to cast their lot with the system that they had for years denounced as racist, in order to gain goods and services for their constituents. Reform, once more, had supplanted rebellion.

7. Reaction: The Demise of the Second Reconstruction, 1976–1982

Without a new vision of ourselves and the world beyond the borders of our persons, many of the events of the 1970s became nothing more than frustrating repetitions of history, new signs of white racism or mystifying novelties and epiphenomena. . . . What kind of a society do we want, and are we willing to struggle for? Without a nationwide pressing of that question among blacks and whites, we surely would not recognize 'integration' if we saw it.

Vincent Harding

Starvation is God's way of punishing those who have too little faith in capitalism.

John D. Rockefeller, Sr.

I

Nothing fails like success. By the mid-1970s, the black nationalist impulse had been effectively splintered, repressed, and removed from political discourse. The black élite was retrieved from its marginal and defensive stance within the black community, and with the election of Carter, had unprecedented access to middle-to-upper levels of the political bureaucracy. The BEOs, like the Old Guard of the NAACP and Urban League, viewed the 1976 election as a kind of public ratification for the body of its own politics. Radicalism and militancy were defeated. Wallace, Maddox and the most overtly

REACTION: DEMISE OF THE SECOND RECONSTRUCTION, 1976–1982   169

racist white Southern governors and representatives either had been removed from public offices or, at least, no longer postured defiantly against desegregation. Jim Crow signs had been removed from public restaurants; federally-sponsored 'affirmative action' programmes brought tens of thousands of blacks into middle-class jobs in both the public and private sectors; blacks were allowed to participate without restrictions within the political marketplace; urban riots had been quelled, and ghetto blacks seemingly succumbed to the quiescence of the dominant society. The general interpretation of the period was, at least for the black élite, one of tremendous optimism. There was no longer a need to march in the streets against the policies of big-city mayors, because blacks were now in virtually every municipal administration across the nation. The total number of blacks in the Congressional Black Caucus had doubled in the eight years before Carter's victory; there was every reason to believe that their numbers would double again in another decade, as more Congressional districts became primarily non-white. Certainly, it was said, the Second Reconstruction was on the verge of success. Black freedom would become a reality through gradual yet meaningful reforms within the existing system.

The prime beneficiary of the gains from the Second Reconstruction was the black élite. It is imperative here to describe in some detail the socio-economic position of this stratum, in order to explain its basically optimistic and reformist outlook. First, and foremost, the black élite was characterised by its relatively modest size. Only about 50,000 black men and 200,000 black women were employed as elementary and secondary schoolteachers in 1977. In that same year, the numbers of black medical and health-care workers were approximately 50,000 men and 116,000 women; professional and technical white-collar workers, 315,000 males and 505,000 women, respectively; and salaried managers and administrators, 180,000 males and 78,000 females, respectively. When contrasted with whites, however, the actual presence of blacks in white-collar jobs was actually quite low when compared to their numbers in the overall labour force. In 1977 again, the actual percentage of blacks to all races within the medical and health-care professions was 3.9 per cent for all men and 8.4 per cent among all women. Among all salaried administrators and managers, only 3.0 per cent of the men were black, and 5.0 per cent of the women employees were black. The figures decline still further when each white-collar category is analysed by specific vocation.

Over 90 per cent of all black women employed in health care were nurses or more commonly para-medics and hospital workers. As late as 1970, the number of black doctors in the US was only 6106, about 2 per cent of the total number of all physicians and surgeons. In the mid-1970s, there were fewer than 5000 practising black attorneys in the US, about 1 per cent of all lawyers.

This élite was in many respects, however, markedly similar in its socio-economic profile with other upwardly mobile white ethnic groups which had advanced in previous decades. Many of these men and women had attended the newly desegregated colleges and universities during the 1960s and 1970s. The Federal government's requirements for affirmative action forced the admission of large numbers of blacks into positions which they had long been denied, solely on the basis of race. Thus, in the early 1970s, the upper fraction of the black labour force experienced a real advance in its absolute incomes. Between 1969 and 1974, for example, the earnings of the top 5 per cent of all non-white families increased from $17,238 to $24,267, about 74 per cent of the level for that of white families of similar background. By 1977, 21 per cent of all black families had incomes between $15,000 and $24,999, and another 9 per cent earned above $25,000. Advances in income were more likely for those black families whose major 'breadwinner' had a college education. The median income of black family heads 25-years-old and over who had acquired one to three years of college training was $13,371 in 1974 and $15,027 in 1976. For black family heads who had graduated from college, median earnings jumped from $17,316 in 1974 to $20,733 in 1976. For one special group, black husband-wife families below the age of 35 who were both income earners, the income gap between themselves and other white families with a similar socio-cultural profile virtually disappeared. In the South, black husband-wife families in this group earned $14,563 in 1976, roughly 90 per cent of the earnings received by white families with the same background. In the North and West, the incomes of young black husband-wife families actually exceeded that of white families, $16,715 to $16,691, in 1976. The traditional income margin of racial inequality, at least for many of the black élite, had been almost eliminated by the mid-1970s.

In other economic aspects, the status of the black élite was remarkably secure. In 1977, for instance, the overall black unemployment rate for civilian workers was 13.1 per cent for men, 14.8 per cent for women. Black professional and technical workers, however, experienced unemployment rates of 6.1 per cent for males, 5.1 per cent for females. Black salaried and self-employed managers and administrators had jobless rates of only 5.3 per cent and 5.6 per cent for males and females respectively. Conversely, in 1977 black males employed as service workers had an unemployment rate of 13.7 per cent; black female blue-collar workers experienced a jobless rate of 16.9 per cent; and 16.4 per cent of all black men who worked as non-farm labourers were without jobs. In the fields of commerce and finance, black entrepreneurs were also registering notable gains. Between 1969 and 1977, the total number of black businesses increased from 163,073 to 231,195; gross receipts of these firms almost doubled, from $4.5 billion to $8.7 billion. Between 1970 and 1975, 24 black-owned banks were founded, compared to only 11 established between 1960 and 1969. Yet even here, the fragility of the economic foundations of the black élite were clearly visible to any researcher. Blacks owned few if any corporations or industries which were most profitable. Fewer than 2 per cent of all US construction firms and manufacturing industries were black-owned. Blacks acquired only a half of 1 per cent of all wholesale trade firms, financial establishments, insurance companies, and real estate firms. Over 80 per cent of all black-owned firms in 1980 did not have a single paid employee, and over one-third of all black-owned establishments failed within twelve months after beginning business. In 1977, only 113 black-owned businesses out of 231,195 had more than 100 paid employees, and another 230 retained only 50 to 99 workers. The upper 0.005 per cent of all black firms hired most of the employees and earned 28.5 per cent of all black businesses' gross receipts.

Considered as a socio-economic group, the black élite – in the fields of banking, commerce, law, education, and medicine – comprised only 7 to 10 per cent of the total Afro-American population. They were set apart from the vast majority of working-class and impoverished blacks by their relative income parity with whites; their educational training and professional advancement; their political moderation and social conformity; their advocacy of the economics of capitalism and corporate upward mobility. In all critical respects, this group had every reason to applaud the gains of the previous years, the destruction of Jim Crow, and the acceptance of affirmative action within the white-collar workforce. This stratum controlled the NAACP, and the Urban League, as well as other civil rights organisations. It owned or influenced the 50 black-owned radio and

television stations which reached into the predominantly black
metropolitan areas; it had access to white politicians, corporate
leaders and influential social institutions; its own leaders were
appointed to President Carter's Administration in a variety of
capacities. The rise and institutionalisation of the black élite during
the 1970s had a profound impact upon white and black societies. For
whites of all income levels, the emergence of thousands of well-
educated, articulate and aggressive black professionals seemed to
require a political 'white backlash'. Whites assumed incorrectly that
the great majority of black Americans were now firmly within the
'middle class'. In growing numbers, whites asked bitterly: 'Why are
blacks still demanding civil rights? Segregation has ended, and with
affirmative action, partially-qualified blacks are now taking jobs
which rightfully belong to better-qualified whites.' Conveniently
ignoring economic data on the burgeoning millions of black unemployed and the poor, many white liberals and civil rights proponents
began to insist that 'too much' had been given to all blacks, and that
some of the political and economic reforms alloted to non-whites had
to be rescinded. On the other side of the colour line, the primary effect
of the black élite was a growing socio-economic and cultural division
among blacks. Thousands of black professionals fled the inner cities
to purchase homes in formerly all-white suburbs. Black middle-class
adults who had once attended segregated black public schools and
universities now sent their children to private schools and white,
upper-class colleges. Many black doctors and attorneys who only a
few years before were confined to the ghetto now serviced a more
affluent clientele which was largely white or primarily black élite.
Desegregation allowed the most gifted black intellectuals, athletes,
artists and musicians to leave black colleges to accept higher-paying
positions within white institutions. Thus in a cruel paradox of history,
many traditional black cultural, economic, social and political
institutions experienced a decline in status, quality and viability
precisely because Jim Crow had been overturned. The objective
social distance between upwardly mobile black professionals and the
great majority of black labourers and the poor had never been greater.

II

While the black élite advanced, the social and economic conditions
for the majority of blacks remained the same, and in some respects

grew worse. Millions of blacks in the South and North lived in dilapidated, rat-infested dwellings. In 1970, 61 per cent of all black families living in rural areas and 8 per cent of black urban households lacked some or all plumbing facilities, compared to only 11 per cent for rural whites and 2 per cent of urban whites; 902,000 black families residing in the South lived in housing units which had either no toilets or incomplete plumbing facilities. Many black families lived in overcrowded apartments or rented houses in which their landlords, who usually were white, denied them adequate heat and other essentials. In urban renter-occupied dwellings, one-fifth of all black homes had a person-per-room ratio above 1.01 persons per room in 1970 – a clear indication of overcrowded conditions. In rural areas and in the South, housing conditions were worse: 29 per cent of all Southern black renters and 19 per cent of Southern black home-owners lived in crowded housing. Among rural blacks who rented their dwellings, overcrowded conditions affected 40 per cent of all families. Almost one-fourth of all rural black renters had an incredible person-per-room ratio above 1.5 persons per room. Given these dire living conditions, it is not surprising that a disproportionately high number of blacks suffer from certain types of illnesses compared to whites. US Census statistics for 1974 revealed that blacks suffered much higher death rates than whites per 100,000 population in many categories: for tuberculosis, blacks had an annual death rate of 4.1 to the white death rate of 1.3; syphilis, 0.5 for blacks, 0.1 for whites; hypertension, 5.3 for blacks, 1.3 for whites; early infancy diseases, 29 for blacks, 11.3 for whites. Overall, by race and gender, blacks' life expectancies from birth were lower than those for whites. Using 1974 statistics, black males' life expectancy was 62.9 years; white males, 68.9 years; black females, 71.2 years; white females, 76.6 years. Black womens' mortality rates during childbirth were 600 per cent higher than among white women in 1970. Out of every thousand, 16.8 black newborn infants died before reaching their first month, compared to only 10.4 white infants in 1975.

The most disturbing social characteristic within black America in the post-segregation period was the upward spiral in the rate of homicide. Trapped in the urban ghettoes of America's decaying inner cities, plagued with higher unemployment rates, disease, bad housing, poor public schools, and inadequate social services, young blacks were filled with a sense of anger, self-hatred, and bitterness. In the 1960s, this black rage lashed out against the symbols of white property, power and privilege. Black Power provided unemployed black youth with an opportunity to vent their collective anger into a political act of defiance. In the wake of the demise of militant black nationalism, and with the flight of the black élite into the safe havens of suburbia, the ghetto's black rage was unleashed against itself. In 1960, the homicide rate per 100,000 blacks was 21.9, slightly less than the black homicide figure of 1910 (22.3). By 1970, the black homicide rate reached 35.5 per cent, compared to a 4.4 figure among American whites. During the Nixon, Ford and Carter Administrations, black fratricidal violence soared. About 55 black males per thousand were the victims of violent crime during the 1970s. Of all black working-class and impoverished households 13 to 16 per cent experienced robberies every year in the decade. Black male homicide rates were between 600 and 900 per cent higher than those for whites by the late 1970s. And by 1980, 50 per cent of all American homicides were black males killing other black males. The rise in urban violent crime allowed white politicians and corporate interests to increase the number of police and law enforcement officers within the black community. US per capita police expenditures jumped 39 per cent between 1970 and 1977. Federal government and local government expenditures for police in 1977 reached $1.4 billion and $8.8 billion, respectively. Despite sizeable increases in police spending, white Americans of all classes became terrified of the omnipresent spectre of the 'black criminal, rapist and burglar'. By 1978, nine out of ten US citizens were convinced that the courts were not attacking crime vigorously enough, and almost half were afraid to walk in their own neighbourhoods. As a result, the urban centres of the nation were rapidly becoming permanently armed camps.

The social consequences of crime and fear were soon manifested in a more authoritarian treatment for blacks within the US criminal justice system. By the late 1970s, over two million black Americans, a figure equalling 8 per cent of the total black population, were arrested every year. Despite vast amounts of money spent to halt crime, almost nothing was done to improve the physical conditions of jails and prisons, or to initiate rehabilitation programmes for persons convicted of crimes. In the state of Illinois, to cite one example, over $160 million was appropriated to the Illinois Department of Corrections in fiscal 1979. Of that sum, only $9000 was spent on improving the facilities in the state's prisons. Many states abandoned 'indeterminate sentencing' in favour of 'mandatory sentences' for specific crimes. American critics of the prison system noted that 'the trend is currently toward warehousing and punishment rather than toward rehabilitation, which is the professed goal of state prisons'.[1] States passed 'habitual offender laws', which ordered the life imprisonment of any person who had been sentenced a second time for certain crimes, including murder, treason, or 'deviate sexual assault'. To intimidate would-be felons, a few state governments experimented with novel methods. In May 1982, the state legislature of Georgia ordered the creation of a 'mobile death wagon'. Georgia's electric chair was literally placed on wheels, as it were, 'so condemned criminals can be executed near the scene' of their alleged crimes.[2] The political demand for law-and-order culminated in a growing web of coercion and terror for blacks, Latinos and low-income whites as well. By December 1981, two million American adults were behind bars, on probation or on parole – about one out of every 83 persons over the age of 18 in the country – 369,000 adults were confined in state and federal prisons; 157,000 were in local jails; over 1.2 million were on probation, and another 224,000 were parolled. About a half of the penal population, at any given time, was black. By June 1982, 1038 persons were awaiting execution, the highest number in American history. Almost half of this group were Afro-Americans. While only 13 of the prisoners on 'Death Row' had black victims, 54 per cent of all US homicide victims in the 1980s were black.

As the social environment continued to deteriorate, many black families began to splinter under the forces of oppression. The number of children born to unmarried black women increased significantly. In 1950, only 88,000 births among non-whites were outside wedlock. In 1975, the figure for blacks reached 250,000, 48.8 per cent of all black births recorded that year. Birth rates, which had declined among blacks between 1900–60, began to increase, especially among the uneducated and the poor. For black married women with an eighth grade education or less, the average number of children increased from 3.6 in 1960 to 4.8 in 1975. Of all black married women between the ages from 35 to 39 years in 1975, 36 per cent had five or more children, and another 46 per cent had two to four children. As birth rates soared, the percentage of black children who lived with both parents dropped. Only 17 per cent of all black children in 1975 lived with both parents in households where the total annual income was below $4000. That same year, 957,100 black children whose families earned between $4000 and $5900 annually lived with only one adult, while only 391,000 children in the same income group lived with both parents. Even for upper-income levels, the tendency for black children to live with only one adult was much greater among blacks than for whites. Of all children from black families earning above $15,000, 86 per cent lived in two-parent households, yet for whites of similar incomes, the figure was 97 per cent. Increasingly, some black women were finding it difficult even to find males of marriageable age in certain metropolitan communities. Nationally, the percentage of black women 14-years-old and over who were married declined from 60 per cent in 1960 to 49 per cent in 1975. The number of black women who were divorced doubled in this fifteen-year period; black households maintained by females with no husband present increased from 843,000 in 1960 to 1,940,000 in 1975. Many black women asked each other – 'Where are the black men?' The answers are found partially in the statistics above, and in others as well: over 10,000 black men were murdered each year; 260,000 were in federal and state penitentiaries by 1980; thousands died prematurely due to hypertension and other illnesses; several million were among the partially employed or unemployed, who could not financially support a household.

By the late 1970s, American social scientists began to describe the process of degeneration taking place in the black community in several ways. University of Chicago sociologist William Julius Wilson accepted the 'illusion' that a majority of blacks had become middle class, or at least would soon become more affluent, in *The Declining Significance of Race*, published in 1978. However, Wilson was forced to acknowledge that there was a growing army of 'lower class blacks' who had been virtually unaffected by civil rights legislation, affirmative action, and Federal government initiatives to diminish unemployment. 'The challenge of economic dislocation in modern industrial society', Wilson suggested, 'calls for public policy programs to attack inequality on a broad class front.'[3] More perceptively, Douglas G. Glasgow's *Black Underclass* described the recent development of a hard-core number of young blacks who had virtually no social or economic prospects for advancement. Unlike previous generations of impoverished blacks, the members of this new social strata 'were jobless and lacked saleable skills and opportunities to get them; they had been rejected and labeled as social problems by the police, the schools, the employment and welfare agencies; they were victims of the new camouflaged racism'. The urban society had become a social nightmare, where black men 'drank, gambled, [and] fought', where 'hustling, quasi-legitimate schemes, and outright deviant activity are also alternatives to work'.[4] Juvenile youth gangs sprang up in many cities, involving the participation of up to one-third of the black teenagers in some places. Drugs such as cocaine and heroin which had been confined to a relatively small portion of the population became endemic among hundreds of thousands of black youth. 'Junkies' – individuals dependent upon illegal drugs – began to be a visible problem in inner city high schools. Some reported instances of junkies were cases as young as 12-years-old. Prostitution and random violence, disease and death became commonplace. Glasgow's 'underclass', or more accurately, the black urban reserve army of labour, was a permanently unemployable strata of society. Several million black adults had never had the opportunity to acquire gainful full-time employment. Now, as the economic prospects of urban centres declined, and as factories and plants began closing and moving to the American Southwest and overseas, these black women, men and youngsters were faced with the prospect that they would never work during their entire lives. City services, slipping in the 1960s, sharply diminished in the 1970s. Uncollected garbage, sewage in open streets, rats and cockroaches, dilapidated apartments, buildings gutted by fire, police brutality, reductions in health care and welfare services – these were only part of the social foundations and physical environment of the black underclass.

III

In the mid-1970s, Vincent Harding notes, 'everything seemed to change, the organic center fell apart'.[5] In this environment of black upper-class success and black working-class poverty and repression, many blacks turned in large numbers to religion. With the overt suppression of revolutionary black nationalist groups, the Nation of Islam was in a position to recapture some of its former power. Most black radicals, influenced heavily by Malcolm X's public separation from and feud with the Nation in 1964–65, still viewed the organisation with a great deal of scepticism. But Elijah Muhammad, the octogenarian who still reigned with an iron hand, was able to regain a degree of allegiance among new generations of urban black youth who were searching for spiritual and political direction. Simultaneously, Muhammad attempted to establish closer links with the US government and other foreign interests in an effort to resolve his group's ongoing political and economic troubles. By making peace with Chicago's political boss, Richard Daley, the Nation was able to eliminate most of the police surveillance and harassment against the sect. Imitating the FBI, Nation of Islam members in Philadelphia destroyed that city's Black Panther Party headquarters in retaliation for the group's public advocacy of Malcolm X's ideas. In 1972, Muhammad negotiated a $3 million interest-free loan from Colonel Muamar Kadafi which was used to expand Black Muslim enterprises. Despite these gains, the Nation of Islam was still plagued by internal dissension. One of the Nation's most dynamic and powerful ministers, Hamaas Abdul Khaalis (Ernest McGhee) denounced the Nation as a corruption of the true faith, Sunni Islam, in 1972. Khaalis declared that Muhammad was 'a lying deceiver' and stated that their leader 'who inspired former dope addicts and prostitutes to monklike lives of sacrifice, discipline and hard work, was instead stealing his followers' money and leading them to hell'.[6] For devout defenders of Muhammad, Khaalis' challenge could not remain unanswered. On 18 January 1973, at least five armed gunmen, all members of the Nation of Islam, entered Khaalis' Washington, DC, home and butchered five members of his family.

With Muhammad's death in 1975, the leadership of the Nation of Islam passed to one of his sons, Wallace. Quickly and efficiently, Wallace Muhammad 'Malcolmised' the organisation within two years. The para-military formation, the Fruit of Islam, was disbanded; the mixture of racial mythology and religious dogma promulgated by Elijah Muhammad was abandoned in favour of the orthodox teachings of Islam; whites were permitted to attend services and in some instances even joined the group. The Nation was renamed the World Community of al-Islam in the West. In other matters, however, Wallace Muhammad did not abandon the overtures of his father towards Arab nations and the American government. In 1976 he obtained a gift of $16 million from Sheikh Sultan Ben Mohammad al-Qasimi, head of Sharjah, United Arab Emirates, to construct a new educational institution and a mosque. The World Community of al-Islam even succeeded in obtaining government contracts with the US Army to package food and supplies for troops. Yet these dramatic changes did not occur without more dissension. Louis Farrakhan, perhaps the most charismatic minister in the Nation after the departure of Malcolm X, quietly left the Nation by 1978. In February 1981, Farrakhan announced the creation of the 'old' Nation of Islam under his direction, following the tenets of Elijah Muhammad. Several thousand blacks soon flocked to Farrakhan's group, while many others simply withdrew from both versions of Islam, disillusioned and embittered. The decline and disintegration of the Nation represented in Harding's view the death of a '[corrupt] and dictatorial organisation that had essentially separated itself from the day-to-day struggles of our people. It means the loss of a community that most blacks never formally joined, but which seemed to exist – sometimes romantically – on behalf of certain unspoken feelings and desires in millions of hearts and minds.'[7]

Growing numbers of poor and dispossessed blacks turned to evangelical Christianity to find some comfort in their shattered lives. The great majority of itinerant preachers who were outside the old-established churches in the black community were simply harmless rogues, plying their rhetorical craft in exchange for modest financial wealth, consoling the poor and the hopeless with a flair for drama and hokum. Others were more dangerous. One dynamic white preacher in Indianapolis, Indiana, James Jones, developed his 'People's Temple' with a predominantly black constituency. Moving his congregation to Ukiah, California, in the mid-1960s, Jones started a series of self-help institutions, an animal shelter, and a farm. Relocating to the black Fillmore district of San Francisco in 1970, Jones quickly established a popular following. Elderly and poor blacks joined People's Temple to benefit from the congregation's impressive array of social services. Almost 2000 people were given free breakfasts and dinners every day at the Temple; young children were educated in the group's day-care programme; teenagers were attracted to the social activities and the church's film workshop, printing press and carpentry workshop. Jones recruited social workers and counsellors to assist members in completing forms to receive welfare benefits, and to aid them with other economic problems.

Within several years, Reverend Jones began to orient the church towards specific political struggles. His sermons and public statements became increasingly linked with other progressive organisations, from the radical American Indian Movement to black community activist groups. People's Temple members were organised into a political machine, registering black and other Third World people, and they mobilised thousands of inner city voters in support of liberal and socialist-leaning Democratic candidates. As a result,

Jones became an influential figure in Northern California politics, and a political ally of two prominent black leaders, California lieutenant governor Mervyn Dymally and state assembly-man Willie Brown of San Francisco. For many white liberals and socialists, 'the Temple was a remarkable institution – a mass political organisation in the form of a revivalist church – and they praised it for bringing many poor blacks to demonstrations and involving them in the daily work of local campaigns'.[8] Thousands of Bay Area residents read Jones' newspaper, the *Peoples Forum*, which claimed a circulation of 600,000. Democratic Party officials and civil rights leaders valued Jones' support, and praised the People's Temple's political activities. Glowing letters of endorsement and support for Jones were written by Wallace Muhammad, San Francisco mayor George Moscone, Roy Wilkins, vice president Walter Mondale and the president's wife, Rosalynn Carter. Jones was appointed to a post in the San Francisco city administration, and was applauded for his members' outstanding and vigorous activities in community services and local politics. Beneath this façade of respectability, however, People's Temple was a veritable haven of fear and corruption: drugs, rape and aberrant sexual behaviour, beatings and psychological torture of members.

In 1976–77 Jones ordered the movement of People's Temple to the South American nation of Guyana. Jones used his massive political credentials, his support from the US vice president and other American dignitaries, to persuade the Guyanese government to allow the settlement to develop. By 1978 People's Temple had established a 3000-acre estate in northwestern Guyana, called 'Jonestown', which was settled by 1000 American citizens. The small town quickly cultivated crops, which were sold to Guyanese, Trinidadian, and Venezuelan markets. To secure his village, Jones and his followers purchased large amounts of arms and military equipment. In this secluded jungle haven, Jones' tendencies towards sexual brutality, paranoia and megalomania were increased tenfold. When an American Congressman investigating rumours of Jones' enterprise visited Jonestown, he and his party were murdered. In desperation, Jones ordered his followers to commit suicide, along with himself and his wife: 912 bodies were recovered in Jonestown by Guyanese authorities; over two-thirds of the victims were Afro-Americans. The tragedy of Jonestown raised many still unresolved questions among US blacks. US medical services personnel performed no autopsies on the corpses; American government officials and politicians who had once been supporters of Jones offered no explanations or views on the mass suicides; rumours which circulated that Jones held up to $12 million in foreign banks were 'suppressed'. One black activist, Jitu Weusi, called on the United Nations to 'perform an investigation into the imminent possibility' that Jonestown was a prelude to black 'genocide. While the act physically occurred in Guyana', the Brooklyn, New York leader declared, 'the architect for mass murder was a product of the decadent society of white, capitalist United States of America. . . . The questions and unexplained circumstances of the Jonestown massacre are entirely too numerous for us as a people to simply ignore and file as the actions of a religious fanatic and his misguided flock.'[9] For white progressives, the entire fiasco called into question their 'particular responsibility' for aiding an evangelical maniac to brutalise sexually, intimidate, and finally to murder innocent people. The editors of *Socialist Review* declared,

> No attempts to blame the Jonestown tragedy on the forces of anomic capitalism or on a paranoid leader who saw himself as the reincarnation of Christ and Lenin, or on the CIA, can free us of the need to explain why the Temple grew and why it was accepted as an ally of progressive movements in a region where the left is as strong as anywhere in the nation. . . . The damage done by Jonestown cannot be repaired; beyond the immediate horrors, it will remain for years a nightmarish vision of socialism as death, as passivity and escapism taken to their limits.[10]

IV

From the beginning, Jimmy Carter seemed an unlikely champion of blacks' rights and political reform. The Georgia peanut farmer was the first candidate to defeat an incumbent president since 1932; he was the first Democrat to be elected from the Deep South since the narrow victory of James K. Polk of Tennessee over Henry Clay in 1844. Carter's election was due to overwhelming black support, but also to his ability to obfuscate essential public policy issues. His entire campaign rested on three 'chief slogans: "I will never lie to you," "The Golden Rule [should] be applied in all public matters," and "It is now a time for healing" – [which] specifically repudiated the deception, rancor, and divisiveness associated with Watergate'.[11] Repeatedly, Carter identified himself to black supporters with the racially egalitarian image of Southern Populism which had flourished three generations earlier. Populist historian Lawrence Goodwyn noted, however, that the president's 'paternal forebears were credit merchants who, like their counterparts elsewhere in the South, managed to acquire title to much of the surrounding countryside. As such, from a Populist perspective, they were part of the problem, not part of the solution'.[12] Indeed, a fuller examination of Carter's own rise to power indicated a close and cordial relationship with corporate interests which had perpetuated world-wide racial oppression and, in earlier years, racial segregation. Carter was a prominent member of the Trilateral Commission, a private organisation of Western European, Japanese and North American financial, corporate and political leaders established in 1973 by the head of the Chase-Manhattan Bank, David Rockefeller. Many of Carter's selections for his administration were drawn from the Trilateral Commission – vice president Walter Mondale, Secretary of State Cyrus Vance, Secretary of the Treasury Michael Blumenthal, Secretary of Defense Harold Brown, and Andrew Young. Other Carter appointees came directly from two of the largest multinational corporations in the world, Coca Cola (based in Atlanta, Georgia) and International Business Machines (IBM): Coca Cola attorneys Griffin Bell, Attorney General, and Joseph Califano, Secretary of Health, Education, and Welfare; IBM board directors Vance, Brown and black attorney Patricia Harris, Secretary of Housing and Development.

For almost five decades, the American political party system, ostensibly characterised by the electoral competition between the Democratic and Republican parties, had actually become marked by three distinct points of view identified by particular social characteristics. They comprised political blocs which cut across orthodox party lines. The first, which comprised about one-quarter to one-third of the US electorate, was 'mass conservatism', which included most of the Republican Party, some conservative Southern Democrats, former segregationists, and most of the corporations and financial interests. In addition, this first bloc included reactionary populist groups which either opposed certain civil rights-type reforms (e.g. court-ordered busing to promote racially integrated public schools) or which advocated legislation to limit the rights of women, homosexuals and political dissidents. The second point of view, 'centrist social liberalism', was slightly less than half of the general electorate. This very broad political bloc included Republican liberals, Eastern corporate leaders and financial interests, the Cold War Liberals in the Democratic Party (Truman, Kennedy), white ethnic workers, moderate and anti-segregationist Southern Democrats (Carter), most trade union leaders, and the more conservative representatives of civil rights groups. The smallest bloc, the 'democratic left', encompassed one-fifth to one-quarter of the vote. This grouping included almost all black and Hispanic organisations, liberal and leftist labour leaders, feminist groups, environmentalists, socialists, and perhaps one-third of the Democratic Party's leaders.

From 1932 until 1980, every American president had been a part of the great 'centrist social liberalism' tendency.[13] Roosevelt and at times Johnson had been in the left wing of this eclectic grouping; Eisenhower and Nixon were to the right, but neither could accurately be described as 'true conservatives'. On a racial axis, the democratic left was a strong proponent of civil rights, extensive social democratic reforms in welfare, public housing, education and social justice; the conservatives were vigorous proponents of racial inequality; the centrists were to be found unevenly distributed between these two poles. Since blacks were chiefly responsible for electing Carter, there was the clear expectation that the new president would embrace a programme of progressive racial reforms and social democracy. This did not occur. If anything, blacks were dismayed to learn, as the administration developed its agenda, that Carter was probably the most conservative Democratic president since Woodrow Wilson, the arch-segregationist of 1913–21. After a short time in office, corporate leaders drew pleasant parallels between Carter and Roosevelt's immediate conservative predecessor in the White House, Herbert Hoover. One aide to Eisenhower suggested that Carter 'ventured no notions in economic philosophy to which [Hoover] could have taken serious exception'. Patrick Caddell, a Carter pollster and assistant, urged the new president 'to co-opt many of [the Republicans'] issue positions and to take away large chunks of their presidential coalition by the right actions in government'. A move to the political right would 'cause rumblings from the left of the Democratic Party', but these could be safely ignored.[14] Thus, blacks and the broader American democratic left had helped to elect a president who had absolutely no intention of carrying out key elements of their programme. Once he had assumed office, Carter began to rescind many of the basic achievements of the Second Reconstruction.

The first real indication that Carter was actually carrying out a

'Nixon-Republican'-style programme came in May 1977, when administration officials declared that no new social welfare, health care or educational programmes would be initiated. Carter protégé Bert Lance, the director of the Office of Management and Budget, stated that inflation, not unemployment, was the chief economic dilemma confronting Americans. Carter's oft-repeated campaign promise to reduce defence expenditures was promptly abandoned, and the 1978 military budget soared to the highest level in US history up to that point, $111.8 billion. Despite the appointments of Young, Harris, John Lewis, and Weldon Rougeau to high administrative posts, relatively few blacks received positions in the executive branch of government. In a fifteen-month period between April–June 1976 and July–September 1977, non-white unemployment rates edged upward, from 12.9 per cent to 13.6 per cent, and non-white youth unemployment increased from 35.5 per cent to 39.2 per cent. In Carter's first year in office, an additional 131,000 black families fell below the Federal government's poverty level – yet the White House remained opposed to any extensive initiatives to address the crisis. Black leaders who had campaigned for the Southern Democrat were now ashamed to meet with their own constituents. In August 1977, a number of black leaders who had campaigned for Carter caucused at the national office of the Urban League in New York City. All of the key participants – including Jesse Jackson, Bayard Rustin, Baltimore Congressperson Parren Mitchell, Urban League leader Vernon Jordan, and the newly elected head of the NAACP, Benjamin Hooks of Memphis, Tennessee – claimed that they had been 'betrayed', and that Carter was practising a policy of 'callous neglect' towards blacks.[15]

Carter's relations with blacks deteriorated still further in 1978–79. On economic policy, the president did not battle aggressively for the Full Employment and Balanced Growth Act of 1976, more popularly termed the Humphrey–Hawkins bill. Denounced by conservatives as 'socialistic', the proposal was a joint effort of blacks, democratic leftists, labour union leaders, and many Cold War Liberals such as Senator Hubert Humphrey. In its original form, the act stated that 'all adult Americans able and willing to work have the right to equal opportunities for useful paid employment at fair rates of compensation', and declared that the Federal government should 'meet human and national needs' such as day care, public housing, and public transportation. The act called for the creation of a 'Job Guarantee

Office' which was 'responsible for actually enforcing the right of all "able and willing" adults to a job'. Humphrey–Hawkins was accurately described by friends and opponents alike as 'the most significant employment legislation to appear in the United States in thirty years'.[16] The act was passed eventually in a radically diluted form, such that the basic social democratic thrust of its proposed reforms was eliminated. Civil rights proponents were disappointed that the president had not used the full weight of the administration to gain a credible piece of legislation. Even Coretta King, who described the new law as 'an important first step in the struggle for full employment' recognised that 'we did not get all of the provisions in the bill that we would have liked'.[17] Carter's imposed reductions in Federal spending for social programmes, combined with a relaxation in laws on the private sector, led to higher corporate profits at the expense of the working class. In January–March 1979, for example, after-tax profits of 552 major US corporations had risen 37 per cent over the preceding year. In a series of blatant overtures to business interests, Carter urged the US Federal Reserve Board 'to raise interest rates and tighten the credit supply, so as to curtail economic expansion'; increased the US military budget by 10 to 15 per cent 'combined with unprecedented slashes in benefits and services to the population'; pushed Congress to pass 'measures to increase the prices of dairy products, grain, meat, and other products, and to "deregulate" transportation industries, fostering monopolization and unrestricted price increases'; and imposed 'wage/price guidelines, aiming to limit wage and benefit increases to 7 percent, in the face of living cost increases exceeding 10 percent.' Liberal, black, and socialist economists condemned the Carter agenda 'for lowering living standards for much of the population' and 'for wiping out many small property owners'.[18] By January 1979, only 33 per cent of all Democrats stated in a national poll that they wanted Carter to serve as their party's nominee in 1980. Political columnist Ken Bode described the president as having 'consciously [moved] the Democratic party away from nearly a half-century of its own history'.[19]

For black social institutions and local governments controlled by blacks, Carter represented an acceleration of the political reaction imposed by Nixon. Black colleges and universities, for example, had received three-fourths of their institutional support from the Federal government's 'Developing Institutions Program', under Title III of the Civil Rights Act during the Nixon–Ford Administrations. Under

Carter, the level of black institutional support was slashed to 53 per cent in 1977, and was down to 18 per cent in 1980. Promises of financial aid to black college students and administrators were never kept. Black political columnist William Raspberry attacked Carter's Secretary of Health, Education and Welfare, Joseph Califano, for his callous disregard for 'the historical rose' of black colleges, and for this '[indifference] to the vital service they perform'.[20] The administration's 'comprehensive national urban policy', which was announced in March 1978, allotted only $1 billion per year to create new public jobs for the ghetto's unemployed, and provided only $150 million for urban social services. Increasingly, black mayors were unable to reconcile their feeble defence of Carter's austerity budget with the economic demands of black working-class constituents. In 1977, Atlanta mayor Maynard Jackson fired 900 mostly black sanitation employees during a strike which was provoked by their lack of a pay increase for over three years. Many of these AFSCME union employees had campaigned extensively for Jackson during his first successful race for mayor in 1973, and were devastated when the black leader swung behind local corporate and anti-working-class interests once he was in office. Detroit mayor Coleman Young, once a leftist and activist in the National Negro Labor Council, formed an active alliance with corporate leader Henry Ford of Ford Motor Company and other executives. Black Detroit residents' city services were reduced; public educational and social programmes were cut; yet corporate property taxes were lowered, to foster a favourable climate for greater business investment. The majority of black mayors were forced to discipline the black public labour force, as a result of Federal government reductions in urban support; the chief beneficiaries in the process were the corporations.

The failure of Carter (and his black élite allies) to resolve the 'pervasive and intractable crisis' of the 'American political system' produced three significant trends, all of which affected the present and future status of Afro-Americans in public life. First, as political theorists John Judis and Alan Wolfe noted, Cold-War Liberalism and the old political coalition of Roosevelt had finally collapsed. There was an 'estrangement of Americans from party politics and governmental authority, demonstrated in flagging turnout at the polls, growing independent registration at the expense of both major parties, and the distrust of politicians and government indicated in many opinion surveys and in declining voting rates'.[21] Centrist social liberalism, as the political centre of US political discourse, was fractured on the left and right. Second, there was a growing and perceptible degree of alienation between the black élite, who still favoured Carter, and the majority of black workers and the poor, who were either neutral or by now completely alienated from the political process. Black labour had once believed that the elevation of a black professional into high public office could resolve its pressing economic and social problems. In the aftermath of Jackson's, Coleman Young's and other black mayors' betrayals of their own constituents, a sobering sense of disillusionment pervaded the black community. Even the black élite was shocked and angered in 1979, however, when Carter pressured UN ambassador Andrew Young to resign after he had held an informal discussion with a representative of the Palestine Liberation Organisation. Finally, there was among the urban underclass, or permanent reserve army of labour, a new degree of volatility, of hopelessness and rage. This became strikingly evident in May 1980, when the residents of Liberty City, Brownsville, and Coconut Grove, the black neighbourhoods of Miami, Florida, rose up in rebellion against local authorities and police. In the most disruptive urban revolt since 1968, between $50 to $100 million worth of property damage occurred in several days. Sixty-seven buildings were damaged; 1250 persons were arrested; 400 persons were injured, and 18 were killed; 3600 National Guardsmen were called into Miami to restore order. When Miami officials asked members of the black élite, including Benjamin Hooks, Jesse Jackson, Andrew Young and Houston Congressperson G. T. Leland, to 'cool off' the black community, they were uniformly told by local black activists that they were viewed as unwelcome collaborators. Blacks in Liberty City, where unemployment among adults reached 50 per cent, 'resent[ed] the way they were called in', one black journalist noted. Hooks, Young, and others 'came because people who had ignored our warnings could not tell us they didn't know what was brewing'.[22] The spectre of black urban rebellion once again had made national headlines. But unlike in the mid-to-late-1960s, the backers of racial inequality and white 'mass conservativism' were infinitely stronger in 1980, and were prepared to repress the rights of all national minorities by whatever means at their disposal.

V

For 100 years, American racists had looked back fondly upon the Ku Klax Klan's central role as the bulwark of white supremacy during 'each and every phase of Radical Reconstruction'. The reaction to the struggle for multicultural democracy in the 1970s now gave the historical opening for Klansmen to employ 'intimidation by any effective means of violence conceivable' against the grandchildren of former slaves.[23] Between 1971 and 1980, the Klan almost tripled its national membership. In January 1977, 250 Klansmen held a public rally in Carter's hometown, Plains, Georgia. In 1978–79, Klansmen engaged in a bloody campaign against blacks. The racists fired shotguns into the homes of several NAACP leaders in the South; on 8 May 1979, Klansmen shot one black man in the face in Carbon Hill, Alabama; the group firebombed black homes, churches and schools in over 100 towns and rural areas. One Klansman, 'Grand Dragon' Thomas Metzger, organised a fascist-oriented, black-uniformed security force in California, which led violent attacks against progressive and inter-racial groups. In 1980, Metzger's support among conservative, southern California white voters was registered in his victory in the Democratic Party primary in the state's forty-third congressional district. Metzger's programme of 'white rights' included promises to end school desegregation, affirmative action, and 'a five-year moratorium on all foreign immigration'.[24] The most outrageous act of Klan violence took place in Greensboro, North Carolina, on 3 November 1979. Seventy-five Klansmen and Nazis attacked an anti-racist rally, leaving five protestors killed and eleven others wounded. Only six of the murderers were tried, and an all-white jury acquitted the racists, despite television videotaped evidence which documented the killings in cold and unambiguous detail. A few black groups responded to Klan violence in the only language that racists understand. In November 1978, Klansmen and Okolona, Mississippi police co-operated in an ambush of members of the United League, a black Southern rights organisation. In the shoot-out, one Klansman was killed, and five others were seriously wounded. United League leader Skip Robinson stated later, 'Over 100 rounds [of ammunition] were fired. The Klan never said anything about it, the police never said anything about it, the press never said anything about it. But after that we never saw no more Klan in Okolona.'[25]

Unfortunately, the Klan and Nazis were only a very small portion of the forces of racism which were unleashed against the black community. Police across the country descended into black neighbourhoods, applying 'excessive force' when making routine arrests, shooting first and asking questions later. During the Miami Rebellion of May 1980, a small gang of white police officers destroyed black suspects' automobiles with billy clubs, rifles and steel pipes. Automobiles were spray-painted with the words 'Looter', 'Thief', and 'I am a Cheap No Good Looter'.[26] In Oakland, California, police officers killed nine black males in 1979 alone, one of whom was a 15-year-old boy. One of the victims was a trade unionist, 37-year-old Charles Briscoe:

> On September 5, 1979, Briscoe was gunned down by a police officer who had been involved in four other fatal shootings. First the officer emptied his shotgun into Briscoe and then finished him off with his service revolver. There were no witnesses to collaborate the officer's story that . . . he had to shoot Briscoe a second time because, after being shot with the shotgun, Briscoe walked towards his van and reached for a weapon. The coroner's report, however, indicated the shotgun blasts had broken both of Briscoe's legs; he couldn't have walked to the van. Nevertheless the district attorney and the police department found the shooting justifiable; a civilian police review board was prohibited from looking into the Briscoe case.[27]

In August 1980, Philadelphia police 'accidentally' killed a 17-year-old black suspect while he was being 'pistol-whipped'. In Detroit, during the summer of 1980, police officers fired on seven black suspects, critically wounding three. Detroit police routinely arrested black women on minor charges, such as speeding, and once in the station house, subjected them to humiliating strip-searches and sexual abuse. In one controversial arrest, police strip-searched and harassed three black female relatives of Detroit mayor Coleman Young. In another Detroit case, 'a young black man died after being tortured by a white officer using [an electric] cattle-prod'.[28] When a white policeman was killed in New Orleans on 8 November 1980, white officers assassinated four blacks in five days, in order to intimidate the black urban community. By the early 1980s, 'for every white person killed by the police' in the US in any year, '22 black persons, are killed'.[29] Surveying police atrocities, Washington, DC black activist Damu Smith drew a direct correlation between police repression and mass conservatism. 'The police have very consciously begun to link up more with the racist right wing movement, organizing for the ruling class in its stepped up assault on the rights of the people', Smith suggested in 1981. 'The police today are working to protect and serve those who are in power as well as those in the right wing movement who are organizing at the behest of those in power.'[30]

The most prevalent form of American racist violence was lynching: hangings, castrations, shootings, and other acts of racially motivated random violence. In 1976, Mobile police harassed a young black businessman and community activist Glen Diamond (Casmarah Mani). After beating him, officers 'placed a noose around his neck' and temporarily strangled him in a downtown public square.[31] A Cleveland, Ohio, white patent attorney shotgunned two 14-year-old black girls. Convicted of felonious assault, the attorney countersued the girls' parents and was awarded $5000. One mother of the girls declared to the press, 'My daughter still has 12 pellets from a 16 gauge shotgun in her neck. It's like telling this man he was within his rights shooting my daughter'.[32] In Arizona, 300 black evangelical Christians purchased a farm to develop a religious retreat. In several months, local whites destroyed their recreation centre and swimming pool. Black members were shot at and 'almost run down by automobiles'. In October 1981, a bomb was planted in their church van which exploded, killing one and injuring eight others.[33] Mississippi whites were responsible for at least twelve separate lynchings of blacks in 1980. On 12 October 1981, the body of Douglas McDonald was pulled from a lake in Eastover, Mississippi: the black man's ears were removed and his sex organs had been hacked off. Black investigators 'could get no information from the mortician, the police nor the family'.[34] In Social Circle, Georgia, the cousin of my wife, Lynn Jackson, was discovered lynched on 8 December 1981. Several months later, Frederick York, a 38-year-old black man, was found hanging from a tree in downtown Atlanta. The two most publicised incidents of random violence against blacks occurred in Buffalo, New York, and Atlanta. In September–October 1980, one or more whites randomly selected black males in Buffalo for murder. Several blacks were executed on street corners; one was nearly choked to death as he sat in a hospital room recovering from surgery. Two black men, 71-year-old Parler W. Edwards and 40-year-old Ernest Jones, were savagely beaten to death and amazingly, had their hearts removed from their corpses by the killer or killers. Twenty-eight black youths were methodically murdered in Atlanta between 1979–82. A black man was arrested and convicted of killing two of the youths in 1981, but the remaining murders were left unresolved. After the initial arrest, the FBI refused to pursue new evidence in the other cases.

COINTELPRO-type repression of black radicals, revolutionary nationalists and Marxists also resurfaced during these years. RNA Deputy Minister of Defense Kamau Kambui was arrested by FBI agents in Mississippi. Charged *'with signing his name incorrectly while purchasing a shotgun'*, he was convicted and sentenced to a five-year prison sentence.[35] After the acquittal of the Nazis and Klansmen, local police arrested eight anti-racist demonstrators in Greensboro, North Carolina, charging them with 'fire-bombing, attempted fire-bombing and conspiracy to fire-bomb'. Black Marxist Nelson Johnson, who had received severe knife wounds during the 1979 attack, was charged with 'felony riot' immediately after the incident. Johnson was later jailed for 20 days on 'contempt' charges.[36] On 1 November 1980, black community activist Yulanda Ward was executed by four armed assailants in Washington, DC. A powerful 0.357 magnum pistol had been fired against her head, and her body was left in the streets of the city. Rodney Johnson, a black communist and San Diego labour activist, was charged with two white workers with 'conspiracy to bomb an electrical transformer' in the National Steel and Shipbuilding Company's shipyards, the largest in the US. Days before his arrest, Johnson had led the fight among black and white workers against hazardous working conditions and low wages.[37] In May 1982, California officials arrested a former Black Panther activist, Michael Zinzun, for statements he had made at a black protest gathering in front of a police station. Charging Zinzun with 'feloniously threatening the lives of five Pasadena, [California] police officers', the district attorney cited a 'rarely-used 110 year-old law' which made it a 'felony to threaten a government worker'. One official admitted that the obscure law was only 'rarely' applied in threats made against tax collectors and Federal marshals, but 'the gravity of Mr. Zinzun's conduct' more than justified his arrest under any possible grounds. An American Civil Liberties Union lawyer argued that Zinzun's arrest was a blatant violation of the rights of free speech covered in the First Amendment to the US Constitution. 'The implications of this kind of law are fairly obvious', Zinzun's attorney complained. 'You can risk a felony prosecution anytime you utter words that the police don't like.'[38]

Even moderate black civil rights leaders were not immune to racist assaults and harassment. Vernon Jordan was shot in the back by a gunman in Fort Wayne, Indiana, on 29 May 1980. Police charged an 'avowed racist', Joseph Paul Franklin, with shooting the Urban League leader. Franklin had previously been charged with shooting two Salt Lake City, Utah, black men in August 1980, and was later sentenced to two life imprisonment terms in the case. During the Jordan trial, one prisoner familiar with Franklin testified that the white racist 'talked of the shooting and identified Jordan by name'. Another witness stated under oath that Franklin came into his Ft. Wayne grocery store and graphically detailed his shooting of Jordan: 'It was about perfect. If it had been a little different it would have gotten him just right.' Franklin himself told the jury that he 'hate[d] the [black] race as a whole'. But on 17 August 1982, an all-white jury declared that Franklin was innocent in Jordan's shooting.[39] Travelling to Anderson, Indiana, on 20 November 1981, Benjamin Hooks discovered a burning cross – the historic symbol of the Ku Klux Klan – at the entrance of a public hall where the NAACP leader was scheduled to lecture. No persons were arrested by police. The incidents of violence, an almost endless list of brutalities which touched the lives of millions of blacks, appeared to many to constitute a pattern of black genocide. 'There is almost a hysteria in black communities because of the belief that there is a [racist] conspiracy', Jesse Jackson stated in November 1980. 'Racism has become fashionable again and feelings of guilt toward blacks have turned to feelings of hostility. This country has taken a definite swing toward fascism.' Former King aide Hosea Williams charged that the Carter Administration was indirectly responsible for 'the mounting KKK's violent activities against blacks all across the country'.[40] Carter's response to the outraged demands of blacks and the democratic left that he should conduct vigorous federal measures against black genocide paralleled his other initiatives on welfare, guaranteed employment for the poor, and public housing – virtually nothing. After all, the blacks had been given too much in previous years.

VI

The rising tide of modern white supremacy on America's streets was

also manifested within the nation's high court and political institu-
tions. During Nixon's term in office, several liberal Supreme Court
Justices retired. Chief Justice Warren was replaced by a Minnesota
Republican, Warren Burger; other doctrinaire conservatives were
later appointed. As a result, throughout the 1970s the Supreme
Court's decisions reflected an increasingly conservative and anti-
black bias. By a narrow five to four margin, the Court ruled against
Brian F. Weber, a white steelworker who sued the Steelworkers
Union and the Kaiser Aluminum and Chemical Corporation in
Gramercy, Louisiana, to halt the company's affirmative action
programme for blacks. But in 1978, the Court overturned the
affirmative action programme of the University of California-Davis
Law School in the *Bakke* decision. After *Bakke*, the number of blacks
recruited and admitted to many professional schools dropped
sharply. As political economist Michael Reich observed, 'many
whites apparently felt that affirmative action programs had taken
away educational opportunities, jobs, and income away from white
families . . . and had given these advantages to undeserving blacks
who had not worked for them. The publicity given to the Bakke
Supreme Court case provided a highly distorted picture of un-
deserved black gains' to many whites, leading 'to charges of "racism in
reverse" '.[41] The logic of Bakke was applied to electoral politics as
well. In 1980, the Court upheld an electoral arrangement which
diluted the voting strength of blacks, the *City of Mobile vs. Bolden*.
Potter Stewart, Associate Justice and an Eisenhower appointee,
argued that the Fifteenth Amendment did not include the 'right to
have black candidates elected'. Political scientists Twiley W. Barker,
Jr., and Lucius J. Barker noted that the decision 'in effect' validated
'electoral arrangements that have a discriminatory impact where the
more stringent requirement of intentional or purposeful discrimination cannot be established. . . . It appears that the Court will be
satisfied as long as the scheme does not abridge or deny the blacks the
right to vote.'[42]

   Against this background of political retreat and racist reaction, of
social malaise and economic disorder, Ronald Reagan rose to public
prominence. As discussed briefly in Chapter 5, Reagan had earned
his credentials on the far-right during the 1960s as governor of
California. In 1976 he had challenged the Republican incumbent,
Gerald Ford, for their party's presidential nomination, and was only
narrowly defeated. For over a decade, Reagan was the darling of mass

conservatism. So much was his 1980 candidacy for the White House identified with the various movements against affirmative action, court-ordered busing, and civil rights for blacks, Latinos, women and others that the entire reactionary political phenomenon was termed 'Reaganism'. Reaganites observed that US military spending had declined from 8.0 per cent of the gross national product (GNP) in 1965–70 to 4.6 per cent of the GNP during the Ford and Carter Administrations. Social spending for food stamps, unemployment compensation, Social Security and other social democratic-type reforms during the same period had increased from 5.1 per cent of the GNP to 8.6 per cent. Thus, Reaganites blamed non-productive Federal expenditures as the root cause of inflation, and charged the Democrats and liberal Republican opponents with being 'weak on defense' and accommodationist towards the Soviets. Business profits, adjusted for inflation, had grown a meagre 3.4 per cent in ten years: therefore, conservatives sought to give massive tax reductions to the corporations, waiving certain environmental protection laws, at the expense of working-class and non-white Americans. The 'ideological glue' of Reaganism was racism. The 69-year-old conservative made this clear in August 1980, at a speech delivered in Philadelphia, Mississippi. Before a cheering white crowd, Reagan pledged that his administration would defend the principle of 'states' rights'.[43] Given that the town was the site of the brutal murders of three desegregation workers in 1964, and that the phrase itself was equated by many Southern whites to mean 'white supremacy', the gravity of Reagan's speech could not be lost upon most blacks. Despite Reagan's overtly racist stance, he was able to attract a small number of black intellectuals and former civil rights leaders to his campaign. Dr Nathan Wright, convenor of the 1968 Black Power conference, announced his support for the Republican. Other 'Black Reaganites' included Thomas Sowell, a Marxist-turned-conservative who served as a fellow at the Hoover Institute at Stanford University, California; economist Walter E. Williams of George Mason University; Republican leader J. A. Y. Parker; and Wendell Wilkie Gunn, assistant treasurer of the Pepsi Cola corporation. The two most influential black converts were King's closest aide, Ralph David Abernathy, and SCLC activist Hosea Williams. Abernathy justified his endorsement of one of King's bitterest opponents by attacking the dismal record of the Carter Administration on economic and civil rights issues.

Most black leaders were positively frightened by Reagan's conservative economic rhetoric and covert appeals to racism, and were especially outraged with Abernathy's actions. Mrs King declared that Reaganism represented the most 'negative' and 'even irrational elements in our society'. One black newspaper called Abernathy a 'modern Judas', a 'senile' turncoat who had forgotten 'the police dogs, Selmas, Birmingham, the marches, the sit-ins, the kneel-ins, the pray-ins, Bull Connor, the jails, the beatings, the bombings and the humiliation. . . .'[44] Historically, Reagan was the first national candidate from the mass conservative tendency of American politics to be nominated since Barry Goldwater, in 1964. This fact alone made the record of Carter seem remarkably enlightened. The overwhelming majority of black élite political organisations, from the NAACP to local civil rights groups, vigorously worked for Carter's re-election. But the black poor and the working class, in spite of their genuine revulsion against Reaganism, could not be mobilised sufficiently to accept a candidate who had done so little to protect, much less expand upon, the legislative gains of the Second Reconstruction. In November 1980, Reagan received 43.3 million popular votes and 489 electoral votes, to Carter's 35 million popular votes and 49 electoral votes. A liberal Republican, Illinois Representative John Anderson, ran an independent race and captured 7 per cent of the popular vote in the general election. Between 85 to 91 per cent of the blacks voted for Carter, a percentage slightly below his 1976 black voter figure. Of 17 million black adults who were eligible to vote in 1980, only 7 million or 40 per cent actually voted. The slippage in black votes for Carter allowed Reagan to carry several closely contested Southern states. Furthermore, most of the other New Deal electoral coalition constituencies had been badly divided. A majority of white trade unionists did not vote for Carter; most of the Jewish vote was split between Anderson and Reagan; and only 54 per cent of Puerto Rican and Mexican-American voters supported Carter. Conservative Republicans captured control of the US Senate for the first time in a quarter-century. Carter was sent back to Plains, Georgia, as blacks and the democratic left pondered with some anxiety what the new administration would mean.

With the rapid legislative manoeuvres reminiscent of Roosevelt's 'Hundred Days' period of 1933, when the nation was faced with the Great Depression, the Reagan Administration sought to construct a conservative and unequal order. Within months, Reagan illustrated that his government, unlike Nixon's, would not tolerate even the slightest concessions to the poor, the dispossessed, racial minorities, and labour. The Occupational Safety and Health Administration (OSHA), founded in 1970 under Nixon, was a modest Federal government initiative which attempted to improve workplace conditions, especially for labourers in industries with a record of dangerous and environmentally unsafe conditions. Reagan named a millionaire construction owner, Thorne Auchter, as OSHA director, and a former CIA employee as Auchter's chief assistant. Heading the administration's Task Force to eliminate federal regulations on corporations was J. C. Miller III, a former academic fellow at a right-wing research centre, who had once 'testified in opposition to the proposed OSHA coke-oven standard intended to limit exposure of coke-oven workers to deadly cancer-causing fumes'. Before Congress, Miller had 'argued that the benefits of protecting coke-oven workers were not worth the cost'.[45] Included within Reagan's broad assault upon the legacy of social centrist liberalism were numerous proposals: the abandonment of the Comprehensive Employment and Training Act programme, funded in 1981 for $3.1 billion, and the elimination of its 150,000 federally funded jobs; the closing of the National Consumer Co-operative Bank, which granted loans to small economic co-operatives; a $2 billion reduction in the federal Food Stamps Program by fiscal 1983; the elimination of the $2 billion Guaranteed Student Loan Program; the reduction of $1.7 billion from child nutrition programmes sponsored by the Federal government by fiscal 1983; the closing of the Neighborhood Self Help and Planning Assistance Programs, which allotted $55 million in fiscal 1981 to aid inner cities. To bolster economic growth and corporate profits, Reagan ordered the severe reduction in federal enforcement of affirmative action regulations. Under Carter, employers with federal contracts had to submit written affirmative action plans if they had at least 50 employees and had a contract at $50,000 or above. Reagan proposed submission of plans 'only for contractors with 250 or more workers and a government contract worth $1 million'. Reagan also reduced 'both eligibility and levels of support' for poor women to receive food stamps and Aid to Families with Dependent Children payments. By August 1981, Congress had ratified most of these proposals, and began to contemplate even more stringent restrictions in the areas of human needs. The New York-based Popular Economic Research Group declared: 'While the nation's leading homemaker – Nancy Reagan – spent over $200,000 to replace the White House china, thousands of other mothers began to wonder not what they would serve dinner on, but whether they would serve it at all. . . . Women and people of color are being forced to bear the burden of Reagan's misguided and destructive economics.'[46]

In the areas of defence foreign policy, Reaganism articulated a vision of white capitalist world supremacy. The president proposed the largest military expenditures in human history, $1.6 trillion over a five-year period. This inconceivable amount came to almost $11,000 for every US citizen who paid taxes on 1979 income. Abandoning the previous administration's public commitment to human rights, Reagan's State Department forged closer relationships with fascist military juntas and racist regimes. During 1982, as black miners and workers staged a series of strikes in South Africa, Reagan authorised the opening of new honorary consulates in three US cities, Seattle, Denver, and Cleveland, for the *apartheid* regime. Reagan asked Congress for $2.3 million to train black South Africans inside South Africa, thereby reinforcing the separate-and-unequal educational system. Export control regulations on such critical items as air ambulances, computers and helicopters were weakened to provide greater support for *apartheid*. The dispatch with which conservative and most centrist politicians passed Reagan's authoritarian military programme was described by an outraged US Representative Dellums in a May 1982 interview:

> Two weeks ago, in the midst of all these polls about people being concerned about the military budget, my colleagues, in four hours and 40 minutes, with time off for lunch in the middle, passed a $255.1 billion military budget. Now, you tell me anybody can intelligently debate a quarter of a trillion-dollar budget in four hours and 40 minutes? The vote was 40 to 3. . . . Do you think, on a ratio of 40 to 3 . . . that the American people want to spend a quarter of a trillion dollars on the military budget? But that's how far away my colleagues are from the American people. Maybe we've arrived at a point where this system does not serve us well. I don't see anything sacrosanct about the two-party system.[47]

The impact of Reaganism was felt across the black community as a series of devastating shocks. The Office of Federal Contracts Compliance Programs, one of the Federal government's desegregation agencies, was ordered to reduce its enforcement activities. Under

Reagan, the Civil Rights Division of the Justice Department filed only 5 lawsuits on racial discrimination issues in its first six months, compared to 17 suits under Carter and 24 suits under Nixon during their first six months' tenure. On 4 September 1981, the US Department of Agriculture reduced the amount of food served to 26 million children in over 94,000 schools across the nation. Dietary allowances were distorted in order to reduce federal expenditures for children's lunches. For three weeks, before they were forced to retract, Reagan's nutrition experts even classified catsup and pickle relish as 'vegetables'. On 1 October 1981, more than 400,000 poor families were removed from federal and state welfare rolls. In one year, Reagan had succeeded where Nixon had failed: he actually expanded poverty in America. Between 1969 and 1974, the total number of black families below the poverty line rose from 1.3 million to 1.5 million. Poor white families in these years actually declined slightly, from 3.6 million to 3.5 million; the total number of persons below the poverty line remained roughly the same for the period, 24.1 million in 1969, 24.2 million in 1974. In Reagan's first year in office, the real median income of all black families declined by 5.2 per cent compared to the 1980 figure. The number of poor Americans increased by 2.2 million in 1981, and the share of black families below the poverty line moved upward from 32.4 per cent to 34.2 per cent. In a single year, 'much of the progress that had been made against poverty in the 1960s and 1970s' had been 'wiped out', according to the *New York Times*.[48] In August 1982, Dr James D. McGhee, the Urban League's Director of Research, warned that Reaganomics had blunted 'the hopes and [dashed] the dreams of millions of the poor', and had seriously threatened 'the existence of an emerging, still fragile black middle-class as well. . . . Programs that accomplished so much are now being eliminated one after another for seemingly ideological rather than budgetary reasons, and America is defaulting on its commitment to assure equal opportunity for all its citizens.'[49] Even Reagan's Federal tax cut, passed by Congress in August 1981, to stimulate consumer savings, was designed to perpetuate racial inequality. The average white household was scheduled to receive $1019 in tax cuts for 1983, and $1369 in 1984, while the average black household would receive only $542 in 1983 and $632 in 1984.

In a sense, the triumph of Reaganism represented a cruel and paradoxical conclusion to part of the rebellious impulse of the late 1960s. No-one expressed this better than Eldridge Cleaver. After returning to the US in 1974, Cleaver was incarcerated for less than a year in jail. By the early 1980s, Cleaver had not only repudiated his old Black Panther ties, but actually had joined forces with racist mass conservatism. In a February 1982 interview, Cleaver declared:

> . . . God came to France and tapped me on my shoulder and said, 'Eldridge, follow me. . . .' [Americans] don't believe or even manifest any awareness of what makes our democratic form of government different from other forms of government. They don't understand and appreciate the great battles and triumphs and victories that were involved in creating this country. We are still the most free and the most democratic country in the world. I think America is the greatest country in the world. I really feel in my heart that America really needs to take control of the world. . . . Black people are notorious for sitting on the sidelines complaining, but they won't get off their butt and go vote and so they are taking no responsibility for what happens except they have full responsibility for not doing anything to make it happen differently. I believe that instead of black people hating the police department, I think they need to join the police department . . . and make it our own.

In Cleaver's 'most democratic country in the world', 23.4 million Americans, or about one out of every five workers, were unemployed in 1981. Of all black workers 30.5 per cent were jobless at some point during the year. In June 1982, Congress voted to cut federal welfare programmes by one-fifth and Medicaid spending by one-sixth, and reduced other domestic programmes, including assistance to state and municipal governments, by a projected $45 billion by 1985. Congress' budgetary actions were aimed specifically to cripple blacks, Hispanics, low-income workers, and the unemployed. The 1982 budget 'goes to the people who were bloodied last year and bloodies them and guts them some more', declared black Congressman Parren Mitchell.[51] Reaganism, racism, and political reaction had made a mockery of democracy.

8. Epilogue: The Vision and the Power

> Because I do not hope to know again
> The infirm glory of the positive hour . . .
> Because I know that time is always time
> And place is always and only place
> And what is actual is actual only for one time
> And only for one place
> I rejoice that things are as they are . . .
> Because I cannot hope to turn again
> Consequently I rejoice, having to construct something
> Upon which to rejoice.
>
> T. S. Eliot, 1930

> Let us not forget that in the Negro people, there sleep and are now awakening passions of a violence exceeding . . . anything among the tremendous forces that capitalism has created. Anyone who knows them, who knows their history, is able to talk with them intimately . . . watches them in their churches, reads their press with a discerning eye, must recognise . . . the hatred of bourgeois society and the readiness to destroy it when the opportunity should present itself, rests among them to a degree greater than in any other section of the population in the United States.
>
> C. L. R. James, 1948

I

American history has repeated itself, in regard to its interpretation of the pursuit of biracial democracy: the first time as 'tragedy', the second time 'as catastrophe'.[1] In the aftermath of the First Reconstruction, white American historians attempted to portray the democratic experiment of 1865–77 as a complete disaster. Writing in 1935, DuBois explained that 'the facts' of the Reconstruction period 'have in the last half century been falsified because the nation was ashamed. The South was ashamed because it fought to perpetuate human slavery. The North was ashamed because it had to call in the black men to save the Union, abolish slavery and establish democracy.'[2] After the Second Reconstruction, a similar process of historical revisionism occurred – led by none other than the president of the United States. In a series of speeches and statements, President Reagan attempted to undermine the last vestiges of institutional equality. At the Denver, Colorado, convention of the NAACP in July 1981, Reagan declared that his programme of budgetary reductions and economic austerity for the poor was 'the surest, most equitable way to ease the pressures on all the segments of our society'. It was time for black Americans to halt their dependency on the Federal government to resolve their economic plight. 'Just as the Emancipation Proclamation freed black people 118 years ago, today we need to declare an economic emancipation', the president suggested. Incredibly, Reagan justified his programme by invoking the legacy of anti-slavery activist Harriet Tubman. 'Tubman's glory was the glory of the American experience. It was a glory which had no color or religious preference or nationality.' In early 1982, the president infuriated blacks by supporting Federal tax exemptions for racially segregated, private schools. At a black high school, Reagan offered as an excuse, 'I didn't know there were any [schools that still practised] segregation'. Speaking later with 40 Mid-western newspaper editors, Reagan was asked for his opinion concerning the major public drive to declare Martin Luther King's birthday a national holiday. 'No, I haven't taken a stand one way or the other, and I certainly understand why the black community would like to do that.' Reagan quickly added, '[however], we could have an awful lot of holidays if we start down that road. It might be that, there's no way we could afford all the holidays'.[3] In a nation that celebrates the birthday of George Washington, slaveholder and slavetrader, and where many states still legally observe the birthdays of Confederate president Jefferson Davis and rebel general Robert E. Lee, Reagan's assertions were for blacks as absurd as they were obnoxious.

Reagan's most controversial attempt to rewrite black history occurred at the National Black Republican Council, which met in

Washington, DC, on 15 September 1982. The president stated that
blacks 'would be appreciably better off today' if Johnson's Great
Society – a series of social democratic reforms in housing, health care,
education, vocational training, and other public services – had never
been started:

> With the coming of the Great Society, Government began eating
> away at the underpinnings of the private enterprise system. The big
> taxers and big spenders in Congress had started a binge that would
> slowly change the nature of our society, and even worse, it
> threatened the character of our people. . . . To pay for all this
> spending, the tax load increased till it was breaking the backs of
> working people, destroying incentive and siphoning off resources
> needed in the private sector to provide new jobs and opportunity.
> Inflation had jumped to double-digit levels, unemployment was
> climbing, and interest rates shot through the roof, reaching 21.5 per
> cent shortly before we took office. . . . By the time the full weight of
> Great Society programs was felt, economic progress for America's
> poor had come to a tragic halt. The poor and disadvantaged are
> better off today than if we had allowed runaway Government
> spending, interest rates and inflation to continue ravaging the
> American economy.[4]

Reagan's speech was delivered several days after the chairmen of 33
state agencies affiliated with the US Commission on Civil Rights had
declared that Reagan was responsible for a 'dangerous deterioration
in the Federal enforcement of civil rights'; it was only hours after a
Washington, DC lawyers' association issued an indictment that
Reagan's Justice Department had 'retreated' from desegregation and
blacks' rights. Many political moderates found the president's
remarks embarrassing. The *New York Times* admitted that Johnson's
welfare programmes were sometimes 'mismanaged', but that on
balance, 'the Great Society was a necessary, imaginative and
productive response to a deeply rooted social conflict'. The president
was attempting 'to justify Reaganomics to massively disaffected black
voters. They are not likely to be so easily fooled'.[5] Gathering in
Washington, DC, for the conference sponsored by the Congressional
Black Caucus on 17–18 September 1982, civil rights leaders and black
elected officials were severely shaken by Reagan's recent statements.

Speaking before the conference, Andrew Young, who had been elected recently as mayor of Atlanta, Georgia, lashed out against Reagan. If the president's remarks were valid, Young stated, then all of the desegregation marches, the sit-ins, and the protests to obtain black equality were meaningless. 'Martin Luther King, Jr., would have died in vain', he declared, his speech stammering. Young pulled away from the podium briefly as tears flooded down his face. Hundreds in the audience began to cry openly. Were all their sacrifices for nothing? The assassinations, the bombings, the jail-ins, the whole wrenching ordeal of a people surging forward towards freedom – were they simply unproductive and futile gestures? Fisk University president Walter J. Leonard described the scene as a 'wake', the mourning time for the dead. Reagan's speech and Andrew Young's public ordeal 'marked the end of the Second Reconstruction'.[6]

As mass conservatism increased its control of the US political system, the trend towards racially motivated random violence continued unchecked. Almost daily throughout 1982, fresh episodes of racial atrocity occurred in virtually every corner of the country. Charles Randolph, Jr., a black retired postal worker, moved his family into a small, rural white town in Connecticut. In short order, he received threatening phone calls, stating 'Nigger, get out of this town or we'll kill you!' Randolph was 'seized by the state troopers and hauled off to a hospital with no warrant or probable cause; oil was dumped in his pond, killing his ducks; sand was poured into the engine of his Volkswagen, ruining it; the family dog was beaten to death in the front yard; his oldest son was chased off the road and his car demolished.'[7] On 19 December 1981, and 16 January 1982, the offices of a black newspaper, the *Jackson Advocate* (Mississippi) were firebombed and shotgunned, and staff members were threatened. On 3 May 1982, Chester Reems, a black man in Durham, North Carolina, was attacked by a racist for 'walking with a white woman'. The white man drove his automobile into Reems, 'throwing him more than 80 feet. Reems was pronounced dead on arrival at [Durham's] hospital, having suffered a broken neck and multiple fractures'.[8] On 26 May 1982, one young black man was killed and another seriously wounded by a gun-wielding white man in Franklinton, North Carolina. Black families in Boston's Hyde Park neighbourhood experienced assaults, racial slurs, and had their homes vandalised during July and August 1982. Much of the racist violence came from

white teenagers and young adults. White students at Chicago's
Bogan High School harassed and attacked young blacks. Between 55
and 73 black teenagers were arrested in the inter-racial fighting, but
police arrested no whites. White youths in Dorchester, Massachusetts, firebombed an apartment building into which black
families had recently moved. On 8 August, a black family driving in
downtown Boston were pursued by four young racists. 'The youths
got out of their car, covered their license plates and, while hurling
racist epithets, began smashing the windows of the [family's] car with
chains and clubs. Fortunately the family escaped with only minor
injuries.'⁹ The most publicised 'lynching' occurred in Brooklyn, New
York, on 22 June. A gang of young whites stopped an automobile
containing three black men. Two of the men were cut and punched,
but managed to escape. The third black man, William Turks, was
brutally beaten to death. White bystanders watched passively as the
angry whites continued to pummel a lifeless black corpse.

The violence against blacks can be explained only through the
prism of history. Immediately following the Compromise of 1877, and
the end of the First Reconstruction, Afro-American people experienced a wave of murderous race hatred and violence, as I have
illustrated in Chapter 1. With the demise of the Second Reconstruction, many whites have returned to the bloody American tradition of
the *auto-da-fé*, mob violence, and criminal behaviour towards peoples
of colour. Ethnocentrism is usually a passive characteristic among all
cultural groups, yet the violence fostered among many thousands and
even millions of white Americans towards blacks transcends simple
prejudice. What we are now witnessing is 'the spirit of the mob': a
desire to inflict punishment at random; to terrorise small children and
their families; to force black people ever backwards, into the darkest
and most obscure corners of political discourse and economic life.
DuBois had seen the ugly face of the mob, as it looted, raped, and
murdered black citizens in Atlanta in the 1906 race riot. He
understood that:

> Back of the writhing, yelling, cruel-eyed demons who break,
> destroy, maim and lynch and burn at the stake, is a knot, large or
> small, of normal human beings, and these human beings at heart
> are desperately afraid of something. Of what? Of many things, but
> usually of losing their jobs, being declassed, degraded, or actually
> disgraced; of losing their hopes, their savings, their plans for their

children; of the actual pangs of hunger, of dirt, of crime. And of all this, most ubiquitous in modern industrial society is that fear of unemployment. It is its nucleus of ordinary men that continually gives the mob its initial and awful impetus. Around this nucleus, to be sure, gather snowball-wise all manner of flotsam, filth and human garbage, and every lewdness of alcohol and current fashion. But all this is the horrible covering of this inner nucleus of Fear.[10]

The mob hates the black man and woman, because it fears the potential strength of united black political power, the danger of being replaced on the job by a black person, the threat of blacks living next door and undermining property values. The mob believes 'the Negro an inferior race', and that 'this inferiority must be publicly acknowledged and submitted to'.[11] Leaders of the 'mob spirit', from the hoodlums in Boston, the firebombers of Mississippi, to the president himself, will distort the lessons of the past to ensure racial inequality in the future.

Confronted by this omnipresent terror, what can Latinos, Afro-Americans, Indians, and other people of colour do to resolve this crisis? In the First Reconstruction, the reign of white supremacy created 'the situation when Booker T. Washington became the leader of the Negro race and advised them to depend upon industrial education and work rather than politics', DuBois writes. As a result, 'the better class of Southern Negroes stopped voting for a generation', and the 'most educated and deserving black man was compelled in many public places to occupy a place beneath the lowest and least deserving of the whites'.[12] Today, a similar dynamic of racial accommodation has emerged amongst a section of the black élite. Two of the most influential representatives of this trend towards compromise are found within the black church. The Reverend Joseph H. Jackson, leader of the 6.3 million member National Baptist Convention, urged his subordinates to create 'a new partnership between management and labor in order to stimulate economic growth'. Speaking at the church's 102nd annual session in Miami Beach, Florida, in August 1982, Jackson deplored the Black Power-inspired notion that US blacks had a nationality identity. 'We are not a Black nation as such, but a community of people with some opportunities to reap some benefits from the American democratic process. . . . The federal Constitution offers the overall power to gain higher goals and benefits and to make both nation and race stronger.'[13] The Reverend Leon Sullivan, founder of an anti-poverty agency, Opportunities Industrial Centers (OIC), is even further to the political right. Sullivan has authored the 'Sullivan Principles', a set of very broad human rights and affirmative action guidelines which permit 'public relations-conscious' corporations to invest in South Africa. Investigations of Sullivan's agency in 1980 revealed that he had received half a billion dollars in federal funds and millions more in corporate support over a sixteen-year period. Only 13 per cent of OIC-trained blacks found employment in training-related jobs. Yet Sullivan's popularity soared under Reaganism: in January 1981, the black minister testified before Congress on behalf of Reagan's nominee for Secretary of State, hard-line anti-communist Al Haig. In 1982, Sullivan announced the creation of the 'Hire One Youth' campaign, which promoted the crudely simplistic idea that massive black youth unemployment could be resolved if US businesses each employed a black person. The economic theory behind Sullivan's activities, *laissez-faire* capitalism, squares neatly with the prevalent mood of Reaganomics, 'self-help', and fiscal austerity. Nathan Wright has matched Sullivan with Booker T. Washington, and calls them 'the two towering racial figures' in black economic history. 'No single American of our present generation has done more in terms of undergirding and advancing our nation's peaceable progress toward productive fulfillment than has Leon Sullivan', Wright proclaimed. 'What a man! What a gift by black people to the ongoing history of the world! His life is a Gift of Love, a Song of Service, a Lesson in Peace, a Promise of Prosperity and a Legacy of Hope for all of God's many children near and far.'[14] This sorry high hosanna for a black accommodationist who defends US investments in *apartheid* is just another indication of the intellectual turpitude of Wright and a significant segment of the contemporary Negro intelligentsia.

Some of the civil rights organisations have followed Sullivan's lead, and have accommodated themselves to the new conservative order; others, like CORE, which is still directed by Innis, are merely shadow structures, with little substance, no programme, and few followers. But even in the era of Reaganism and reaction, flames of protest could be found. In 1980, two progressive black nationalist formations emerged, the National Black United Front (NBUF) and the National Black Independent Political Party (NBIPP). The former organisation grew out of anti-racist struggles within Brooklyn during the late

1970s, and developed into a national network of local protest and political groups under the leadership of the Reverend Herbert Daughtry. NBIPP evolved from a core of progressive black community organisers, revolutionary nationalists, socialists and Marxists from the remnants of the National Black Political Assembly. The founding convention of NBIPP, held in Philadelphia three weeks after Reagan's election, brought almost 2000 black activists together to debate new strategies for the black freedom movement. The Reverend Ben Chavis, recently released from his North Carolina prison cell, Assembly leader Ron Daniels and other veterans of black-community-based campaigns helped to co-ordinate the meeting. In 1981 and 1982, both NBUF and NBIPP engaged in numerous local efforts to contain the impact of Reaganism, and by their actions, kept alive the vision of the 1972 Gary Convention.

Scarcely documented by the mainstream American media, black nationalists, workers, students and the poor participated in several hundred demonstrations and marches against racism and Reaganism in 1982. In a scene 'reminiscent of the 1960s civil rights campaigns when black and white activists defiantly marched through the streets to protest anti-black violence', hundreds of demonstrators marched in Brooklyn on 18 July 1982, to denounce the murder of William Turks.[15] In Athens, Georgia, over 400 University of Georgia students held a vigil against the Ku Klux Klan, sponsored by the National Anti-Klan Network, in May. In two separate demonstrations, hundreds of blacks and whites from church, university and community groups protested against the training of El Salvadorian troops in Fayetteville, North Carolina. For two months, the SCLC led a nation-wide march from Tuskegee, Alabama, to Washington, DC, to oppose the Reagan Administration's attempts to weaken the 1965 Voting Rights Act. When Reagan visited the state capitol in Nashville, over 1000 people, led by the NAACP and the United Furniture Workers, demonstrated against his budgetary reductions in human services. In Louisville, Kentucky, hundreds of unemployed black youths marched in the city streets demanding jobs. Almost 2000 blacks participated in a political convention held in New York's City College on 21 August, to discuss strategies to confront 'racial discrimination, unemployment, poor housing, crime and the lack of significant influence in the political arena'. The widely diverse group, which included black 'corporate executives and the unemployed, elected politicians and those who scorn the traditional political

system', was united in its 'belief that the current political economic
and social trends had thrown blacks into a state of crisis'.[16] Despite
Reaganism, the triumph of mass conservatism, and the capitulation
of many black élites and sections of the Old Guard integrationists to
reaction, the majority of blacks had not submitted mildly to the forces
of inequality. The vast potential of black protest still exists, and the
reasons for resistance have never been more clear. The twilight of the
Second Reconstruction could bring the dawning of yet another wave
of political unrest, activism, and power among blacks, as well as all
minority groups in America.

II

Was the Second Reconstruction a failure? Our judgment would be a
resounding and unconditional 'no'. Legal Jim Crow is permanently
dead. The American State is committed to equal opportunity under
the law for all Americans. DuBois' characterisation of the First
Reconstruction as 'a splendid failure' does not seem to apply to the
period 1945–82. The growth rate of black elected officials has declined
since 1970, but the increase of black officeholders and administrators
has continued. The black consumer market has grown dramatically
in two decades, from $30 billion in 1960 to over $125 billion in 1980.
Blacks currently occupy, as of this writing, positions as mayors in a
number of major US cities: Los Angeles, New Orleans, Atlanta,
Detroit, Birmingham, and Newark. Certainly, when the profile of the
black élite is under consideration, the whole struggle for desegregation must be viewed as a dramatic success. It is in the tradition of
American policy-makers, politicians, and corporate executives to
applaud the relative gains that Afro-Americans have made in the
pursuit of equality: no person or class which has historically exploited
another is likely to do otherwise. Similarly, the black élite now has an
absolute material interest to defend the economic and political status
quo. They may, upon occasion, offer a stinging rebuke to representatives of mass conservatism. For the black élite comprehends that its
marginal influence upon public policy can be best maintained only
when more liberal politicians of the centre dominate the State.
    The ideological limitations impressed upon black thought and
politics during the Cold War are still operative upon the current black
leadership. The black élite will promulgate an economic programme
which mirrors the right-wing tendencies of Social Democracy in most

of the Western world's nations, but beyond that invisible boundary, they will go no further left. In short, the black élite calls for federal initiatives to provide employment for the poor, but will not advocate a clearly socialist agenda which would severely restrict the prerogatives of private capital. They denounce the growing trend of racist violence, but they will not see that such violence is a manifestation of a more profound crisis within the capitalist political economy. The élite has no viable solutions for the proliferating and permanent black reserve army of labour, or the deterioration of the inner cities. They are simply ready to administer the crisis, but are ill-prepared to resolve it.

Their failure, in brief, is one of vision. The Old Guard constantly manoeuvres, responding to minor political crises, but they are hopelessly inept in projecting a constructive programme to transform the larger society. They react, rather than act; they imitate, rather than create; they plead, rather than demand. Theirs is a failure within a qualified and compromised success, and as the decade of the 1980s progresses, it has become obvious that the result of their limited vision has been the creation of a temporary yet quite real barrier between the immediate political agenda of the élite and the black majority. With DuBois, I must agree that many critical failures of both Reconstructions were the result of the blacks' leadership 'by the blind. We fell under the leadership of those who would compromise with truth in the past in order to make peace in the present and guide policy in the future'.[17] Such a judgment may be considered excessively harsh. Of course, as an Afro-American and a socialist, I cannot write this brief study without a clear and passionate belief in the central humanity of my people, without some degree of political commitment towards justice and a decent life for those on the edge of poverty and degradation, and without some sense of outrage for the many crimes that have been and are still being committed against blacks. 'But, too, as a student of science, I want to be fair, objective and judicial; to let no searing of the memory by intolerable insult and cruelty make me fail to sympathize with human frailties and contradiction, in the eternal paradox of good and evil.'[18] The story of the Second Reconstruction has no moral, other than the simple truth that an oppressed people will not remain oppressed forever. What have sustained black courage in the past are several basic ideals – democracy, equality and freedom – that have enabled millions of Americans to endure beatings, imprisonment, torture and harassments of every conceivable kind.

The prevailing attitude among most black leaders during the First and Second Reconstructions was a belief in the essential applicability of the American democratic system to the plight of the Afro-American. The US Constitution was viewed as being 'color-blind', despite the corpus of laws which validated black bondage for centuries. The majority of black activists fighting for desegregation desired the incorporation of the Negro into the existing system. It rarely occurred to them that a *biracial democracy* was impossible to create unless there was also a concomitant transition in the character of the capitalist economic system of the society. In 1945, DuBois suggested that any government which described itself as a democracy must have, as its guiding principles, the goals of 'the abolition of poverty, the education of the masses, protection from disease, and the scientific treatment of crime'. A democratic state should express in its public policies 'the right and the capacity' for peoples of colour to 'share in human progress' equally, without artificial barriers. It must outlaw any and all restrictions based on colour or gender. Using these criteria, a genuine democracy has never existed in the United States for a majority of the population.[19] DuBois was more frank in his assessment of the American State several years later, in a series of articles for the *National Guardian*. Democracy in the US was not 'obsolete'; it had never been tried because of racism and the powerful control of corporate capital over the lives of working-class people. Democracy for blacks and other oppressed minorities was dependent upon the socialisation of the economy, a massive reorganisation of wealth and power. If blacks chose to reject the economic patterns of private capital, and forged coalitions with the labouring and impoverished white classes, they would 'loose for future civilization the vast energy and potentialities of the mass of human beings now held in thrall by poverty, ignorance and disease.'[20] Given the evolution of capitalism, racism, and democracy in America, a truly anti-racist democratic state must of necessity also be a socialist democracy.

The goal of equality was certainly a part of the desegregation movement. But in the minds of many leaders, equality meant *parity*, or equal access, to the positions of political and economic affluence in America. Behind affirmative action is the notion that blacks were denied historically certain opportunities for advancement within the existing system solely on the basis of race. Technically, this still remains true. However, as a critical framework of analysis for black liberation, it reveals a limited vision of what remains to be done. The demand for racial parity within a state apparatus and economy which is based on institutional racism and capital accumulation at the expense of blacks and labour is fatally flawed from the outset. Racism and capitalist exploitation are logical and consistent by-products of the American system. Thus, as we review the modest successes of the black élite after 1970, we can observe that a racist/capitalist state can co-opt a small segment of the oppressed community, 'in the name of equal opportunity', and manipulate it against the material concerns and demands of the masses of black labour and the unemployed. Under Reaganism, a small number of blacks have been appointed within the administration to carry out essentially racist policies which are devastating to the great majority of blacks. The black movement must reorient itself to view the demand for equal opportunity as a necessary but only initial step in the pursuit of biracial democracy. Real equality, which I have defined previously in other works as the realisation of human fairness, connotes not the passage of laws, but the transferral of power from propertied élites to those who create all wealth, the working class. The problem of police brutality within American ghettoes will not be resolved simply by appointing additional numbers of black police officers, or by blacks controlling their municipal governments alone; it will cease only when black workers and the poor, along with other oppressed labourers, have the effective power to control their own neighbourhoods. Unemployment would not disappear with the passage of a Humphrey–Hawkins Bill; only the empowerment of workers at the point of production, and the general reallocation of wealth, will provide an effective barrier to the perpetual plight of black joblessness.[21]

In late twentieth-century America, capital is 'free' and labour is 'unfree'. That is, there is a remarkable degree of freedom for the owners of corporations and factories to transfer their wealth into various forms, without regard to the broader social impact that such transfers have upon the majority of the American population. Failing corporations appeal to the Federal government to provide loans or guarantees for their continued fiscal viability, yet profits accrued from sales remain private. Plant closings in 1982 alone were responsible for the loss of almost 500,000 American jobs. As the perpetual bottom of the labour market, blacks and Latinos are caught in a never-ending economic vice – 'the last hired' during an economic upturn, 'the first fired' during cyclical recession. Freedom for black workers must connote the assertion of a job as an absolute human right; the community's control over factory closings or relocations; the freedom from the fear created by poor medical facilities in inner cities and rural areas; the right to free public education from pre-school levels through to the universities; the right to decent housing. Such a definition of freedom is alien to the norms and traditions of America's racist/capitalist state. Martin and Malcolm, DuBois and Robeson, all in their own unique manner, came to this realisation. There cannot be peaceful and productive race relations in the US, unless there is economic justice; and without justice, there can be no peace. The vision of a society freed from bigotry and hunger, freed from unemployment and racial violence, will be realised only through a Third Reconstruction which seeks the empowerment of the labouring classes, national minorities, and all of the oppressed. The 'freedom' of capital must be restricted for the common good.

A Third Reconstruction will arise in the not-too-distant future, to fulfil the lost promises of the first and second social movements. Its vision is quite clear. It is now only a question of power.

Notes

1. PROLOGUE: THE LEGACY OF THE FIRST RECONSTRUCTION

1. W. E. B. DuBois, *Black Reconstruction in America, 1860–1880* (New York: Atheneum, 1971), p. 59.
2. Ibid., p. 378.
3. Lawrence Goodwyn, *The Populist Moment: A Short History of the Agrarian Revolt in America* (New York: Oxford University Press, 1978), pp. 5–6.
4. C. Vann Woodward, *The Strange Career of Jim Crow* (New York: Oxford University Press, 1974), p. 118.
5. DuBois, *Black Reconstruction*, p. 703.

2. THE COLD WAR IN BLACK AMERICA, 1945–1954

1. Harold Cruse, *Rebellion or Revolution?* (New York: William Morrow, 1968), p. 12.
2. Philip S. Foner, *Organized Labor and the Black Worker, 1619–1973* (New York: International Publishers, 1974), p. 270.
3. Henry Lee Moon, *Balance of Power: The Negro Vote* (New York: Doubleday, 1948), pp. 9, 18.
4. Isaac Deutscher, *Stalin: A Political Biography* (New York: Oxford University Press, 1949), pp. 573, 575.
5. David Caute, *The Great Fear: The Anti-Communist Purge Under Truman and Eisenhower* (New York: Simon and Schuster, 1979), pp. 539–40.
6. Richard Pollenberg, *One Nation Divisible: Class, Race, and Ethnicity in the United States Since 1938* (New York: Penguin Books, 1980), pp. 87–8.
7. Lillian Hellman, *Scoundrel Time* (Boston: Little, Brown, 1976).
8. Pollenberg, *One Nation Divisible*, p. 106.
9. Caute, *The Great Fear*, p. 15.
10. Ibid., p. 11.
11. Foner, *Organized Labor and the Black Worker, 1619–1973*, p. 279.
12. On Randolph's political career, see William H. Harris, *Keeping the Faith: A. Philip Randolph, Milton P. Webster, and the Brotherhood of Sleeping Car Porters* (Urbana, Illinois: University of Illinois Press, 1977); Theodore Kornweibel, 'The Messenger Magazine, 1917–1928' (PhD dissertation, Yale University, 1971); Manning Marable, *From the Grassroots: Social and Political Essays Towards Afro-American Liberation* (Boston: South End Press, 1980), pp. 59–85.
13. Pollenberg, *One Nation Divisible*, p. 112.
14. Hanes Walton, Jr., *Black Politics: A Theoretical and Structural Analysis* (Philadelphia: J. B. Lippincott, 1972), p. 66.
15. Foner, *Organized Labor and the Black Worker*, p. 280.

16. W. E. B. DuBois, *The Autobiography of W. E. B. DuBois* (New York: International Publishers, 1968), p. 293.

17. Ibid., p. 334. The shift in the NAACP's position on the Soviet Union and the American left in general can be observed by analysing the attitudes of James Weldon Johnson. Johnson, who was not a leftist, wrote this passage in 1934:

> Soviet Russia [is] a land in which there is absolutely no prejudice against Negroes. . . . I hold no brief against Communism as a theory of government. I hope that the Soviet experiment will be completely successful. . . . If America should turn truly Communistic, . . . if the capitalistic system should be abolished and the dictatorship of the proletariat established, with the Negro aligned, as he naturally ought to be, with the proletariat, race discriminations would be officially banned and the reasons and feelings back of them would finally disappear.

See Johnson, *Negro Americans, What Now?* (New York: Viking Press, 1962).

18. W. E. B. DuBois, 'The Negro and Radical Thought', *Crisis*, 22 (July 1921), 204.

19. W. E. B. DuBois, 'My Evolving Program for Negro Freedom', in Rayford Logan (ed.), *What the Negro Wants* (Chapel Hill, North Carolina: University of North Carolina Press, 1944), pp. 31–70.

20. Pollenberg, *One Nation Divisible*, pp. 112–13.

21. C. Vann Woodward, *The Strange Career of Jim Crow* (New York: Oxford University Press, 1974), p. 136. Once out of office, Truman was absolutely candid about his opposition to blacks' civil rights. At a Cornell University lecture in 1960, Truman charged that 'Communists' were 'engineering the student sit-downs at lunch counters in the South'. King and Wilkins deplored the former president's statement, and demanded that he provide details. Truman replied that he had no proof: 'But I know that usually when trouble hits the country the Kremlin is behind it'. Caute, *The Great Fear*, p. 35.

22. August Meier and Elliott Rudwick, *CORE: A Study in the Civil Rights Movement, 1942–1968* (New York: Oxford University Press, 1973), p. 35.

23. Woodward, *The Strange Career of Jim Crow*, p. 142.

24. Jessie Parkhurst Guzman (ed.), *Negro Year Book: A Review of Events Affecting Negro Life, 1941–1946* (Tuskegee Institute, Alabama: Tuskegee Institute, Department of Records and Research, 1947), pp. 270–1.

25. Pollenberg, *One Nation Divisible*, p. 159.

26. V. O. Key, Jr., *Southern Politics in State and Nation* (New York: Vintage, 1949), p. 649.

27. Meier and Rudwick, *CORE*, pp. 64–5.

28. Pollenberg, *One Nation Divisible*, p. 113.

29. DuBois, *Autobiography*, p. 369.

30. Ibid., p. 370.

31. Caute, *The Great Fear*, p. 418.

32. Ibid., pp. 120, 128–9, 190, 193.

33. Foner, *Organized Labor and the Black Worker*, pp. 293–311.

34. Caute, *The Great Fear*, pp. 192, 198–9, 209–10.

35. W. A. Swanberg, *Norman Thomas: The Last Idealist* (New York: Charles Scribner's Sons, 1976), pp. 353–5, 479–80.

36. Thomas Sowell, *Race and Economics* (New York: Longman, 1975), p. 94.

37. Mario T. Garcia, 'On Mexican Immigration, the United States, and Chicano History', *Journal of Ethnic Studies*, 7 (Spring 1979), 85.

38. Key, *Southern Politics in State and Nation*, pp. 272–5.

39. Stan Steiner, *La Raza: The Mexican-Americans* (New York: Harper and Row, 1970), pp. 232–3.

40. Roxanne Dunbar Ortiz, 'Land and Nationhood: The American Indian Struggle for Self-Determination and Survival', *Socialist Review*, 12 (May–August 1982), 109.

41. William Loren Katz, *The Black West* (Garden City, New York: Anchor Books, 1973), pp. 201–14.

42. S. J. Makielski, Jr., *Beleaguered Minorities: Cultural Politics in America* (San Francisco: W. H. Freeman, 1973), p. 56.

43. Ortiz, 'Land and Nationhood', p. 116.

44. Makielski, *Beleaguered Minorities*, p. 57.

45. Richard A. Garcia, 'The Chicano Movement and the Mexican-American Community, 1972–1978: An Interpretative Essay', *Socialist Review*, 8 (July–October 1978), 123.

46. Guzman (ed.), *Negro Year Book*, pp. 182–3.

3. THE DEMAND FOR REFORM, 1954–1960

1. C. Vann Woodward, *The Strange Career of Jim Crow* (New York: Oxford University Press, 1974), pp. 146–7.

2. Ibid., p. 144; Carl N. Degler, *Affluence and Anxiety, 1945–Present* (Glenview, Illinois: Scott, Foresman, 1968), p. 96.

3. Numan V. Bartley and Hugh D. Graham, *Southern Politics and the Second Reconstruction* (Baltimore: Johns Hopkins Press, 1975), p. 67. Wallace's metamorphosis as a racist demagogue merits serious examination, because it helps to explain the relationship between racism and American politics. When Wallace began his political career, he urged friends not to oppress local blacks. 'You know, we just can't keep the colored folks down like we been doin' around here for years and years', he argued in 1946. 'We got to quit. We got to start treatin' 'em right. They just like everybody else.' On economic issues, Wallace was a progressive populist, a supporter of extensive state programmes for public schools, medical clinics, and welfare. In 1958, Wallace's opponent for governor accepted the public support of the Klan. Wallace promptly issued a denunciation of the Klan. After that, he won the support of 'the substantial Jewish minority in Alabama [and] the NAACP'. Wallace's defeat in 1958, losing by 65,000 votes, made him into the South's most notorious bigot. In 1962, 1970 and 1974 Wallace was elected governor of Alabama on a racist programme. In 1982, as huge numbers of blacks were now voters, and a black man, Richard Arrington, served as mayor of Alabama's largest city, Birmingham, Wallace ran successfully for governor for a fourth term – this time, as an economic liberal and racial moderate. In doing so, he managed to attract about one-third of the black voters in the state's Democratic primary race. See Marshall Frady, *Wallace* (New York: New American Library, 1976), pp. 126–7, 137, 141.

4. Woodward, *The Strange Career of Jim Crow*, pp. 156–8.

5. Ibid., pp. 165–6.

6. Richard Wright, 'A Blueprint for Negro Writing', *New Challenge*, 11 (1937), 53–65.

7. Richard Wright, *The Outsider* (New York: Harper and Row, 1953), p. 366.

8. Langston Hughes, 'Un-American Investigators', in Dudley Randall (ed.), *The Black Poets* (New York: Bantam, 1972), pp. 79–80.

9. Harold Cruse, *The Crisis of the Negro Intellectual* (New York: William Morrow, 1967), pp. 267–84.

10. LeRoi Jones, *Black Music* (New York: William Morrow, 1970), pp. 21, 37–40, 56–57, 69–73.

11. Martin Luther King, quoted in Cruse, *Rebellion or Revolution?*, pp. 60–1.

12. DuBois, *The Autobiography of W. E. B. DuBois*, pp. 399–401.

13. Herbert Hill, 'Race and Labor: The AFL–CIO and the Black Worker Twenty-Five Years After the Merger', *Journal of Intergroup Relations*, 10 (Spring 1982), 14.

14. Philip S. Foner, *Organized Labor and the Black Worker, 1619–1973* (New York: International Publishers, 1974), pp. 314–15.

15. Gus Tyler, 'Contemporary Labor's Attitude Toward the Negro', in Julius Jacobson (ed.), *The Negro and the American Labor Movement* (Garden City, New York: Anchor, 1968), p. 367.

16. Ibid., p. 363.

17. Hill, 'Race and Labor', p. 20.

18. Foner, *Organized Labor and the Black Worker*, pp. 330–1.

19. Hill, 'Race and Labor', p. 25.

20. C. Eric Lincoln, *The Black Muslims in America* (Boston: Beacon Press, 1961), pp. x, 251.

21. Ibid., pp. 147–8.

22. Malcolm X and James Farmer, 'Separation or Integration: A Debate', *Dialogue Magazine*, 2 (May 1962), 14–18.

23. Cruse, *The Crisis of the Negro Intellectual*, p. 352.

24. Robert F. Williams, 'USA: The Potential of a Minority Revolution', *The Crusader Monthly Newsletter*, 5 (May–June) 1964), 1–7.

25. David Caute, *The Great Fear: The Anti-Communist Purge Under Truman and Eisenhower* (New York: Simon and Schuster, 1979), p. 59.

26. G. William Danhoff, *Who Rules America?* (Englewood Cliffs, New Jersey, Prentice-Hall, 1967), pp. 74–86.

4. WE SHALL OVERCOME, 1960–1965

1. August Meier and Elliott Rudwick, *CORE: A Study in the Civil Rights Movement, 1942–1968* (New York: Oxford University Press, 1973), p. 101.

2. Debbie Louis, *And We Are Not Saved: A History of the Movement as People* (Garden City, New York: Anchor, 1970), p. 51.

3. Ibid., p. 32.

4. Vincent Harding, *The Other American Revolution* (Los Angeles: Center for Afro-American Studies, 1980), p. 159.

5. Clayborne Carson, *In Struggle: SNCC and the Black Awakening of the 1960s* (Cambridge, Mass.: Harvard University Press, 1981), p. 68.

6. Ibid., p. 78.

7. Meier and Rudwick, *CORE: A Study in the Civil Rights Movement, 1942–1968*, p. 209.

8. Carson, *In Struggle*, p. 105.

9. Harding, *The Other American Revolution*, p. 167.

10. C. Vann Woodward, *The Strange Career of Jim Crow* (New York: Oxford University Press, 1974), pp. 175–6.

11. William Robert Miller, *Martin Luther King, Jr.: His Life, Martyrdom and Meaning for the World* (New York: Avon Books, 1968), p. 147.

12. Ibid., p. 150.

13. Martin Luther King, Jr., *Why We Can't Wait* (New York: Harper and Row, 1964), Chapter 5.

14. Woodward, *The Strange Career of Jim Crow*, p. 181.

15. Harding, *The Other American Revolution*, p. 172.

16. Miller, *Martin Luther King, Jr.*, pp. 67, 173–8.

17. Meier and Rudwick, *CORE: A Study in the Civil Rights Movement, 1942–1968*, p. 214.

18. Miller, *Martin Luther King, Jr.*, pp. 161–2.

19. Carson, *In Struggle*, pp. 106–7, 136–7.

20. Bayard Rustin, 'The Meaning of the March on Washington', *Liberation*, 8 (October 1963), 11–13.

21. W. E. B. DuBois, *The Education of Black People: Ten Critiques, 1906–1960* (New York: Monthly Review Press, 1973), pp. 149–58.

22. G. Plekhanov, quoted in Isaac Deutscher, *The Prophet Outcast: Trotsky: 1929–1940* (New York: Vintage, 1963), pp. 242–3.

23. Louis Lomax, *To Kill a Black Man* (Los Angeles: Holloway House, 1968), pp. 113–18.

24. James Baldwin, 'The Dangerous Road Before Martin Luther King', *Harper's Magazine* (February 1961).

25. August Meier, 'On the Role of Martin Luther King', *New Politics*, 4 (Winter 1965), 52–9.

26. Manning Marable, *From the Grassroots: Social and Political Essays Towards Afro-American Liberation* (Boston: South End Press, 1980), pp. 53–4.

27. Miller, *Martin Luther King, Jr.*, p. 206

28. Harding, *The Other American Revolution*, p. 181.

29. Robert L. Allen, *Black Awakening in Capitalist America: An Analytic History* (Garden City, New York: Anchor, 1969), p. 111.

30. Meier, 'On the Role of Martin Luther King', pp. 52–3.

31. Steven F. Lawson, *Black Ballots: Voting Rights in the South, 1944–1969* (New York: Columbia University Press, 1976), p. 300.

32. Ibid., pp. 321, 329, 331; Woodward, *The Strange Career of Jim Crow*, pp. 182–3.

33. Louis, *And We Are Not Saved*, pp. 132–3.

34. Numan V. Bartley and Hugh D. Graham, *Southern Politics and the Second Reconstruction* (Baltimore: Johns Hopkins Press, 1975), pp. 106–7, 112–13, 117, 123, 126.

35. Woodward, *The Strange Career of Jim Crow*, pp. 186–7.

36. Louis, *And We Are Not Saved*, p. 173.

37. Allen, *Black Awakening in Capitalist America*, p. 70.

38. Carson, *In Struggle*, pp. 185–6.

39. Harding, *The Other American Revolution*, pp. 183, 185.

5. BLACK POWER, 1965–1970

1. Walter Rodney, 'Guyana: The making of the labour force', *Race and Class*, 22 (Spring 1981), 331.

2. Malcolm X, *The Autobiography of Malcolm X* (New York: Grove Press, 1965), pp. 201–2, 204, 213.

3. Ibid., pp. 202, 219.

4. Ibid., pp. 240–1.

5. Ibid., p. 246.

6. Ibid., p. 301.

7. George Breitman, *The Last Year of Malcolm X: The Evolution of a Revolutionary* (New York: Schocken, 1968), p. 19.

8. Malcolm X, *The Autobiography of Malcolm X*, p. 375.

9. Breitman, *The Last Year of Malcolm X*, p. 33.

10. Ibid., p. 57.

11. August Meier and Elliott Rudwick: *CORE: A Study in the Civil Rights Movement, 1942–1968* (New York: Oxford University Press, 1973), p. 206.

12. Ibid., p. 331.

13. Carson, *In Struggle: SNCC and the Black Awakening of the 1960s* (Cambridge, Mass.: Harvard University Press, 1981), p. 100.

14. Ibid., p. 136.

15. There is a great amount of evidence which indicates that the US government may have had direct responsibility for the slaying of Malcolm X, and in the two-decade-long 'cover up' about the identity of his killers. See George Breitman, Herman Porter and Baxter Smith (eds), *The Assassination of Malcolm X* (New York: Pathfinder Press, 1976); Peter L. Goldman, *The Death and Life of Malcolm X* (New York: Harper and Row, 1973); William Seraile, 'The Assassination of Malcolm X: The View From Home and Abroad', *Afro-Americans in New York Life and History*, 5 (January 1981), 43–58.

16. Breitman, *The Last Year of Malcolm X*, pp. 83, 87, 93–4; Malcolm X, *The Autobiography of Malcolm X*, pp. 443, 444, 447, 454.

17. Malcolm X, *The Autobiography of Malcolm X*, pp. 443, 444, 447, 454.

18. Baldwin, quoted in Stokely Carmichael and Charles V. Hamilton, *Black Power: The Politics of Liberation in America* (New York: Vintage, 1967), p. 155.

19. Herbert J. Gans, 'The Ghetto Rebellions and Urban Class Conflict', in Robert H. Connery (ed.), *Urban Riots: Violence and Social Change* (New York: Vintage, 1969), pp. 45–54.

20. Kenneth Clark, *Dark Ghetto* (New York: Harper and Row, 1965), pp. 63–4.

21. David Lewis, *King: A Critical Biography* (Baltimore: Penguin, 1969), p. 323.

22. Carson, *In Struggle*, pp. 209–10.

23. Meier and Rudwick, *CORE*, p. 417.

24. Roy Wilkins, 'Whither "Black Power?" ' *Crisis* (August–September 1966), 354.

25. Carson, *In Struggle*, p. 220.

26. Ibid., pp. 220–1; and Harold Cruse, *Rebellion or Revolution?* (New York: William Morrow, 1968), p. 200.

27. Martin Luther King, *Where Do We Go from Here: Chaos or Community* (New York: Harper and Row, 1967), pp. 51–2.

28. August Meier and Elliott Rudwick, *CORE: A Study in the Civil Rights Movement, 1942–1968* (New York: Oxford University Press, 1973), pp. 412, 414–15.

29. Carmichael and Hamilton, *Black Power*, pp. vi, vii. Cruse's comments on Carmichael and Hamilton's *Black Power* are quite critical. Cruse argued that by 1965

the urban militants who had listened with rapt attention to the message of Malcolm X realized that militant-protest integrationism had reaped the last dregs of the rewards of diminishing returns. The moment the slogan 'Black Power' was sounded, it signalled a turning inward, a reversal of self-motivated aims in the direction of 'Black Economic and Political Control' of Black communities. . . . That [*Black Power*] failed to present anything so advanced . . . was only a very real reflection of the collective state of Black consciousness in force at the 'Black Power' juncture of the Sixties. . . . Whatever occurred after publication of *Black Power* was simply anti-climactic. The book's analysis was not of the quality that it could have lent meaningful guidance to the movements which were visibly running out of steam in the late Sixties. These movements were infused with the methodology of militant pragmatism, and rife with the competing clash of varying consensuses. There was no general consensus as to where the competing factions of the Black militant *élites* wanted to lead the Black masses.

Cruse, 'The Little Rock National Black Political Convention', *Black World*, 23 (October 1974), 10–17, 82–8.

30. Meier and Rudwick, *CORE*, p. 423.

31. Robert L. Allen, *Black Awakening in Capitalist America: An Analytic History* (Garden City, New York: Anchor, 1969), p. 59.

32. Cruse, *Rebellion or Revolution?*, p. 198.

33. James Boggs, *Racism and the Class Struggle: Further Pages from a Black Worker's Notebook* (New York: Monthly Review Press, 1970), pp. 54–8. Even the American Communist Party, what was left of it following years of governmental suppression and the departure of thousands of members due to the reaction against the Soviet Union's intervention into Hungary in 1956, was generally favourable towards Black Power. Black Communist leader Claude Lightfoot recognised in early 1968 that the phrase 'means many things to different people. . . . But the central reason why the slogan has been embraced by most people is the recognition of the necessity for black people to have a greater share of economic and political power'. Black Power was 'not only violence in the streets in response to provocations, but a revolt at the polls, a revolt to change the composition of government and to enforce the laws involving the rights of black people'. In general, Lightfoot, like Boggs and other black socialists, tended to underestimate the capitalist thrust of many Black Powerites. Claude M. Lightfoot, *Ghetto Rebellion to Black Liberation* (New York: International Publishers, 1968), pp. 17, 19.

34. Allen, *Black Awakening in Capitalist America*, pp. 163–4, 228–9.

35. Cruse, *Rebellion or Revolution?*, pp. 201, 206–7, 213–14. Cruse adds that 'the conference steering committee refused to allow the paper to be presented, so I had no real motivation for attending in any event. It all added up to another of a long series of misadventures with the Marxists, with whom I am forever at odds' (p. 25).

36. Ibid., p. 197.

37. Debbie Louis, *And We Are Not Saved: A History of the Movement as People* (Garden City, New York: Anchor 1970), pp. 296–7.

38. 'Crisis and Commitment', *Crisis* (November 1966), 474–9.

39. George Breitman (ed.), *By Any Means Necessary: Speeches, Interviews and a Letter by Malcolm X* (New York: Merit, 1970), p. 162.

40. 'SNCC press release: Statement on Vietnam', in Clyde Taylor (ed.), *Vietnam and Black America: An Anthology of Protest and Resistance* (Garden City, New York: Anchor, 1973), pp. 258–9.

41. Stokely Carmichael, 'At Morgan State', in Taylor, *Vietnam and Black America*, p. 271.

42. Julian Bond, 'The Roots of Racism and War', in Taylor, *Vietnam and Black America*, pp. 108–9.

43. Ronald Dellums, 'Involvement in Indochina is Number One Priority', in Taylor, *Vietnam and Black America*, pp. 103–4.

44. Addison Gayle, Jr., 'Hell, No, Black Men Won't Go!'; James Baldwin, 'The War Crimes Tribunal'; S. E. Anderson, 'Junglegrave'; and Robert Hayden, 'Words in the Mourning Time', in Taylor, *Vietnam and Black America*, pp. 45, 101–2, 139, 143.

45. Lewis, *King*, pp. 310–11.

46. Ibid., p. 354.

47. Ibid., p. 360.

48. Ibid., p. 376.

49. Ibid., p. 387. The great tragedy of monumental historical figures is that their legacy is left to their followers, many of whom often have no real insights into his/her political praxis. King provides a fitting example of this phenomenon. Vincent Harding cites an interview with one of King's closest advisers, given several years after the 1968 assassination. The adviser stated, 'In a way, it was probably best for many of us who worked with Martin that he was killed when he was, because he was moving into some radical directions that few of us had been prepared for. And I don't think that many of us would have been ready to take the risks of life, possessions, security, and status that

such a move would have involved. I'm pretty sure I wouldn't have been willing.' Vincent Harding, *The Other American Revolution* (Los Angeles: Center for Afro-American Studies, 1980), p. 212.

50. Nikki Giovanni, *Black Feeling, Black Talk, Black Judgement* (New York: William Morrow, 1970), pp. 19–20.

51. Ibid., p. 83.

52. Allen, *Black Awakening in Capitalist America*, p. 166.

53. Julius Nyerere, *Ujamaa – Essays on Socialism* (New York: Oxford University Press, 1968), pp. 39, 42.

54. David Caute, *Frantz Fanon* (New York: Viking Press, 1970), pp. 104–5.

55. Addison Gayle, Jr., *The Black Situation* (New York: Delta, 1970), pp. 84–7.

56. 'What we want now! What we Believe', in John H. Bracey, Jr., August Meier and Elliott Rudwick (eds), *Black Nationalism in America* (Indianapolis: Bobbs-Merrill, 1970), p. 526.

57. Ibid., p. 528. Relations between the Black Panthers and the 'New Left' of the 1960s were not always harmonious. The largest white left formation, the Students for a Democratic Society (SDS), opposed the Panthers' claims that they represented the true 'vanguard' of the socialist movement. At the National Conference for a United Front Against Fascism, held in Oakland in July 1969, Bobby Seale declared sternly that the Panthers would administer 'disciplinary actions' against 'those little bourgeois, snooty nose SDS's' if they got 'out of order'. See John P. Diggins, *The American Left in the Twentieth Century* (New York: Harcourt, Brace, Jovanovich, 1973), pp. 175–6.

58. Lennox S. Hinds, *Illusions of Justice: Human Rights Violations in the United States* (Iowa City, Iowa: School of Social Work, University of Iowa, 1978), p. 88.

59. Carson, *In Struggle*, p. 256.

60. Donald McDonald, 'Nixon's Record Revealed', in Melvin Steinfield (ed.), *Our Racist Presidents* (San Ramon, California: Consensus Publishers, 1972), pp. 283–96.

6. BLACK REBELLION: ZENITH AND DECLINE, 1970–1976

1. Philip S. Foner, *Organized Labor and the Black Worker, 1619–1973* (New York: International Publishers, 1974), pp. 418–19.

2. Ibid., p. 431.

3. Ibid., p. 435.

4. Herbert Hill, 'Race and Labor: The AFL–CIO and the Black Worker Twenty-five Years After the Merger', *Journal of Intergroup Relations*, 10 (Spring 1982), 40–41.

5. Ibid., p. 47.

6. Marguerite Ross Barnett, 'The Congressional Black Caucus: Illusions and Realities of Power', in Michael B. Preston, Lenneal J. Henderson, Jr., and Paul Puryear (eds), *The New Black Politics: The Search For Political Power* (New York: Longman, 1982), p. 35.

7. William Strickland, 'The Gary Convention and the Crisis of American Politics', *Black World*, 21 (October 1972), 18–26; and Imamu Amiri Baraka, 'Toward the Creation of Political Institutions for all African Peoples', *Black World*, 21 (October 1972), 54–78. The Gary Convention's statement was one of the most politically advanced statements produced by black Americans in history:

We come to Gary in an hour of great crisis and tremendous promise for Black America. While the white nation hovers on the brink of chaos, while its politicians offer no hope of real change, we stand on the edge of history and are faced with an amazing and frightening choice: We may choose in 1972 to slip back into the decadent white politics of American life, or we may press forward, moving relentlessly from Gary to the creation of our own Black life. The choice is large, but the time is very short. . . . If we have never faced it before, let us face it at Gary: The profound crisis of Black people and the disaster of America are not caused by men nor will they be solved by men alone. These crises are the crises of basically flawed economics and politics, and of cultural degradation. None of the Democratic candidates and none of the Republican candidates – regardless of their vague promises to us or to their white constituencies – can solve our problems or the problems of this country without radically changing the systems by which it operates.

See Strickland, 'The Gary Convention and the Crisis of American Politics', pp. 20, 24.

8. Carl N. Degler, *Affluence and Anxiety 1945 – Present* (Glenview, Illinois, Scott, Foresman, 1968), p. 192.

9. William E. Nelson, Jr., and Philip J. Meranto, *Electing Black Mayors: Political Action in the Black Community* (Columbus, Ohio: Ohio State University Press, 1977), p. 336.

10. Ibid., pp. 343–51.

11. Bureau of the Census, *Social Indicators III: Selected data on social conditions and trends in the United States* (Washington, DC: US Government Printing Office, 1980), p. 237.

12. Mary F. Berry, *Black Resistance: White Law: A History of Constitutional Racism in America* (Englewood Cliffs, New Jersey: Prentice-Hall, 1971), p. 228.

13. Lennox S. Hinds, *Illusions of Justice: Human Rights Violations in the United States* (Iowa City, Iowa: School of Social Work, University of Iowa, 1978), pp. 119–22.

14. Ibid., pp. 258–63.

15. Ibid., p. 168.

16. Angela Davis, *With My Mind on Freedom: An Autobiography* (New York: Bantam, 1975), p. 15.

17. Robert Chrisman, 'George Jackson', *Black Scholar*, 3 (October 1971), 2–4.

18. Eric Mann, *Comrade George: An Investigation into the Life, Political Thought, and Assassination of George Jackson* (New York: Harper and Row, 1972), p. 144.

19. Ibid., pp. 28, 146–9; anonymous, 'Episodes From The Attica Massacre', *Black Scholar*, 4 (October 1972), 34–9.

20. Richard Polenberg, *One Nation Divisible: Class, Race, and Ethnicity in the United States Since 1938* (New York: Penguin Books, 1980), pp. 252–3.

21. William Strickland, 'Watergate: Its Meaning For Black America', *Black World*, 23 (December 1973), 4–14.

22. Vincent Harding, *The Other American Revolution* (Los Angeles: Center for Afro-American Studies, 1980), pp. 216–17.

23. Barnett, 'The Congressional Black Caucus', p. 35.

24. Harold Cruse, 'The Little Rock National Black Political Convention', *Black World*, 23 (October 1974), 13.

25. Ladun Anise, 'The Tyranny of a Purist Ideology', *Black World*, 24 (May 1975), 18–27. Anise added with emphasis,

The argument that a collective identity of over 300 million Black people is a parochial identity fit for the zoo constitutes an intolerable misreading of history. Oppression wears many faces under many hats. No single, variable explanatory theory or model will ever provide a reasonable functional analysis of the problem. The constant proclivity toward extreme polarities is nothing more than a sophisticated escapism born of either a distorted view of history, ignorance or insecurity projected as power or tough-mindedness (p. 24).

26. Kalamu Ya Salaam, 'Tell No Lies, Claim No Easy Victories', *Black World*, 23 (October 1974), 18–34.

27. Alkalimat wrote in November 1969,

> The ofay has sinned against God. We are God's righteous warriors and must rise as Gods ourselves. The Black revolution must burn the earth rid of the white boys' curse so that love can reign and we can become who we were really meant to be . . . When we rebel and become our true African selves we will then have started acting out our true role in the post-American future of the world.

In stark contrast, in September 1974, Alkalimat declared that capitalism was

> the fundamental cause of the problems facing black people. . . . The imperialism which exploits and oppresses Africa is rooted in the system of U.S. monopoly capitalism. . . . Thus, while the black working class must of necessity lead the black liberation struggle – because of its unwavering militancy and because it has the firmest grip of the levers of social change of any sector of the black community – all progressive forces truly interested in the liberation of black people have a definite and important role to play.

See Alkalimat, 'What Lies Ahead for Black Americans?' *Negro Digest*, 19 (November 1969), 21; Peoples College, 'Imperialism and Black Liberation', *Black Scholar*, 6 (September 1974), 38–42.

28. Haki Madhubuti, 'The Latest Purge: The Attack on Black Nationalism and Pan-Afrikanism by the New Left, the sons and daughters of the Old Left', *Black Scholar*, 6 (September 1974), 43–56.

29. Maglanbayan and Walters quoted in Haki Madhubuti, 'Enemy: From the White Left, White Right and In-Between', *Black World*, 23, (October 1974), 36–47.

30. Mark Smith, 'A Response to Haki Madhubuti', *Black Scholar*, 6 (January–February, 1975), 45–52.

31. Hoyt Fuller, 'Another Fork in the Road', *Black World*, 23 (October 1974), 49–50, 97.

32. Stanley Aronowitz, 'Remaking the American Left, Part One: Currents in American Radicalism', *Socialist Review*, 13 (January–February 1983), 20.

33. Among a large number of recent texts which document the economic and political plight of the American Indian since the 1950s are: Wilcomb E. Washburn, *The Indian in America* (New York: Harper and Row, 1975); Stan Steiner, *The New Indians* (New York: Harper and Row, 1968), and a book which reached a more popular audience, Vine DeLoria's *Custer Died for Your Sins: An Indian Manifesto* (New York: Macmillan, 1969).

34. Dennis Banks, 'Interview', *Black Scholar*, 7 (June 1976), 33.

35. Roxanne Dunbar Ortiz, 'Land and Nationhood: The American Indian Struggle for Self-determination and Survival', *Socialist Review*, 12 (May–August 1982), 11.

36. Banks, 'Interview', p. 29.

37. Ortiz, 'Land and Nationhood', pp. 111–12.

38. Thomas Sowell, *Race and Economics* (New York: Longman, 1975), pp. 111–13. For a detailed analysis of the political economy of Chicanos, see Mario T. Garcia, 'Radical Dualism in the El Paso Labor Market, 1880–1920', *Atzlán*, 6 (Fall 1975), 197–218; Tomás Almaguer, 'Historical Notes on Chicano Oppression: The Dialectics of Racial and Class Oppression in North America', *Atzlán*, 5 (Spring and Fall 1974), 27–56; Marietta Morrisey, 'Ethnic Stratification and the Study of Chicanos', *Journal of Ethnic Studies*, 10 (Winter 1983), 71–99; and Mario Barrera, *Race and Class in the Southwest* (Notre Dame, Indiana: University of Notre Dame, 1979).

39. Cesar Chavez, 'The California Farm Workers' Struggle', *Black Scholar*, 7 (June 1976), 16.

40. S. J. Makielski, Jr., *Beleaguered Minorities: Cultural Politics in America* (San Francisco: W. H. Freeman, 1973), p. 68.

41. Ibid., p. 70.

42. Richard A. Garcia, 'The Chicano Movement and the Mexican-American Community, 1972 – An Interpretative Essay', *Socialist Review*, 8 (July–October 1978), 120–1.

43. Gutierrez's political coup in Crystal City, Texas, is documented in a study by John Shockley, *Chicano Revolt in a Texas Town* (Notre Dame, Indiana: University of Notre Dame Press, 1974). Other general studies which explore modern Chicano nationalism are Rodolfo Acuna, *Occupied America: The Chicano's Struggle toward Liberation* (San Francisco: Canfield Press, 1972); and Richard A. Garcia's sweeping account, *The Chicanos in America, 1540–1974* (Dobbs Ferry, New York: Oceana Press, 1977).

44. Garcia, 'The Chicano Movement and the Mexican-American Community, 1972–1978', p. 119.

45. Ibid., p. 121.

46. Ibid., pp. 131, 135.

47. Chuck Stone, 'Black Political Power in the Carter Era', *Black Scholar*, 8 (January–February 1977), 6–15.

48. Eddie N. Williams, 'Black Impact on the 1976 Elections', *Focus*, 4 (November 1976).

49. Stone, 'Black Political Power in the Carter Era', p. 9.

7. REACTION: THE DEMISE OF THE SECOND RECONSTRUCTION, 1976–1982

1. Jim Thomas, David Stribling, Ra Rabb Chaka, Edmond Clemons, Charlie Secret and Alex Neal, 'Prison Conditions and Penal Trends', *Crime and Social Justice*, No. 15 (Summer 1981), 49–50.

2. Franklin H. Williams, 'On Death Cars', *Milwaukee Courier* (12 June 1982).

3. William Julius Wilson, *The Declining Significance of Race: Blacks and Changing American Institutions* (Chicago: University of Chicago Press, 1978), *passim*.

4. Douglas G. Glasgow, *The Black Underclass: Poverty, Unemployment and the Entrapment of Ghetto Youth* (New York: Vintage, 1981), pp. 1–9.

5. Vincent Harding, *The Other American Revolution* (Los Angeles: Center for Afro-American Studies, 1980), p. 221.

6. Askia Muhammad, 'Civil War in Islamic America', *Nation*, 224 (11 June 1977), 721.

7. Harding, *The Other American Revolution*, p. 222.

8. Barbara Easton, Michael Kazin and David Plotke, 'Desperate Times: The Peoples Temple and the Left', *Socialist Review*, 9 (March–April 1979), 64.

9. Jitu Weusi, 'Jonestown Massacre – An Act of Genocide?' *Black Thoughts*, 10 (May–June 1979), 1, 30–1.

10. Easton, Kazin and Plotke, 'Desperate Times: The Peoples Temple and the Left', pp. 63, 74.

11. Richard Polenberg, *One Nation Divisible: Class, Race and Ethnicity in the United States Since 1938* (New York: Penguin Books, 1980), pp. 258–9.

12. Lawrence Goodwyn, 'Jimmy Carter and "Populism",' *Southern Exposure*, 5 (Spring 1977), 45.

13. David Plotke, 'The Politics of Transition: The United States in Transition', *Socialist Review*, 11 (January–February 1981), 21–72.

14. Ken Bode, 'Carter's Chosen Path', *New Republic*, 180 (27 January 1979), 13.

15. Manning Marable, *From The Grassroots: Social and Political Essays Towards Afro-American Liberation* (Boston: South End Press, 1980), p. 30.

16. Elliott Currie, 'The Politics of Jobs: Humphrey–Hawkins and the Dilemmas of Full Employment', *Socialist Review*, 7 (March–April 1977), 93–4, 103–4.

17. Marguerite Ross Barnett, 'The Congressional Black Caucus: Illusions and Realities of Power,' in Preston, Henderson and Puryear (eds), *The New Black Politics: The Search for Political Power* (New York: Longman, 1982), p. 45.

18. Victor Perlo, 'Carter's Economic Prescription: Bitter Medicine for the People', *Political Affairs*, 58 (January 1979), 1.

19. Ken Bode, 'Carter's Chosen Path', *New Republic*, 180 (27 January 1979), 12–14.

20. Manning Marable, *Blackwater: Historical Studies in Race, Class Consciousness, and Revolution* (Dayton, Ohio: Black Praxis Press, 1981), pp. 151–2.

21. John Judis and Alan Wolfe, 'American Politics at the Crossroads: The Collapse of Cold-War Liberalism', *Socialist Review*, 7 (March–April 1977), 9.

22. Marable, *Blackwater*, p. 133.

23. John Hope Franklin, *Reconstruction After the Civil War* (Chicago: University of Chicago Press, 1961), pp. 155, 157.

24. Baxter Smith, 'The Resurgence of the KKK', *Black Scholar*, 12 (January–February 1981), 29.

25. Andrew Marx and Tom Tuthill, 'Resisting the Klan: Mississippi Organizers', *Southern Exposure*, 8 (Summer 1980), 27.

26. Marable, *Blackwater*, p. 130.

27. Brenda Payton, 'Police Use of Deadly Force in Oakland', *Black Scholar*, 12 (January–February 1981), 62.

28. Herb Boyd, 'Blacks and the Police State: A Case Study of Detroit', *Black Scholar*, 12 (January–February 1981), 60.

29. Payton, 'Police Use of Deadly Force in Oakland', p. 64.

30. Damu Smith, 'The Upsurge of Police Repression: An Analysis', *Black Scholar*, 12 (January–February 1981), 43.

31. Leonard Sykes, Jr., 'Jim Crow, Lynchings and a Return to Business As Usual', *Black Books Bulletin*, 7 (Fall 1981), 20.

32. Joe Gilyard, 'White Man Who Shot Two Black Girls Is Awarded $5,000 For His Trouble', *Cleveland Call and Post* (17 October 1981).

33. Chinta Strausberg, 'White Sheriff Denies Rights to Black Religious Group', *Chicago Defender* (22 September 1981).

34. Demetri Brown, 'Black Man Found Near Lake Stirs Rumors', *Jackson Advocate* (15–21 October 1981).

35. Chokwe Lumumba, 'Short History of the U.S. War on the R.N.A.', *Black Scholar*, 12 (January–February 1981), 77.

36. Janice Bevien, 'Notes on Current Struggles Against Repression', *Black Scholar*, 12 (January–February 1981), 82; Manning Marable, 'Justice is on Trial in Greensboro', *San Francisco Sun Reporter* (10 September, 1981).

37. Bevien, 'Notes on Current Struggles Against Repression', p. 84.

38. John L. Marshall, '1872 Law Used to Prosecute Police Gadfly: Ex-Black Panther Accused of Trying to Turn Crowd Against Police', *Los Angeles Times* (6 May 1982).

39. Marable, *Blackwater*, pp. 149, 157.

40. Ibid., pp. 149, 157.

41. Michael Reich, *Racial Inequality: A Political-Economic Analysis* (Princeton, New Jersey: Princeton University Press, 1981), pp. 5–6.

42. Twiley W. Barker, Jr. and Lucius J. Barker, 'The Courts, Section 5 of the

Select Bibliography

BOOKS (including books not mentioned in the Notes)

Rodolfo Acuna, *Occupied America: The Chicano's Struggle toward Liberation* (San Francisco: Canfield Press, 1972).

Robert L. Allen, *Black Awakening in Capitalist America: An Analytic History* (Garden City, New York: Anchor, 1969).

Rob Backus, *Fire Music: A Political History of Jazz* (Chicago: Vanguard Books, 1978).

Imamu Amiri Baraka (LeRoi Jones), *Black Music* (New York: William Morrow, 1970).

——, *Three Books by Imamu Amiri Baraka: The System of Dante's Hell; Tales; The Dead Lecturer* (New York: Grove Press, 1975).

E. D. Barbour (ed.), *The Black Power Revolt* (Boston: Sargent Press, 1968).

Mario Barrera, *Race and Class in the Southwest* (Notre Dame: Indiana: University of Notre Dame Press, 1979).

Numan V. Bartley and Hugh D. Graham, *Southern Politics and the Second Reconstruction* (Baltimore: Johns Hopkins Press, 1975).

Derrick Bell, *Race, Racism and American Law* (Boston: Little, Brown, 1973).

Lerone Bennett, Jr., *Confrontation Black and White* (Baltimore: Penguin Books, 1965).

Robert F. Berkhofer, Jr., *The White Man's Indian: Images of the American Indian From Columbus to the Present* (New York: Alfred A. Knopf, 1978).

Mary F. Berry, *Black Resistance, White Law: A History of Constitutional Racism in America* (Englewood Cliffs, New Jersey: Prentice-Hall, 1971).

Nelson Blackstock, *COINTELPRO: The FBI's Secret War Against Political Freedom* (New York: Random House, 1976).

James Boggs, *Racism and the Class Struggle: Further Pages from a Black Worker's Notebook* (New York: Monthly Review Press, 1970).

John H. Bracey, Jr., August Meier and Elliott Rudwick (eds), *Black Nationalism in America* (Indianapolis: Bobbs-Merrill, 1970).

George Breitman, *The Last Year of Malcolm X: The Evolution of a Revolutionary* (New York: Schocken, 1968).

—— (ed.), *By Any Means Necessary: Speeches, Interviews and a Letter by Malcolm X* (New York: Merit, 1970).

George Breitman, Herman Porter and Baxter Smith (eds), *The Assassination of Malcolm X* (New York: Pathfinder Press, 1976).

Thomas R. Brooks, *Toil and Trouble: A History of American Labor* (New York: Delta, 1971).

Bureau of the Census, 'Selected Characteristics of Persons and Families of Mexican, Puerto Rican and Other Spanish Origins, March, 1971', *Current Population Reports* (Washington, DC: US Government Printing Office, 1971).

——, *Social Indicators III: Selected data on social conditions and trends in the United States* (Washington, DC: US Government Printing Office, 1980).

——, *The Social and Economic Status of the Black Population in the United States: An Historical View, 1790–1978* (Washington, DC: Government Printing Office, 1980).

Peter Camejo, *Racism, Revolution, Reaction, 1861–1877: The Rise and Fall of Radical Reconstruction* (New York: Pathfinder Press, 1976).

Clayborne Carson, *In Struggle: SNCC and the Black Awakening of the 1960s* (Cambridge: Harvard University Press, 1981).

Wilfred Cartey and Martin Kilson (eds), *The Africa Reader: Colonial Africa* (New York: Vintage, 1970).

David Caute, *Frantz Fanon* (New York: Viking Press, 1970).

——, *The Great Fear: The Anti-Communist Purge Under Truman and Eisenhower* (New York: Simon and Schuster, 1978).

Barbara Christian, *Black Women Novelists: The Development of a Tradition, 1892–1976* (Westport, Connecticut: Greenwood Press, 1980).

Kenneth B. Clark, *Dark Ghetto* (New York: Harper and Row, 1965).

—— (ed.), *The Negro Protest: James Baldwin, Malcolm X, Martin Luther King Talk with Kenneth B. Clark* (Boston: Beacon Press, 1963).

Ramsey Clark and Roy Wilkins, *Search and Destroy* (New York: Harper and Row, 1973).

Eldridge Cleaver, *Post-Prison Writings and Speeches* (New York: Vintage, 1969).

Dick Cluster (ed.), *They Should Have Served That Cup of Coffee: Seven Radicals Remember the Sixties* (Boston: South End Press, 1979).

John Collier, *The Indians of the Americas* (New York: Norton, 1947).

Robert H. Connery (ed.), *Urban Riots: Violence and Social Change* (New York: Vintage, 1969).

Harold Cruse, *Rebellion or Revolution?* (New York: William Morrow, 1968).

——, *The Crisis of the Negro Intellectual: From Its Origins to the Present* (New York: William Morrow, 1967).

Angela Y. Davis (ed.), *If They Come in the Morning* (New York: New American Library, 1971).

——, *With My Mind on Freedom: An Autobiography* (New York: Bantam, 1975).

Carl N. Degler, *Affluence and Anxiety, 1945–Present* (Glenview, Illinois: Scott, Foresman, 1968).

Vine DeLoria, *Custer Died for Your Sins: An Indian Manifesto* (New York: Macmillan, 1969).

——, *We Talk, You Listen, New Tribes, New Turf* (New York: Macmillan, 1970).

Roberta Yancy Dent (ed.), *Paul Robeson: Tributes and Selected Writings* (New York: Paul Robeson Archives, 1977).

Isaac Deutscher, *Stalin: A Political Biography* (New York: Oxford University Press, 1949).

——, *The Prophet Outcast: Trotsky: 1929–1940* (New York: Vintage, 1963).

John P. Diggins, *The American Left in the Twentieth Century* (New York: Harcourt, Brace, Jovanovich, 1973).

Leonard Dinnerstein and David M. Reimers, *Ethnic Americans: A History of Immigration and Assimilation* (New York: New York University Press, 1977).

G. William Domhoff, *Who Rules America?* (Englewood Cliffs, New Jersey: Prentice-Hall, 1967).

W. E. B. DuBois, *Black Reconstruction in America, 1860–1880* (New York: Atheneum, 1971).

——, *Color and Democracy: Colonies and Peace* (New York: Harcourt, Brace and Company, 1945).

——, *The Autobiography of W. E. B. DuBois: A Soliloquy on Viewing My Life from the Last Decade of Its First Century* (New York: International Publishers, 1968).

——, *The Education of Black People: Ten Critiques, 1906–1960* (New York: Monthly Review Press, 1973).

——, *The World and Africa* (New York: International Publishers, 1946).

Chester E. Eisinger (ed.), *The 1940s: Profile of a Nation in Crisis* (Garden City, New York: Anchor, 1969).

Archie Epps (ed.), *The Speeches of Malcolm X at Harvard* (New York: William Morrow, 1968).

Les Evans and Allen Myers, *Watergate and the Myth of American Democracy* (New York: Pathfinder Press, 1974).

James Farmer, *Freedom – When?* (New York: Random House, 1966).

William Faulkner, Benjamin E. Mays and Cecil Sims, *The Segregation Decisions* (Atlanta: Southern Regional Council, 1956).

Stanley Feldstein and Lawrence Castello (eds), *The Ordeal of Assimilation: A Documentary History of the White Working Class* (Garden City, New York: Anchor Books, 1974).

Philip S. Foner, *Organized Labor and the Black Worker, 1619–1973* (New York: International Publishers, 1976).

—— (ed.), *The Black Panthers Speak* (Philadelphia: J. B. Lippincott, 1970).

James Forman, *The Making of Black Revolutionaries* (New York: Macmillan, 1972).

Marshall Frady, *Wallace* (New York: New American Library, 1976).

John Hope Franklin, *From Slavery to Freedom: A History of Negro Americans* (New York: Vintage Books, 1969).

Richard Freeman, *Black Elite: The New Market for Highly Qualified Black Americans* (New York: McGraw-Hill, 1977).

Herbert Garfinkel, *When Negroes March* (New York: Atheneum, 1969).

Richard A. Garcia (ed.), *The Chicanos in America, 1540–1974* (Dobbs Ferry, New York: Oceana Press, 1977).

Addison Gayle, Jr., *The Black Situation* (New York: Delta, 1970).

Irene L. Gendzier, *Frantz Fanon: A Critical Study* (New York: Pantheon, 1973).

Eugene D. Genovese, *In Red and Black: Marxian Explorations in Southern and Afro-American History* (New York: Vintage, 1971).

Dan Georgakas and Marvin Surkin, *Detroit: I Do Mind Dying, A Study in Urban Revolution* (New York: St. Martin's Press, 1975).

James Geschwender, *Class, Race and Worker Insurgency: The League of Revolutionary Black Workers* (New York: Cambridge University Press, 1977).

Nikki Giovanni, *Black Feeling, Black Talk, Black Judgement* (New York: William Morrow, 1970).

Douglas G. Glasgow, *The Black Underclass: Poverty, Unemployment and the Entrapment of Ghetto Youth* (New York: Vintage, 1981).

Nathan Glazer, *Beyond the Melting Pot* (Cambridge: MIT Press, 1963).

Peter L. Goldman, *The Death and Life of Malcolm X* (New York: Harper and Row, 1973).

Robert J. Goldstein, *Political Repression in Modern America, 1870 to the Present* (New York: Two Continents Publishing Group, 1978).

Charles Goodell, *Political Prisoners in America* (New York: Random House, 1973).

Lawrence Goodwyn, *The Populist Moment: A Short History of the Agrarian Revolt in America* (New York and London: Oxford University Press, 1978).

Leo Grebler, Joan W. Moore and Ralph C. Guzman, *The Mexican-American People: The Nation's Second Largest Minority* (New York: Free Press, 1971).

Bertram Gross, *Friendly Fascism: The New Face of Power in America* (New York: M. Evans, 1980).

Jesse Parkhurst Guzman (ed), *Negro Year Book: A Review of Events Affecting Negro Life, 1941–1946* (Tuskegee Institute, Alabama: Tuskegee Institute, Department of Records and Research, 1947).

Morton H. Halperin, Jerry J. Berman, Robert L. Borosage and Christine M. Marwich, *The Lawless State: The Crimes of the U.S. Intelligence Agencies* (New York: Penguin, 1976).

Richard Handyside (ed), *Revolution in Guinea: Selected Texts by Amilcar Cabral* (New York: Monthly Review Press, 1969).

Vincent Harding, *The Other American Revolution* (Los Angeles: Center for Afro-American Studies, 1980).

Celia S. Heller, *Mexican-American Youth: Forgotten Youth at the Cross-Roads* (New York: Random House, 1966).

Lillian Hellman, *Scoundrel Time* (Boston: Little, Brown, 1976).

Florette Henri, *Black Migration: Movement North, 1900–1920* (Garden City, New York: Anchor Books, 1976).

John Hillson, *The Battle of Boston: Busing and the Struggle for School Desegregation* (New York: Pathfinder Press, 1970).

Lennox S. Hinds, *Illusions of Justice: Human Rights Violations in the United States* (Iowa City, Iowa: School of Social Work, University of Iowa, 1978).

Bell Hooks, *Ain't I A Woman: Black Women and Feminism* (Boston: South End Press, 1981).

Edwin P. Hoyt, *Paul Robeson: the American Othelllo* (Cleveland: World, 1967).

Paul Jacobs and Saul Landau (eds), *The New Radicals: A Report with Documents* (New York: Vintage, 1966).

Sylvia M. Jacobs (ed.), *Black Americans and the Missionary Movement in Africa* (Westport, Connecticut: Greenwood Press, 1982).

Julius Jacobson (ed.), *The Negro and the American Labor Movement* (Garden City, New York: Anchor, 1968).

James Weldon Johnson, *Negro Americans, What Now?* (New York: Viking Press, 1962).

Marcus E. Jones, *Black Migration in the United States with Emphasis on Selected Central Cities* (Saratoga, California: Century Twenty One Publishing, 1980).

V. O. Key, Jr., *Southern Politics in State and Nation* (New York: Vintage, 1949).

Martin Luther King, Jr., *Strength to Love* (New York: Pocket Books, 1964).

——, *The Trumpet of Conscience* (New York: Harper and Row, 1967).

——, *Where Do We Go From Here: Chaos or Community* (New York: Harper and Row, 1967).

——, *Why We Can't Wait* (New York: Harper and Row, 1964).

Harry H. L. Kitano, *Japanese Americans* (Englewood Cliffs, New Jersey: Prentice-Hall, 1969).

Frank Kofsky, *Black Nationalism and the Revolution in Music* (New York: Pathfinder Press, 1970).

Judith Kramer, *The American Minority Community* (New York: Crowell, 1970).

Mark Lane and Dick Gregory, *Code Name Zorro: The Murder of Martin Luther King, Jr.* (New York: Prentice-Hall, 1977).

Steven F. Lawson, *Black Ballots: Voting Rights in the South, 1944–1969* (New York: Columbia University Press, 1976).

Robert Lefcourt (ed.), *Law Against the People* (New York: Vintage, 1971).

Murray B. Levin, *Political Hysteria in America: The Democratic Capacity for Repression* (New York: Basic Books, 1971).

David Lewis, *King: A Critical Biography* (Baltimore: Penguin, 1969).

Claude M. Lightfoot, *Ghetto Rebellion To Black Liberation* (New York: International Publishers, 1968).

C. Eric Lincoln (ed.), *Martin Luther King, Jr.: A Profile* (New York: Hill and Wang, 1970).

——, *My Face is Black* (Boston: Beacon Press, 1964).

——, *The Black Muslims in America* (Boston: Beacon Press, 1961).

Louis E. Lomax, *The Negro Revolt* (New York: Harper, 1963).

——, *To Kill a Black Man* (Los Angeles: Holloway House, 1968).

——, *When The Word is Given* (Cleveland: World Publishing Company, 1963).

Debbie Louis, *And We Are Not Saved: A History of the Movement as People* (Garden City, New York: Anchor, 1970).

John Lukcas, *A New History of the Cold War* (Garden City, New York: Anchor Books, 1966).

William Madsden, *The Mexican-Americans of South Texas* (New York: Holt, Rinehart, and Winston, 1964).

S. J. Makielski, Jr., *Beleaguered Minorities: Cultural Politics in America* (San Francisco: W. H. Freeman, 1973).

Malcolm X, *Malcom X on Afro-American History* (New York: Pathfinder Press, 1970).

——, *The Autobiography of Malcolm X* (New York: Grove Press, 1965).

Eric Mann, *Comdrade George: An Investigation into the Life, Political Thought, and Assassination of George Jackson* (New York: Harper and Row, 1972).

Manning Marable, *Blackwater: Historical Studies in Race, Class Consciousness, and Revolution* (Dayton, Ohio: Black Praxis Press, 1981).

——, *From The Grassroots: Social and Political Essays Towards Afro-American Liberation* (Boston: South End Press, 1980).

——, *How Capitalism Underdeveloped Black America: Problems in Race, Political Economy and Society* (Boston: South End Press, 1983).

Gene Marine, *The Black Panthers* (New York: New American Library, 1969).

Stanley Masters, *Black-White Income Differentials* (New York: Academic Press, 1975).

Donald R. McCoy, *Coming of Age: The United States during the 1920s and 1930s* (New York: Penguin, 1973).

August Meier, *Negro Thought in America, 1880–1915: Racial Ideologies in the Age of Booker T. Washington* (Ann Arbor, Michigan: University of Michigan Press, 1963).

August Meier and Elliott Rudwick, *CORE: A Study in the Civil Rights Movement, 1942–1968* (New York: Oxford University Press, 1973).

——, *From Plantation to Ghetto*, Revised Edition (New York: Hill and Wang, 1970).

William Robert Miller, *Martin Luther King, Jr.: His Life, Martyrdom and Meaning for the World* (New York: Avon Books, 1968).

Joan W. Moore, *Mexican-Americans* (Englewood Cliffs, New Jersey: Prentice-Hall, 1970).

Wayne Moquin and Charles van Doren, *Documentary History of the Mexican American* (New York: Praeger, 1972).

Robert Mullen, *Blacks in America's Wars: The Shift in Attitudes from the Revolutionary War to Vietnam* (New York: Pathfinder Press, 1974).

Benjamin Muse, *The American Negro Revolution* (Bloomington, Indiana: University of Indiana Press, 1968).

Michael Myerson, *Nothing Could be Finer* (New York: International Publishers, 1978).

William E. Nelson, Jr., and Philip J. Meranto, *Electing Black Mayors: Political Action in the Black Community* (Columbus, Ohio: Ohio State University Press, 1977).

Herbert Northrup (ed.), *Negro Employment in Basic Industry: A Study of Racial Policy in Six Industries* (Philadelphia: University of Pennsylvania Press, 1970).

Julius Nyerere, *Ujamaa – Essays on Socialism* (New York: Oxford University Press, 1968).

Earl Ofari, *The Myth of Black Capitalism* (New York: Monthly Review Press, 1970).

Elena Padilla, *Up from Puerto Rico* (New York: Columbia University Press, 1958).

Nelson Perry, *The Negro National Colonial Question* (Chicago: Workers Press, 1975).

Frances Fox Piven and Richard Cloward, *Regulating the Poor: The Functions of Public Welfare* (New York: Random House, 1971).

Richard Polenberg, *One Nation Divisible: Class, Race, and Ethnicity in the United States Since 1938* (New York: Penguin Books, 1980).

Michael B. Preston, Lenneal J. Henderson, Jr. and Paul Puryear (eds.), *The New Black Politics: The Search for Political Power* (New York: Longman, 1982).

Dudley Randall (ed.), *The Black Poets* (New York: Bantam, 1972).

Mark Reisler, *By the Sweat of their Brow: Mexican Immigrant Labor in the United States, 1900–1940* (Westport, Connecticut: Greenwood Press, 1976).

Feliciano Rivera, *The Chicanos: A History of Mexican Americans* (New York: Hill and Wang, 1972).

Caroline Ross and Ken Lawrence, *J. Edgar Hoover's Detention Plan: The Politics of Repression in the United States, 1939–1976* (Jackson, Mississippi: Anti-Repression Resource Team, 1978).

John R. Salter, Jr., *Jackson, Mississippi: An American Chronicle of Struggle and Schism* (Hicksville, New York: Exposition-Banner, 1979).

Don A. Schanche, *The Panther Paradox: A Liberal's Dilemma* (New York: D. McKay, 1970).

Bobby Seale, *Seize the Time* (New York: Vintage, 1970).

Mario Seton, *Paul Robeson* (London: Dobson, 1958).

John Shockley, *Chicano Revolt in a Texas Town* (Notre Dame, Indiana: University of Notre Dame Press, 1974).

James W. Silver, *Mississippi: The Closed Society* (New York: Harcourt, Brace and World, 1966).

Thomas Sowell, *Ethnic America: A History* (New York: Basic Books, 1981).

——, *Markets and Minorities* (New York: Basic Books, 1981).

——, *Race and Economics* (New York: Longman, 1975).

Charles Spencer, *Blue Collar: An Internal Examination of the Workplace* (Chicago: Workers Press, 1978).

Stan Steiner, *La Raza: The Mexican Americans* (New York: Harper and Row, 1970).

——, *The New Indians* (New York: Harper and Row, 1968).

Melvin Steinfield (ed.), *Our Racist Presidents* (San Ramon, California: Consensus Publishers, 1972).

Gerald D. Suttles, *The Social Order of the Slum* (Chicago: University of Chicago Press, 1968).

W. A. Swanberg, *Norman Thomas: The Last Idealist* (New York: Charles Scribner's Sons, 1976).

Clyde Taylor (ed.), *Vietnam and Black America: An Anthology of Protest and Resistance* (Garden City, New York: Anchor, 1973).

Athan Theoharis, *Spying on America: Political Surveillance from Hoover to the Houston Plan* (Philadelphia: Temple University Press, 1978).

US Commission on Civil Rights, *Racism in America* (Washington, DC: US Government Printing Office, 1970).

Thomas Wagstaff (ed.), *Black Power* (Beverly Hills, California: Glencoe Press, 1969).

Hanes Walton, Jr., *Black Politics: A Theoretical and Structural Analysis* (Philadelphia: J. B. Lippincott, 1972).

——, *The Political Philosophy of Martin Luther King, Jr.* (Westport, Connecticut: Greenwood Press, 1971).

Robert Penn Warren, *Who Speaks for the Negro?* (New York: Random House, 1965).

Wilcomb E. Washburn, *The Indian in America* (New York: Harper and Row, 1975).

Chancellor Williams, *The Destruction of Black Civilization* (Dubuque, Iowa: Kendall/Hunt, 1971).

Daniel T. Williams and Carolyn L. Redden, *The Black Muslims in the United States: A Selected Bibliography* (Tuskegee, Alabama: Tuskegee Institute, 1964).

John A. Williams and Charles F. Harris (eds.), *Amistad 2* (New York: Vintage, 1971).

Walter E. Williams, Loren A. Smith and Wendell Wilkie Gunn, *Black America and Organized Labor: A Fair Deal?* (Washington, DC: Lincoln Institute for Research and Education, 1980).

William Julius Wilson, *The Declining Significance of Race: Blacks and Changing American Institutions* (Chicago: University of Chicago Press, 1978).

Robert L. Woodson (ed.), *Black Perspectives on Crime and the Criminal Justice System* (Boston: G. K. Hall, 1977).

C. Vann Woodward, *The Strange Career of Jim Crow* (New York: Oxford University Press, Third Revised Edition, 1974).

ARTICLES

Hussein M. Adam, 'Frantz Fanon: His "Understanding",' *Black World*, 21 (December 1971), 4–14.

Muhammad Ahmad (Max Stanford), 'We Are All Prisoners of War', *Black Scholar*, 4 (October 1972) 3–5.

Abdul Alkalimat (Gerald McWorter), 'What Lies Ahead for Black Americans?' *Negro Digest*, 19 (November 1969), 21.

Mark Allen, 'James E. Carter and the Trilateral Commission: A Southern Strategy', *Black Scholar*, 8 (May 1977), 2–7.

Robert L. Allen, 'A Reply to Harold Baron', *Socialist Review*, 8 (January–February 1978), 120–4.

——, 'Black Liberation and the Presidential Race', *Black Scholar*, 4 (September 1972), 2–6.

——, 'Politics of the Attack on Black Studies', *Black Scholar*, 6 (September 1974), 2–7.

——, 'Racism and the Black Nation Thesis', *Socialist Revolution*, 6 (January–March 1976) 145–50.

Tomás Almaguer, 'Chicano Politics in the Present Period', *Socialist Review*, 8 (July–October 1978), 137–41.

——, 'Historical Notes on Chicano Oppression: The Dialectics of Racial and Class Combination in North America', *Atzlán*, 5 (Spring and Fall 1974), 27–56.

S. E. Anderson, 'Black Students: Racial Consciousness and the Class Struggle, 1960–1976', *Black Scholar*, 8 (January–February 1977), 35–43.

Ladun Anise, 'The Tyranny of a Purist Ideology', *Black World*, 23 (October 1974), 18–34.

Anonymous, 'Episodes From The Attica Massacre', *Black Scholar*, 4 (October 1972) 34–9.

Obi Antarah, 'A Blueprint for Black Liberation', *Black World*, 22 (October, 1973), 60–6.

Earl Anthony, 'Interview: Eldridge Cleaver', *Players*, 8 (February 1982), 27–35.

Stanley Aronowitz, 'Remaking the American Left, Part One: Currents in American Radicalism', *Socialist Review*, 13 (January–February 1983), 9–51.

James Baldwin, 'The Dangerous Road Before Martin Luther King', *Harper's Magazine* (February 1961).

Barbara Banks, 'Wanted: Killer of Black Men Still At Large in City', *Buffalo Challenger* (2 October 1980).

Dennis Banks, 'Interview', *Black Scholar*, 7 (June 1976) 29–36.

Imamu Amiri Baraka (LeRoi Jones), 'Black Nationalism: 1972', *Black Scholar*, 4 (September 1972), 23–9.

——, 'The National Black Assembly and the Black Liberation Movement', *Black World*, 26 (March 1975), 22–7.

——, 'Toward the Creation of Political Institutions for all African Peoples', *Black World*, 21 (October 1972), 54–78.

Harold Baron, 'The Retreat from Black Nationalism: A Response to Robert L. Allen', *Socialist Review*, 8 (January–February 1978), 109–19.

Bruce Bartlett, 'Assault on Federal Spending', *Society*, 19 (July–August 1982), 39–43.

A. H. Beller, 'The economics of enforcement of an anti-discrimination law: Title VII of the Civil Rights Act of 1964', *Journal of Law and Economics*, 21 (October 1978), 359–80.

Lerone Bennett, Jr., 'SNCC: Rebels With a Cause', *Ebony*, 20 (June 1965), 146–53.

Janice Bevien, 'Notes on Current Struggles Against Repression', *Black Scholar*, 12 (January–February 1981), 82–4.

Ken Bode, 'Carter's Chosen Path', *New Republic*, 180 (27 January 1979), 12–14.

——, 'Glad Old Party', *New Republic*, 180 (17 February 1979), 13–15.

Benjamin P. Bowser, 'Black People and the Future: A Summary of the Major Trends', *Black Books Bulletin*, 4 (Summer 1976), 6–10.

Herb Boyd, 'Blacks and the Police State: A Case Study of Detroit', *Black Scholar*, 12 (January–February 1981), 58–61.

Anne Braden, 'Lessons From a History of Struggle', *Southern Exposure*, 8 (Summer 1980), 8–13.

Demetri Brown, 'Black Man Found Near Lake Stirs Rumors', *Jackson Advocate* (15–21 October 1981).

Robert Brown, 'Black Land Loss: The plight of black ownership', *Southern Exposure*, 2 (Fall 1974) 112–21.

Tony Brown, 'Is Integration Killing Black Colleges?' *African-American News and World Report* (5 September 1980).

Pat Bryant, 'Justice vs. the Movement', *Southern Exposure*, 8 (Summer 1980), 31–9.

Herrington J. Bryce, 'Are Most Blacks in the Middle Class?' *Black Scholar*, 5 (February 1974), 32–6.

Jim Campen, 'Economic Crisis and Conservative Economic Policies: US Capitalism in the 1980s', *Radical America*, 15 (Spring 1981), 33–54.

Rodney Carlisle, 'Black Nationalism: An Integral Tradition', *Black World*, 22 (February 1973), 4–10.

Frank Carroll, 'OSHA Under the Gun', *Political Affairs*, 60 (September 1981), 28–33.

Cesar Chavez, 'The California Farm Workers' Struggle', *Black Scholar*, 7 (June 1976), 16–19.

Robert Chrisman, 'George Jackson', *Black Scholar*, 3 (October 1971), 2–4.

Imani Clairborne, 'Racial Violence as Reported in the Black Press During the Autumn of 1981', *Racially Motivated Random Violence*, 1 (November–December 1981), 1–11.

John Henrik Clarke, 'The Rise of Racism in the West', *Black World*, 19 (October 1970), 4–10.

Eldridge Cleaver, 'On Lumpen Ideology', *Black Scholar*, 4 (November–December 1972), 2–10.

Mark Colvin, 'The Contradictions of Control: Prisons in Class Society', *Insurgent Sociologist*, 10 (Summer–Fall 1981), 33–45.

M. R. Cramer, 'Race and Southern white worker's support for unions', *Phylon*, 39 (December 1978), 311–21.

Harold Cruse, 'Black and White: Outlines of the Next Stage', *Black World*, 20 (January 1971), 19–41, 66–71.

——, 'The Little Rock National Black Political Convention', *Black World*, 23 (October 1974), 10–17, 82–8.

——, 'The Methodology of Pan-Africanism', *Black World*, 24 (January 1975), 4–20.

Elliott Currie, 'The Politics of Jobs: Humphrey–Hawkins and the Dilemmas of Full Employment', *Socialist Review*, 7 (March–April 1977), 93–114.

Ronald V. Dellums, interview, 'Peace, Justice, and Politics', *Plain Speaking* (16–31 May 1982).

Elaine Douglas, 'The Conversion of Eldridge Cleaver', *Encore*, 2 (2 February 1976), 9–15.

St. Clair Drake, 'The Black Diaspora in Pan-African Perspective', *Black Scholar*, 7 (September 1975), 2–13.

W. E. B. DuBois, 'A History of the Negro Vote', *Crisis*, 40 (June 1933), 128–9.
——, 'Bound by the Color Line', *New Masses*, 58 (12 February 1946), 8.
——, 'Civil Rights Legislation Before and After the 14th Amendment', *Lawyers' Guild Review*, 6 (November–December 1946), 640–2.
——, 'Negroes and the Crisis of Capitalism in the United States', *Monthly Review*, 4 (April 1953), 478–85.
——, 'Reconstruction and Its Benefits', *American Historical Review*, 15 (July 1910), 781–99.
——, 'Reconstruction, Seventy-Five Years After', *Phylon*, 4 (1943), 205–12.
——, 'The Choice That Confronts America's Negroes', *National Guardian* (13 February 1952).
——, 'The Negro in America Today', Five-part Essay, *National Guardian* (16, 23, 30 January; 13 February; 5 March 1956).
——, 'The Thirteenth, Fourteenth and Fifteenth Amendments', *Lawyers' Guild Review*, 9 (Spring 1949), 92–5.
——, 'There Must Come a Vast Social Change in the United States', *National Guardian* (11 July 1951).
Barbara Easton, Michael Kazin and David Plotke, 'Desperate Times: The Peoples Temple and the Left', *Socialist Review*, 9 (March–April 1979), 63–73.
Frank Elam, 'Attacks on Blacks: Death Toll Climbs', *Guardian* (22 October 1980).
Glen Ford, 'Reagan and South Africa', *Black Communicator*, 1 (Spring 1981), 15–16.
——, 'The Need for a Black Women's Movement', *Black Communicator*, 1 (Spring 1981), 4–7.
Raymond S. Franklin, 'The Political Economy of Black Power', *Social Problems*, 16 (Winter 1969), 286–301.
Jeff Frieden, 'The Trilateral Commission: Economics and Politics in the 1970s', *Monthly Review*, 29 (December 1977), 1–18.
Hoyt Fuller, 'Another Fork in the Road', *Black World*, 23 (October 1974), 49–50, 97.
Mario T. Garcia, 'On Mexican Immigration, the United States and Chicano History', *Journal of Ethnic Studies*, 7 (Spring 1979), 80–8.
——, 'Racial Dualism in the El Paso Labor Market, 1880–1920', *Atzlán*, 6 (Fall 1975), 197–218.
Richard A. Garcia, 'The Chicano Movement and the Mexican-American Community, 1972–1978: An Interpretative Essay', *Specialist Review*, 8 (July–October 1978), 117–36.
James Garrett, 'A Historical Sketch: The Sixth Pan African Congress', *Black World*, 26 (March 1975), 4–20.
Joe Gilyard, 'White Man Who Shot Two Black Girls Is Awarded $5,000 For His Trouble', *Cleveland Call and Post* (17 October 1981).
Nathan Glazer, 'Ethnicity – North, South, West', *Commentary* 73 (May 1982), 73–8.
Lawrence Goodwyn, 'Jimmy Carter and "Populism",' *Southern Exposure*, 5 (Spring 1977), 45–6.
A. James Gregor, 'Black Nationalism: A Preliminary Analysis of Negro Radicalism', *Science and Society*, 26 (Fall 1963), 415–32.
Bertram M. Gross, 'Profits Without Honor: The Secret Success of Jimmy Carter', *Nation*, 228 (2 June 1979), 623–4.
Bob Hall, 'Jimmy Carter: Master Magician', *Southern Exposure*, 5 (Spring 1977), 43–4.
Charles V. Hamilton, 'Black Americans and the Modern Political Struggle', *Black World*, 19 (May 1970), 5–9, 77–9.
Nathan Hare, 'A Critique of Black Leaders', *Black Scholar*, 3 (March–April 1972), 2–5.
Richard G. Hatcher, 'Black Politics in the 70s', *Black Scholar*, 4 (September 1972), 17–22.

L. J. Henderson, 'The impact of the Equal Employment Opportunity Act of 1972 on employment opportunities for women and minorities in municipal government', *Policy Studies Journal*, 7 (Winter 1978), 234–43.

John Herbers, 'Poverty Rate, 7.4% Termed Highest Since '67', *New York Times* (26 July 1982).

Herbert Hill, 'Race and Labor: The AFL–CIO and the Black Worker Twenty-Five Years After the Merger', *Journal of Intergroup Relations*, 10 (Spring 1982), 5–78.

James J. Horgan, 'Voter Literacy Tests: Hail the Passing, Guard the Tomb', *Southern Exposure*, 10 (July–August 1982), 62–6.

Mathew Hutchins and Lee Sigelman, 'Black Employment in State and Local Governments: A Comparative Analysis', *Social Science Quarterly*, 62 (March 1981), 79–87.

Florence B. Irving, 'The Future of the Negro Voter in the South', *Journal of Negro Education*, 26 (Summer 1957), 390–9.

C. L. R. James, 'Kwame Nkrumah: Founder of African Emancipation', *Black World*, 21 (July 1972), 4–10.

Jacquelyne Johnson Jackson, 'Death Rates of Aged Blacks and Whites, United States, 1964–1978', *Black Scholar*, 13 (January–February 1982), 36–48.

John Judis and Alan Wolfe, 'American Politics at the Crossroads: The Collapse of Cold-War Liberalism', *Socialist Review*, 7 (March–April 1977), 9–37.

Maulana Ron Karenga, 'Black Art: A Rhythmic Reality of Revolution', *Negro Digest*, 17 (January 1968), 5–9.

——, 'Overturning Ourselves: From Mystification to Meaningful Struggle', *Black Scholar*, 4 (October 1972), 6–14.

Kaidi Kasirika and Maharibi Muntu, 'Prison or Slavery', *Black Scholar*, 3 (October 1971), 6–12.

Muhammad Isaiah Kenyatta, 'The Impact of Racism on the Family as a Support System', *Catalyst*, 2 (1980), 37–44.

Martin Kilson, 'Black Power: Anatomy of a Paradox', *Harvard Journal of Negro Affairs*, 2 (1968), 30–4.

Martin Luther King, Jr., 'Behind the Selma March', *Saturday Review*, 16 (3 March 1965), 16–17.

——, 'Fumbling on the New Frontier', *Nation*, 194 (3 March 1962), 190–3.

——, 'Let Justice Roll Down', *The Nation*, 206 (15 March 1965), 269–74.

——, 'Next Stop: The North', *Saturday Review*, 16 (13 November 1965), 33–5.

B. Sung Lee, 'A differential index of black/white income inequality, 1965–74', *Review of Black Political Economy*, 9 (Fall 1978), 90–4.

Edward A. Leonard, 'Ninety-Four Years of Non-Violence', *New South*, 20 (April 1965), 4–7.

Kirk Loggins and Susan Thomas, 'The Menace Returns', *Southern Exposure*, 8 (Summer 1980), 2–6.

Chokwe Lumumba, 'Short History of the U.S. War on the R.N.A.', *Black Scholar*, 12 (January–February 1981), 72–81.

Clifford M. Lytle, 'The History of the Civil Rights Bill of 1964', *Journal of History*, 51 (October 1966), 275–96.

Haki Madhubuti (Don L. Lee), 'Enemy: From the White Left, White Right and In-Between', *Black World*, 23 (October 1974), 36–47.

——, 'The Death Walk Against Afrika', *Black World*, 22 (October 1973), 28–36.

——, 'The Latest Purge: The Attack on Black Nationalism and Pan-Afrikanism by the New Left, the sons and daughters of the Old Left', *Black Scholar*, 6 (September 1974), 43–56.

Malcolm X (Malcolm Little) and James Farmer, 'Separation or Integration: A Debate', *Dialogue Magazine*, 2 (May 1962), 14–18.

Manning Marable, 'Black Conservatives and Accommodation: Of Thomas Sowell and Others', *Negro History Bulletin*, 45 (April–June 1982), 32–5.

——, 'Justice is on Trial in Greensboro', *San Francisco Sun Reporter* (10 September 1981).

——, 'Martin Luther King's Ambiguous Legacy', *WIN* magazine, 18 (15 April 1982) 15–19.

——, 'Reaganomics', *Umoja Sasa*, 3 (Spring 1981), 25, 28.

——, 'The Crisis of the Black Working Class: An Economic and Historical Analysis', *Science and Society*, 46 (Summer 1982), 130–61.

——, 'The Question of Genocide', *Journal of Intergroup Relations*, 10 (Autumn 1982), 19–29.

John L. Marshall, '1872 Law Used to Prosecute Police Gadfly: Ex-Black Panther Accused of Trying to Turn Crowd Against Police', *Los Angeles Times* (6 May 1982).

Andrew Marx and Tom Tuthill, 'Resisting the Klan: Mississippi Organizes', *Southern Exposure*, 8 (Summer 1980), 25–8.

August Meier, 'Negro Protest Movements and Organizations', *Journal of Negro Education*, 32 (Fall 1963), 437–50.

——, 'On the Role of Martin Luther King', *New Politics*, 4 (Winter 1965), 52–9.

——, 'The Dilemmas of Negro Protest Strategy', *New South*, 21 (Spring 1966), 1–18.

——, 'The Revolution Against the NAACP', *Journal of Negro Education*, 32 (Spring 1963), 146–52.

Martin B. Miller, 'Sinking Gradually into the Proletariat: The Emergence of the Penitentiary in the United States', *Crime and Social Justice*, No. 14 (Winter 1980), 37–43.

David Moberg, Alexander Cockburn and James Ridgway, 'Cult Politics Comes of Age', *Santa Barbara News and Review* (30 November 1978).

Dhoruba Moore, 'Strategies of Repression Against the Black Movement', *Black Scholar*, 12 (May–June 1981), 10–16.

D. R. Morgan and M. R. Fitzgerald, 'A casual perspective on school segregation among American States: A Research Note', *Social Forces*, 58 (1979), 329–35.

Marietta Morrissey, 'Ethnic Stratification and the Study of Chicanos', *Journal of Ethnic Studies*, 10 (Winter 1983), 71–99.

Askia Muhammad (Rolland Snellings), 'Behind the Washington Siege: Civil War in Islamic America', *Nation*, 224 (11 June 1977), 721–4.

C. Lynn Munro, 'LeRoi Jones: A Man in Transition', *CLA Journal*, 17 (September 1973), 58–78.

Samuel L. Myers and E. Kenneth Phillips, 'Housing segregation and black employment: another look at the ghetto dispersal strategy', *American Economic Review*, 69 (May 1979), 298–301.

Julius K. Nyerere, 'Capitalism or Socialism? The Rational Choice', *Black World*, 23 (March 1974), 38–48.

Imari Obadele (Richard Henry), 'The Struggle of the Republic of New Africa', *Black Scholar*, 5 (June 1974), 32–41.

J. K. Obatala, 'How Carter Should Pay His Debt', *Nation*, 223 (27 November 1976), 550–2.

John H. O'Connell, Jr., 'Black Capitalism', *Review of Black Political Economy* (Fall 1976), 67–84.

Earl Ofari, 'Black Labor: Powerful Force For Liberation', *Black World*, 22 (October 1973), 43–7.

——, 'W. E. B. DuBois and Black Power', *Black World*, 19 (August 1970), 26–8.

Alexander Okanlawon, 'Africanism – A Synthesis of the African World-View', *Black World*, 21 (July 1972), 40–4.

John O'Loughlin, 'Black Representation and the Seat-Vote Relationship', *Social Science Quarterly*, 60 (June 1979), 72–86.

Roxanne Dunbar Ortiz, 'Land and Nationhood: The American Indian Struggle for Self-Determination and Survival', *Socialist Review*, 12 (May–August 1982), 105–20.

Alfred E. Osborne, Jr., 'A Note on Black Well-Being in the North and West', *Review of Black Political Economy*, 7 (Fall 1976), 85–92.

Brenda Payton, 'Police Use of Deadly Force in Oakland', *Black Scholar*, 12 (January–February 1981), 62–4.

Peoples College, 'Imperialism and Black Liberation', *Black Scholar*, 6 (September 1974), 38–42.

T. F. Pettigrew, 'Racial change and social policy', *Annals of the American Academy of Political and Social Science*, 441 (January 1979), 114–31.

Kenneth Porter, 'Relations Between Negroes and Indians Within the Present Limits of the United States', *Journal of Negro History*, 17 (July 1932), 287–367.

Alejandro Portes, 'Illegal Immigration and the International System: Lessons From Recent Legal Mexican Immigrants to the United States', *Social Problems*, 26 (April 1979), 425–38.

Popular Economics Research Group, 'Barefoot and Pregnant Women and Reaganomics', *WIN* magazine, 18 (15 April 1982), 12–14.

A. Philip Randolph Institute, 'An Appeal by Black Americans for United States Support of Israel', *Black World*, 19 (October 1970), 42–4.

Jack L. Roach and Janet K. Roach, 'Mobilizing the Poor: Road to a Dead End', *Social Problems*, 26 (December 1978), 160–71.

Gene Roberts, 'The Story of Snick: From "Freedom Rides" to "Black Power",' *New York Times Magazine* (25 September 1966), 27–9.

Paul Robeson, 'Voting for Peace', *Masses and Mainstream* (January 1952), 7–14.

E. O'Neill Robinson, 'Jury Convicts Utah Murderer of Joggers', *Baltimore Afro-American* (26 September 1981).

Walter Rodney, 'Guyana: The making of the labour force', *Race and Class*, 22 (Spring 1981), 331–52.

Sheila Rule, 'Black Middle Class Slipping, Study by Urban League Says', *New York Times* (4 August 1982).

——, 'New York Blacks Focusing on Equal Opportunity', *New York Times* (22 August 1982).

Bayard Rustin, ' "Black power" and Coalition Politics', *Commentary*, 42 (September 1966), 35–40.

——, 'The Meaning of the March on Washington', *Liberation*, 8 (October 1963), 11–13.

Kalamu ya Salaam, 'In the Face of Oppression: A Case Study of New Orleans', *Black Scholar*, 12 (January–February 1981), 65–7.

——, 'Tell No Lies, Claim No Easy Victories', *Black World*, 23 (October 1974), 18–34.

William Seraile, 'The Assassination of Malcolm X: The View from Home and Abroad', *Afro-Americans in New York Life and History*, 5 (January 1981), 43–58.

Mohan L. Sharma, 'Martin Luther King: Modern America's Greatest Theologian of Social Action', *Journal of Negro History*, 53 (July 1968), 257–63.

Baxter Smith, 'New Evidence of FBI "Disruption" Program', *Black Scholar*, 6 (July–August 1975), 43–8.

——, 'The Resurgence of the KKK', *Black Scholar*, 12 (January–February 1981), 25–30.

Damu Smith, 'The Upsurge of Police Repression: An Analysis', *Black Scholar*, 12 (January–February 1981), 35–57.

Mark Smith, 'A Response to Haki Madhubuti', *Black Scholar*, 6 (January–February 1975), 45–52.

Frederic Solomon, Walter L. Walker, Garrett J. O'Connor and Jacob R. Fishman, 'Civil Rights Activity and Reduction in Crime among Negroes', *Archives of General Psychiatry*, 12 (1965), 227–36.

Yusufu Sonebeyatta (Joseph F. Brooks), 'Ujamaa For Land and Power', *Black Scholar*, 3 (October 1971), 13–20.

Thomas Sowell, 'Myths About Minorities', *Commentary*, 68 (August 1979), 33–7.

——, 'The Uses of Government for Racial Equality', *National Review*, 33 (4 September 1981), 1009–16.

Johnny Spain, 'The Black Family and the Prisons', *Black Scholar*, 4 (October 1972), 18–31.

Robert Staples, 'Black Manhood in the 1970s: A Critical Look Back', *Black Scholar*, 12 (May–June 1981), 2–9.

Chuck Stone, 'Black Political Power in the Carter Era', *Black Scholar* 8 (January–February 1977), 6–15.

Chinta Strausberg, 'White Sheriff Denies Rights to Black Religious Group', *Chicago Defender* (22 September 1981).

William Strickland, 'The Gary Convention and the Crisis of American Politics', *Black World*, 21 (October 1972), 18–26.

——, 'Watergate: Its Meaning For Black America', *Black World*, 23 (December 1973), 4–14.

D. H. Swinton, 'A labor force competition model of racial discrimination in the labor market', *Review of Black Political Economy*, 9 (Fall 1978), 5–42.

Leonard Sykes, Jr., 'Jim Crow, Lynchings and a Return to Business As Usual', *Black Books Bulletin*, 7 (Fall 1981), 18–20.

Abigail M. Thernstrom, 'The odd evolution of the Voting Rights Act', *Public Interest*, No. 55 (Spring 1979), 49–76.

Jim Thomas, David Stribling, Ra Rabb Chaka, Edmond Clemons, Charlie Secret and Alex Neal, 'Prison Conditions and Penal Trends', *Crime and Social Justice*, No. 15 (Summer 1981), 49–55.

June Manning Thomas, 'Miami: Harbinger of Rebellion?' *Catalyst*, 3 (1981), 37–56.

John Trinkl, 'Racist acquitted in Jordan Shooting', *Guardian* (1 September 1982).

Kenneth N. Vines, 'Courts and Political Change in the South', *Journal of Social Issues*, 22 (January 1966), 59–62.

K. Vinodgopal, 'Anti-Black attacks rise in Boston', *Guardian* (1 September 1982).

Don Wallace, 'The Political Economy of Incarceration Trends in Late U.S. Capitalism: 1971–1977', *Insurgent Sociologist*, 10 (Summer–Fall 1981), 59–65.

Ronald Walters, 'African-American Nationalism: A Unifying Ideology', *Black World*, 22 (October 1973), 9–27, 84.

Hanes Walton, Jr., 'The Political Leadership of Martin Luther King, Jr.', *Quarterly Review of Higher Education Among Negroes*, 36 (July 1968), 163–71.

Joseph R. Washington, Jr., 'Black Nationalism: Potentially Anti-Folk and Anti-Intellectual', *Black World*, 22 (July 1973), 32–9.

Richard A. Wasserstrom, 'Federalism and Civil Rights', *University of Chicago Law Review*, 33 (Winter 1966), 411–13.

J. C. Webb, 'Weber, Sears and the Fight for Affirmative Action', *Political Affairs*, 58 (June 1979), 13–16.

Bernard L. Weinstein and John Rees, 'Reaganomics, Reindustrialization, and Regionalism', *Society*, 19 (July–August 1982), 33–8.

Steven R. Weisman, 'Reagan Says Blacks Were Hurt by Works of the Great Society', *New York Times* (16 September 1982).

Jitu Weusi, 'Jonestown Massacre – An Act of Genocide?', *Black Thoughts*, 10 (May–June 1979), 1, 30–1.

Roy Wilkins, 'Whither "Black Power?" ', *Crisis* (August–September 1966), 354.

Roy Wilkins *et al.*, 'Crisis and Commitment', *Crisis* (November 1966), 474–9.

Eddie N. Williams, 'Black Impact on the 1976 Elections', *Focus*, 4 (November 1976).

Franklin H. Williams, 'On Death Cars', *Milwaukee Courier* (12 June 1982).

Robert F. Williams, '1957: The Swimming Pool Showdown', *Southern Exposure*, 8 (Summer 1980), 22–4.
——, 'USA: The Potential of a Minority Revolution', *The Crusader Monthly Newsletter*, 5 (May–June 1964), 1–7.
Ann Withorn, 'Retreat From The Social Wage: Human Services in the 1980s', *Radical America*, 15 (Spring 1981), 23–31.
M. Frank Wright, 'The National Question: A Marxist Critique', *Black Scholar*, 5 (February 1974), 43–53.
Nathan Wright, Jr., 'Another Look At Leon Sullivan: A Leader Among Us', *Fort Lauderdale Westside Gazette* (2 September 1982).
Richard Wright, 'A Blueprint for Negro Writing', *New Challenge*, 11 (1937), 53–65.
Robert L. Zangrando, 'From Civil Rights to Black Liberation: The Unsettled 1960s', *Current History*, 62 (November 1969), 281–6, 299.
Howard Zinn, 'Registration in Alabama', *New Republic*, 149 (26 October 1963), 11–12.
Sam Zuckerman, 'House backs "soak-the-poor" budget', *Guardian* (23 June 1982).

Index

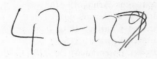

241